D0793168

Muscle Management for Musicians

Elizabeth Andrews

The Scarecrow Press, Inc.
Lanham, Maryland • Toronto • Oxford
2005

SCARECROW PRESS, INC.

Published in the United States of America
by Scarecrow Press, Inc.
A wholly owned subsidary of
The Rowman & Littlefield Publishing Group, Inc.
4501 Forbes Boulevard, Suite 200, Lanham, Maryland 20706
www.scarecrowpress.com

PO Box 317
Oxford
OX2 9RU, UK

British Library Cataloguing in Publication Information Available

Library of Congress Cataloging-in-Publication Data

Andrews, Elizabeth, 1943–
  Muscle management for musicians / Elizabeth Andrews.
    p.   cm.
  Includes bibliographical references and index.
  ISBN 0-8108-5134-2 (pbk. : alk. paper)
  1. Music—Physiological aspects. 2. Musicians—Health and hygiene
3. Kinesiology. I. Title.
ML3820.A63   2005
613.7′1′02478—dc22   2004013781

Contents

Preface

The idea behind this book is to follow up on *Healthy Practice for Musicians* (Rhinegold 1997), to introduce and support musicians and those medical and alternative medical professionals who care for them, to applied kinesiology. The material presented here in its simplest form is to be used as a means to improve performance and promote self-help, responsibility, and injury prevention.

I do not presume to claim any of these techniques as my own nor to be the first to describe them to nonchiropractors. I am simply translating and updating material already made available by John Thie in plain English, together with my experience of them, in musician's terms. Beyond these, applied kinesiology should *never* be used on its own without the background knowledge of a chiropractic, osteopathic, medical, or dental practitioner. I have purposely omitted much technical data that applied kinesiology embraces, such as the acupuncture five element law, complicated nutritional advice, and manipulative techniques. They are, of course, extremely relevant, but the musician should seek a specialist, an applied kinesiologist, for these. What I have included concentrates on simplicity, is safe to use, and works brilliantly well to empower the musician to reach greater heights in performance.

This book is my final gift to the music profession on my retirement from fifteen years as a chiropractor specializing in musicians' injuries. I would therefore like to thank those who supported me through twenty-five years as a freelance musician, those members of the Amadeus Quartet and the professors at the Moscow Conservatorium, and fellow freelance musicians. The greatest among those who encouraged and inspired me in applied kinesiology are George Goodheart, DC, who founded and developed applied kinesiology and John Thie, DC, for his *Touch for Health* version, but there are also countless others too numerous to mention. I am most grateful to Ron Colyer for his considerable Alexander technique contributions to the text and to my patients and the staff at the British Association for Performing Arts Medicine.

I would like to thank Lettice Lachlin for proofreading, and I could not have done the illustrations and typing without the IT help from Sara Lafferty, who deserves huge thanks, nor published the book without Bruce Phillips and Jeffrey Wolf at Scarecrow Press.

Introduction

I wrote this book because a letter to *Classical Music* magazine stated that "only a minority of musicians are beset by problems physical and psychological." In response I wrote:

> While I agree that playing a musical instrument is hardly a dangerous sport, I must protest etc. at the quote above. Research published in *Medical Problems of Professional Artists Magazine* USA, shows that 75% of professional musicians do have a problem that stops them playing sometime during their careers.
>
> The small number calling the British Performing Arts Medicine Trust is not indicative of the size of the problem, but [due to] the fact that the trust is not so well known as it might be, or should be.
>
> In addition to my general chiropractic work, I saw musicians at the Trusts' premises in London. The small numbers calling are also due to fear in the freelance market of being seen as unreliable, and the sports mentality of "no gain without pain" betraying simple ignorance—ignorance not only as to availability of specialist help in crisis management, but also basic anatomy and physiology in teacher training, of injury prevention and self-help and not least of efficient practice methods.
>
> As a professional musician for 25 years, I was taught none of these, and as a chiropractor specialising in musicians' injuries for 15 years I see the lack in every patient. The most frequent comment from them is: "That's so obvious and simple, why did nobody tell me before?" It makes no sense just to rest after an injury, if when you start playing again you make the same mistakes. To assist matters I spend as much time educating as treating; I wrote *Healthy Practice for Musicians* (Rhinegold 1997)—long sold out—and many articles for music

magazines and lectured extensively to music colleges and academies, universities, orchestras and music societies in UK and New Zealand.

The above letter epitomizes the reasons for writing this book—to update my last book (*Healthy Practice for Musicians*) and integrate some Alexander technique ways of thinking with contributions to the sections on circulatory aspects, equilibrium, voluntary and involuntary nerve pathways, prerequisites for fine motor control, reflexes, and breathing misconceptions by my colleague, violinist and Alexander teacher Ron Colyer.

Most problems seem to occur in the first and final years at music college, and then from the age of forty onward. While updating, therefore, it seemed sensible to confine ourselves more narrowly to muscles and what affects them as the main subject, thus giving room to include more techniques, so as to be relevant to doctors, physiotherapists and masseuses, teachers, and college welfare officers who might come in contact with ailing musicians, as well as the musicians themselves.

Slowly, slowly the message is getting through. In the United Kingdom, there are now very new postgraduate courses for music teachers on matters beyond instrumental technique and musical interpretation. I believe the main ideas in this book should be part of the standard undergraduate course in every music college (as it has been in Norway for years), so that all teachers and performers have at least some awareness of such matters.

I make no apology for using plain English.

1

How to Use This Book

Have no fear, this is not yet another book about how to play your instrument or about new instrumental techniques. It is about how you can best do what you want to do—play.

HOW TO USE THIS BOOK MOST EFFICIENTLY

- Read the contents page to see how the book is laid out and where the main blocks of information are.
- Flick through page by page. This will only take a few minutes and will give you an overview of what is available, the format, and the diagrams.
- Skim read (but beware of relying on this for memory). Mark the pages relevant to you.
- Reread this chapter carefully.
- Do the above four things NOW.
- At leisure, read each of the remaining chapters thoroughly; especially read about what you can do if the only time available is a fifteen-minute rehearsal break or the odd few minutes stuck in a traffic jam.
- If none of the techniques in the book work for you, then either you are not following the instructions carefully enough or you need

professional help from an applied kinesiologist, a chiropractor or osteopath, a doctor, a dentist, or a physiotherapist.

Twenty-five years freelancing in music and fifteen as a practitioner in various kinds of complementary medicine, including various sorts of chiropractic and osteopathy, together with the Alexander technique, teaching gifted children, and lecturing have taught us two things—not only that there is so much that can be discussed between musician, medics, and complementary therapists, but also that much can be done by musicians to help themselves to prevent injury. It is also equally important to recognize when expert or medical professional help is needed, and we hope this is made clear within these pages. Even more can be done when all parties understand each other and speak the same language, and with that aim, plain English is used throughout and jargon from all sides avoided. In doing this, however, it must be made clear that the information is no less effective and the techniques are the same as used by professionals from all sides of the discussion. We have just been careful to omit any techniques that, if misused, could cause harm or necessitate specialized knowledge beyond the scope of this book. The aim is (a) to give only safe information for use as self-help (on the understanding that there is a great deal more available that requires years of devoted study) and (b) for the book to be used as a resource for asking good, searchingly useful questions of practitioners of whatever school of thought. It's not the number of questions so much as the quality of the questions and their relevance.

Everyone has good and bad technical abilities, good and bad luck, and each of us tends to think that others have it easier. Actually there is no "normal" life. But there is a fulfilled life if one can have courage, be responsible for oneself, and have an awareness of all the chances, opportunities, and choices that are out there, even if they are not decked out in Piccadilly-bright lights.

The aim is to dissuade musicians from the "no pain, no gain" attitude and from inappropriate use of excess pain killers, alcohol, or Beta-blockers. The aim is also to encourage musicians to be more responsible for caring for their bodies as well as their instruments and to be able to sort out their problems before those problems become chronic and lead to a victim mentality. Prevention is always far better and cheaper than cure.

As a musician, the most important thing to remember, in whatever method of self-help you choose, is that, since you live with yourself twenty-four hours a day, you know better than anyone else how you feel. That alone makes you an expert on yourself. None of the techniques in this book will harm you if used as described and in moderation. Nor will it harm you to ask for professional advice. Whether or not you take that advice is still *your choice*. However, we have to include an All-Purpose Disclaimer that:

> Before following the advice given in this book, readers are urged to give careful consideration to the nature of their particular health problem and to consult a competent physician if in any doubt. This book should not be regarded as a substitute for professional medical treatment, and while every care is taken to ensure the accuracy of the content, the authors and publishers cannot accept legal responsibility for any problem arising out of experimentation with the methods described.

We aim only to bring to your attention the nature and purpose of pain and the cost to yourself of ignoring it. This is certainly not a book for those who don't want to be responsible for the health of their muscles, or for those who want someone else to "fix" their problems, so they can go and *repeat the same destructive patterns* that caused the problem in the first place. It is a book for those who, despite the occupational hazards, want to go on doing their job successfully in an environment that is as benign as they can make it. You are your greatest asset and best investment.

Although this is essentially a self-help book, you might need another person to help you with the muscle testing to find out exactly which muscle needs help so you can work on the massage and holding points yourself. If you follow the techniques as described here, your innate survival mechanism and healing ability is then able to do an expert job, if left alone to get on with it. These methods are particularly good at removing that last residue of hesitancy and doubt in performance left after injury or surgery. There is no mention of strapping and bandaging, and nothing that conflicts with conventional medicine or physiotherapy. The techniques come way before or way after all that.

When looking for a practitioner of any description, understand that passing exams with yards of letters after the name does not necessarily make a good practitioner; it only makes a good academic who may live in an ivory tower, without an understanding of or a sensitivity to a musician's needs. While exams do guarantee a certain level of knowledge and code of ethics, don't judge a practitioner by the politeness of his or her receptionist, the waiting room décor, or the number of machines with flashing lights. "Some patients equate the use of advanced technology with 'good' care and may be disappointed, surprised or concerned if a thoughtful physician does not order a battery of tests" (Parmley 1995). What you need is someone who understands what you, the musician, are talking about. The better you understand what has gone wrong, the sooner you can find the cause and seek out really appropriate first-class help by giving the right information and asking the right questions of the most appropriate expert.

Whatever advice you take, you will not derive the full benefit from it unless you follow it 100 percent. Don't half do it, or mess about doing a bit of this and a bit of that. Certainly don't double up what you have been advised to do, either, in the mistaken idea that more equals better/faster. If you are dissatisfied with the treatment you have been given, remember that *there will have been good reason for the prescription being given you exactly as it was.* Find out what that reason was. Perhaps you have now progressed beyond it. By all means ask for a second opinion, look things up, ask lots more questions. But don't go around collecting opinions and rubbishing all the previous practitioners you have visited. They will have done their best for you, particularly if you were as clear and specific as possible when you went to see them for the first time.

WHAT IS APPLIED KINESIOLOGY?

To assist medical understanding, the following description is included. Applied kinesiology (AK) is to apply the study of motion, and it is pronounced kin-easy-ology. George Goodheart, DC, introduced AK in 1964. It has been developing and evolving ever since through input from chiropractors, osteopaths, doctors, dentists, psychiatrists, podiatrists, acupuncturists, and homeopaths from all over the world providing many additional dimensions.

Experience over thirty-five years has shown that when using accurate muscle testing, the body reacts and never lies. Because the body functions as a whole, it must be tested as such. AK uses basic manual muscle testing as a diagnostic tool to look at the whole body. It evaluates how well the structural, physical, chemical, and emotional aspects are integrated by looking at the circulation, nervous system, organs and glands, nutrition and food sensitivities, body alignment, muscles, joints, and bones, coordination, and acupuncture meridian energies.

If the body malfunctions in one area, many other parts of the body can also be affected. So, rather than treat the signs and symptoms of disease, AK aims to find and treat the cause of the problem—the imbalances arising through lack of stimulation or overload. AK promotes the body's natural self-healing ability, assisting return to dynamic and integrated health.

AK fosters patients' responsibility for their own health, demonstrating what is physically, nutritionally, and emotionally appropriate. Musicians of all ages, including children with learning difficulties, have all been able to discover why their muscles have become weak, tense, or uncoordinated by working with simple techniques learned at AK sessions. Coordination and precision improve, helping athletes win at Olympic levels and musicians perform at their best.

Where appropriate, AK can be used in conjunction with standard diagnostic tests (history, blood tests, X-rays, and any other relevant investigation). AK examinations enhance standard diagnostic tests and are enhanced by standard diagnosis. Treatment may involve gentle manipulation, guidance in self-help, and nutritional, homeopathic, or herbal support.

AK can treat structural problems such as: headaches and migraines, neck and shoulder pain, arm and hand pain, back pain and sciatica, postural abnormalities, nerve root irritation, and sports and musicians' injuries. It can also alleviate repetitive strain injuries and overuse syndromes, cramps and muscle spasm, and sprains and strains. Allergies, eczema, food intolerance, and irritable bowel syndrome can be investigated. Premenstrual tension, menopause and hormone-related problems, sleep disorders, poor coordination and dyslexia, occupational stresses, stage fright and exam nerves all fall under the AK treatment umbrella.

Membership in the International College of Applied Kinesiology is restricted to practitioners of chiropractic, osteopathic, medical, dental, or veterinary medicine. Each full member must have completed a basic

100 course in applied kinesiology and must have completed the test of clinical competence. Only those techniques that can be safely used by practitioners who do not have a license to diagnose have been included in this book. All manipulation and pharmaceutical information has been omitted, but that still leaves much that the musician can use to help himself or herself. Most of the techniques can be found in "Touch for Health" manuals. Here they are specifically applied to musicians.

Music colleges do a wonderful job as places of focus on youth and music. Their priorities are to teach instrumental technique (maybe to a specific method), repertoire, and academic studies such as composition and research. There will usually be instrumental tuition, orchestral and ensemble work, possibly some tax and business advice, some counselling, and some Alexander technique available. But no one seems to teach musicians to look at and after themselves and their physical attributes or teach them how to prevent injury for the rest of their lives in a way relevant to playing and performance.

Alexander was an actor and lecturer. He didn't have to cope with an instrument outside himself, or play in an orchestral pit. Classical Alexander technique, as most musicians experience it, only goes as far as the musician learning to get out of a chair efficiently without his or her instrument; consequently, all good intentions fly to the winds as soon as he or she has to play in what he or she perceives as the "real" world. If you go to an Alexander teacher, find one who plays your particular instrument and who has an understanding of its postural problems.

Seventy-five percent of musicians have injuries severe enough to stop them playing sometime in their career. Peaks occur at year one and year four at college and in the 40+ age group. Problems in year one occur because there is a sudden increase in playing time, from one to eight or more hours a day. There may be a new instrument, a new professor with a new method, and any small previously unimportant faults will become magnified by increased workload and stress. It may be the first time away from home in strange digs and there are problems of travel and finance to face for the first time. In year four, there are competitions, auditions, and exams to be gotten through and suddenly having to face earning a living.

The body might even have coped up to age forty but slight bad habits previously compensated for and tolerated by the young body now become a real nuisance. By now the musician knows no other way to play and is too busy to look for help until pain forces a stop.

There is an enormous sports medicine lobby and dancers have good support both during college and afterward performing, but with a performing career usually at least twice as long as sports people and dancers, musicians only have crisis management, administered by general practitioners (GPs) and the like who are not players themselves. In the United Kingdom, both the British Performing Arts Medicine Trust and the Association of Medical Advisers to British Orchestras systems are excellent as far as they go, but too few freelancers know there is expert help available and you can't take your GP on tour with you (unless you are a member of one of the large UK orchestras).

An average doctor's training is about *reductionist* scientific methodology (concentrating on the area of complaint and not the whole person), statistical proof, medical diagnosis, and symptom suppression, and failing that, rest, psychiatry, or physiotherapy or surgery as a last resort. Because of a lack of understanding about the precision of muscle movement needed to play a specific musical instrument, GPs can be dismissive of musicians' complaints, especially if symptoms are deemed to be within normal range. This is because they prescribe for normal people, not musicians. They *never* see the musician playing, the one-sided body use, the awful chairs, sloping stages and orchestra pits, the disruptive desk partner, the exhaustion of touring, and the fear of being thought unreliable through injury and of not being booked to play again.

Terms such as thoracic outlet syndrome, carpal tunnel syndrome, repetitive strain injury, tendinitis, and bursitis don't describe the cause and don't actually help musicians. The diagnosis is medically related, not musically related. The general public thinks touring is rather glamorous, equating it with a musician's holiday. Although doctors are wiser, they might not realize the sort of schedule that often has to be followed to make a tour pay. Consider the following schedule.

A typical concert tour goes like this. You have six concerts in eight days (fewer would be uneconomical). Get up at 6 A.M., make sure everything is packed, grab breakfast and leave at 7 A.M. to get a bus or train at 8 A.M. to get to the airport at 9 A.M. for an 11 A.M. takeoff. A two-hour flight and then a bus ride gets you to your hotel at 1:30 P.M. (if there is no continental time change), but you can't get into your room—it is not ready yet. So, hungry, you search the local streets for a meal—either a McDonalds or strange food in a strange town that is expensive because the hotel is near the tourist traps. You have no time to look further as the bus leaves for the concert hall in one hour.

Rehearsal, from 3–6 P.M., is needed even if the entire band can play the program in its sleep, because the acoustics, stage, or seating arrangements are different in each hall and you might have differing programs or soloists or daft spotlights to contend with.

Back at the hotel—it's 6:30 P.M. already. At least you can get into your room and hang out your clothes, take a quick snooze, grab a room-service sandwich, shower, and change, hoping the creases have come out of your concert wear. A 7:30 P.M. bus takes you back to the hall for the 8 P.M. concert.

After the concert, there is often a late reception given by the sponsor that you would rather not go to because you are tired, but you can't refuse because next year's tour may depend on it. Back to your room long after midnight, and up again at 6 A.M. as the next day repeats the schedule—and does so for each of the eight days of the tour, as you live out of a suitcase and sleep in a different bed every night.

If you have time off, it's a Sunday or a Saint's day, so everything is shut and if it's neither of these, it's pouring with rain and you are just too tired to sightsee. You become an expert in airports, buses, and back stages of concert halls and at living out of a suitcase. It's hardly a glamorous holiday!

MUSICIANS' INJURIES

Who gets the most injuries among musicians and where do they get them? Upper strings most frequently get neck, wrist, shoulder, and back problems. Lower strings get back, left-hand stretch and thumb problems, and right-hand index and shoulder problems. Piano and organ players get neck, shoulder, and lower-back problems and may have hemorrhoids. All of these frequently interfere with musicians' breathing because many hold their breath or even stop breathing temporarily while playing. Wind players and singers get neck problems; mouth, jaw joint, and teeth problems; hyperventilation; and diaphragm and eating problems. Brass players have similar problems but may also have deafness to cope with and percussionists have ear and back problems. *All* frequently have to cope with adverse heat and light conditions, restricted room to play, and performance nerves.

Most of this dreadful list could have been prevented if simple rules of injury prevention had been taught early on. Musicians should be taught that their problems will arise in three main areas:

1. *Musician versus instrument*—integration with it, and musicians' personal physique, size, and posture; instrument failure, breakage, and theft.
2. *Musician versus environment*—stand height, desk partner and lack of room to play properly; chairs and sloping stages; wearing high heels or putting one foot up on a stool while performing; living out of a suitcase and carrying it as well as carrying instrument cases and heavy music; noise and spotlights; draughts and excessive heat; and touring (with all the inherent frustrations).
3. *Musician versus self*—emotional stress, family problems, practicing (especially while on tour), activities of daily living, and activities that mitigate against playing such as typing, gardening, and house decorating.

The next assumption is that once all the orthopedic and neurological tests have been done there is nothing else that can be done to help. Since these tests are almost *never done with a musician's musical instrument in playing position*, readings are frequently inaccurate. There is also the unbalanced use of muscles—some are very highly trained by playing (such as arm and chest muscles), but most others (lower body and back muscles) on a musician's body are very unused and unfit. Frequently musicians take their bodies for granted until pain occurs, and then they try to play through the pain because they don't want to be seen as unreliable.

Musicians tend to have very little body awareness below the arms unless they were lucky enough to have Alexander or Feldenkreis lessons. No one has educated musicians that there are always possibilities and alternatives as to posture and instrument position on the playing side. On the medical side, musicians don't ask about side effects of drugs or ask their dentists to x-ray their embouchure position before extraction. Some musicians warm up for a few minutes before playing, but almost none have time to cool down as any sensible sports person would.

No one educated them about the main causes of injury in musicians—new instrument; a change in technique; uncoordinated, excessive activity or repetition; straining or even being forced to use a "method" not suited to them physically. They may be compensating physically for other postural faults, nerve entrapments, psychological tension, or stress, or they may be playing when overtired or run down. Extra nonplaying activities, such as sports, gardening, typing, and house decorating, are often ignored as possible contributory and accumulative causes to the injury.

THE TRIAD OF HEALTH

No one explained to musicians the interconnected and downward spiral that can occur mentally, physically, and chemically, or that stress is a reaction in "us" to circumstances "out there." They are not told that there should be a balance between the sympathetic nervous system (SNS) controlling the fight-or-flight reflexes and the parasympathetic nervous system (PNS) controlling repair and absorption. The spiral works like this: Increased stress leads to increased SNS dominance causing the fight-or-flight reactions and consequently decreased PNS function. This depresses the restorative, digestive, and absorptive bodily functions. A repeated high SNS state can mean dyspepsia (especially when eating strange foods on tour), Irritable Bowel Syndrome, and increased allergic and food intolerance reactions. This increased chemical stress means poor nutrition through poor absorption of improperly digested foods. This can lead to adrenal stress and/or exhaustion over time. Adrenal stress leads to physical stress through decreased accuracy of function, poor sleep, vulnerability to muscle spasm and cramps, or overuse syndromes because of practicing extra hard to overcome the decreased accuracy.

Frequently musicians have a typical sports attitude of no pain, no gain, but in contrast to sports people, there is usually no back-up trainer once they leave college and no incentive to seek help because they know that the GP may well not understand musicians' problems. There is no real reintegration into playing after injury, only to normal standards of use. GPs tend to ignore the mental/physical/chemical triad of health—how a failure in one area will produce problems in the other two areas, or that problems are cumulative because they are concerned to suppress symptoms in each area separately.

Musicians are taught predominantly as soloists one to one, yet mostly end up as team players in an orchestra, and they are expected to cope. If they do make it as soloists, they may well be expected to play "freak" repertoire (i.e., violinists often have to play Paganini Caprices written by a sufferer of Erhlers Danlos disease, which causes very lax joints). Pianists with normal hands are expected to cope with works by Rachmaninov who had Marfan's syndrome and consequently a very long back, limbs, and fingers. These are but two examples of unreasonable expectations.

This unhappy stressed state of affairs then becomes associated with performance, and fear of performance starts the stress spiral off again on its downward way. Maslow and Selye encapsulated the idea of a stress spiral where a negative thought, if repeated, causes a negative attitude, which then becomes a negative way of being. This way of being is then defended and defensive tension builds up in the muscles, causing poor posture. Poor posture as a habit squashes internal organs compromising their function and giving a predisposition to acute disease—which, untreated, becomes chronic disease.

There are two types of nervous system. The first type is considered the educated part that learns secondhand from outside experience and is used to think, reason, and judge. The second system, the innate automatic system, responds to survival needs for life. The brain combines autonomic, which automatically responds to input with the sensory systems' information to restore and accomplish homeostatic balance (i.e., health).

The body does not actually know how to get ill, it simply responds perfectly to trauma and toxicity, either by healing itself or by protecting itself from what can't be healed. Its response to unresolved negative thoughts is to act them out. It takes things literally when the mind has not solved the problem. Phrases such as "pull yourself together," "backed into a corner," "put your back into it," "shouldering burdens," "stiff upper lip," "stiff necked," "get your finger out," and "it leaves ones hands tied" are clearly mirrored in the posture and the aches and pains displayed, so that "I can't stand it" may manifest as low back pain, "can't take it in" as indigestion, "sit tight" as clenched buttocks, and "grin and bear it" as jaw joint problems.

No one explains to musicians why the neck is so important—to them it is just something you get a crick in between the head and the body. Simple examination reveals that in every neck, however thin and elegant, there are bones and muscles to support the heaviest part of the body, blood vessels to supply the brain and sense organs, nerve supply between the brain and the body, and passages for all the air, food, and drink you take in. As well as the obvious contents of the neck, several balance mechanisms coordinate between ear, eye, and neck. Just above the neck, extending between the spinal cord and the thinking part of the brain, is the brain stem. This is the oldest part of the brain, dealing with basic instinctive coordination and survival mechanisms. Finally, despite all this extraordinarily important content, the neck has to be incredibly flexible to turn the head to be able to see in all directions and to compensate for any gravitational pulls because of movement, holding an instrument, or poor posture. Alexander was right to think the neck is the primary area to free.

CIRCULATORY ASPECTS

The word *circulation* usually refers to the cardiovascular system, in which blood is pumped by the heart into every nook and cranny of our body. However, other circulatory systems are in the body. If we take a wider view of them all, we could say that we really do consist very largely of fluid of one sort or another.

There is not only the blood but also cranio-sacral fluid (CSF), which is produced in the brain and surrounds the spinal cord along its entire length. In addition, fluid is the main part of our connective tissue (a complex network pervades the whole body that includes the membranous envelopes containing and separating organs, muscles, tendons and ligaments, and the fibrous structures that strengthen the skin and enable it to adhere strongly to the structures beneath). This fluid varies from very liquid to a more gel-like consistency, depending on where it is and what structures and functions it supports. In some cases, the consistency can change according to the demands of the moment.

Intercellular fluids diffuse from blood vessels to cells to nourish them. Metabolic waste then diffuses back into capillaries and lymph vessels to be eventually eliminated. Synovial fluid is also contained in the tough capsules that surround joints. It separates and supports the bones hydraulically, helping to make free movement possible.

Let us imagine a plastic bag filled with water. Put it on the floor and it sags and flattens immediately. But tie it in a few well-chosen places—and it will gain shape and firmness and begin to counteract the flattening force of gravity. It would not be too far-fetched to regard the human form as such a water bag, with the muscles and connective tissue as a complex trussing system of cords and bands to provide support.

The opposing forces of the compressing bands and the expanding tendency of the fluid content contribute very significantly to our anti-gravity capabilities and must in part be responsible for the wonderful sense of lightness and upward flow that we can experience at the hands of an Alexander teacher, when we are centered in a tai chi sense or when we succeed at letting go of our habitual tendencies to collapse or brace ourselves.

This kind of opposition—compression versus expansion, tension versus relaxation, contraction versus stretch, up versus down, and so on—can be found in all parts and all aspects of ourselves, right down to cellular levels, and as a fundamental principle in our universe. Alexander called it *antagonistic action*; ancient Chinese wisdom speaks of Yin and Yang. It is implicit in the concept of balance and equilibrium. If the balance of forces is disturbed by excessive or insufficient tension, the body's built-in mechanisms for maintaining internal space will be compromised. The effects of this can be far-reaching, affecting not only joint freedom, but also circulation, digestion (and therefore nutrition), elimination, and even transmission of signals through the nervous system.

Peripheral nerve tissue (that is, everything in the nervous system other than in the brain and spinal cord) lies within or is surrounded by muscle. The nerves are irrigated by fluids and rely on them for nourishment and waste disposal. Muscles in proper tone supply the necessary squeegee-like pumping system for them (the heart only pumps blood). If the muscles are flaccid and underused, the pumping action is weakened. On the other hand, chronically tense muscles restrict circulation, they constrict any nerves that pass through or underneath, and they constrict capillaries that supply nutrients and extract waste products. This creates an oxygen shortage and waste build up, irritating the nerves and causing further muscular contraction. Electrical activity in the nerves will be adversely affected, bringing pain such as sciatica or facial neuralgia.

Meanwhile, on the blood flow front, constricted capillaries demand higher and higher blood pressure to make them function. They may either burst from the excess pressure or collapse from the squeezing of the overtense muscles around them. Such local devastation may cause scar tissue, permanently affecting circulation in the area, and the higher blood pressure becomes established as a norm.

You can see from these examples that there is a complex interdependence between the various systems within our body, whether mechanical, chemical, or electrical. In this constant interplay, muscle plays an arguably dominant role. Of course, we are subject also to the effects of aging, illness, and accidental injury, but clearly, the way we use our muscles must be a central issue in health and well-being.

A NEW PARADIGM OF HEALTH

What is needed is a new paradigm of health—the assertion that you are basically healthy, but you are also responsible for looking after yourself. Cardinal questions should be: What do I want and What's efficient and in balance with my body? This sort of questioning is not about oughts and shoulds—which lead to negativity, resentment, diets abandoned, victim attitudes, and hardening of the "oughteries." It's about knowing and understanding yourself well; knowing the options of your instrument together with conventional medicine, homeopathy, and food; and knowing what works for your physique—and then you can choose for yourself. This book is not about fads and fancies, it's about common sense.

First, it might be useful to review how we become ill as musicians. Just as our body posture reflects mood, so too, body conditions create mental conditions. It's often as though we had closely followed these instructions:

1. Don't pay any attention to your body. Eat plenty of junk food, drink too much, take drugs, and above all feel guilty about it.

2. If you are overstretched and overtired, keep pushing yourself to "win through." Cultivate the experience of your life as it is at the moment as meaningless and of little value. Do the things you don't like and avoid what you really want, making certain to follow everyone else's opinions and advice rather than your own.

3. Worry as often as you can; be resentful and hypercritical about your playing, filling your mind with dreadful pictures of all the times you have made mistakes and then obsess over them, wearing hairshirt, sackcloth, and ashes.

4. Cut yourself off from others, regard yourself as a pariah and contemplate death. Blame others for all your problems and avoid lasting intimate relationships; be depressed, self-pitying and angry, but do not express your feelings openly and honestly—others won't appreciate it. If at all possible, don't even know what your feelings are.

5. Shun everything that resembles humor and make sure you read articles, books, and newspapers; watch TV programs; and listen to people who reinforce the point of view that there's no hope, that the world is a dreadful place, and that you are powerless to influence your fate. Hate yourself for having destroyed your life.

6. Don't take care of yourself, get others to do it for you and then resent them for not doing a good job. Complain about your symptoms, rehearse and reinforce them by comparing notes with as many people as possible who have the same symptoms—especially if they are unhappy and embittered. Go to see lots of doctors. Run from one to another, spend half your days in waiting rooms and get lots of conflicting opinions and lots of experimental drugs, then start one program after another without sticking to any.

You might laugh—but have a look at yourself and see how much is true! What can you do that is plain, simple, and safe? Consider the contents of chapter 2.

REFERENCES

Barlow, W. *The Alexander Principle*. London: Arrow Books Ltd., 1973.
Beighton, P. *The Ehlers-Danlos Syndrome*. London: William Heinneman Medical Books, 1990.

Chaitow, L. *Osteopathy*. New York: Harper Collins, 1974.

Connelly, D. *Traditional Acupuncture: The Law of the Five Elements*. Laurel, Md.: Center for Traditional Acupuncture Inc., 1979.

Fry, H. Overuse Syndrome in Musicians: Prevention and Management. *The Lancet* (September 27, 1986): 728–731.

Goodheart, G. (Ed.). *The Acceptance of Applied Kinesiology (A short monograph of articles)*. Geneva, Ohio: Author, 1964–1979.

Goodheart, G., and W. Schmitt. *Applied Kinesiology*. Grosse Pointe Woods, Mich.

Lambert, C. Clinical Review. Hand and Upper Limb Problems of Instrumental Musicians. *British Journal of Rheumatology* 31 (1992): 265–271.

La Tourelle, M., and A. Courtenay. *Thorson's Introductory Guide to Kinesiology*. London: Thorsons, Harper Collins, 1992.

Lederman, R. Neuro-Muscular Problems in the Performing Arts. AAEM Mimeograph 43 *Muscle and Nerve* (June 1994).

Lederman, R. Peripheral Nerve Disorders in Instrumentalists. *American Neurological Association Journal of Occupational Health and Safety* 26 (November 1989): 640–646.

Mandel, S. Overuse Syndrome in Musicians. *Post Graduate Medicine* 88, no. 2 (1990).

Moulton, B., and S. Spense. Site-Specific Muscular Hyperactivity in Musicians with Occupational Upper Limb Pain. *Behavioural Res. Ther.* 30, no. 4 (1991): 375–386.

Norris, R. *The Musician's Survival Manual: A Guide to Preventing and Treating Injuries in Instrumentalists*. St Louis, Mo.: International Conference of Symphony and Orchestral Musicians, 1993.

Owen, E. Instrumental Musicians and Repetition Strain Injuries. *Journal of Occupational Health and Safety* 1 (1985): 135–139

Parmley, W. The Decline of the Doctor-Patient Relationship. *Journal of the American College of Cardiology* 26, no. 1 (July 1995): 287–288.

Spaulding, C. Before Pathology. *Medical Problems for Performing Artists* (December 1998): 135–139.

Thie, J. *Touch for Health*. Marina del Rey, Calif.: DeVorss & Co., 1979.

Winspur, I. The Professional Musician and the Hand Surgeon. *Performing Arts Medicine News* 13, no. 3 (Autumn 1995).

2

Growth and Development

It is essential to understand some general anatomy and physiology—not in medical terminology, but in plain English. It seems sensible to start with the basic frame of the body—the skeletal system—before discussing muscles.

GROWTH AND DEVELOPMENT

1. In the beginning, you, the fetus, were just a collection of rapidly dividing cells that had no obvious form.
2. At some point early on, the fetus decided that there should be a head end and a tail end, so there was a very basic orientation.
3. Your body gained a shape by means of differentiating the contents of the soup of chemicals in each cell. The cells with more calcium migrated together into cartilaginous shapes, to provide stiffening, and then turned into protective shields for the vulnerable organs and the spinal cord. They act as spacers to give the fetus a more definite shape and later provide anchorage for muscles.
4. However, this meant that the rest of the cells outside the cartilage were bereft of contact with the important bits, so fibers from the spinal cord grew through the calcified protection, extended themselves, and eventually became nerves.

17

5. The more calcium there is in a collection of cells, the stiffer the
   body tissues they make up tend to be, so organ cells have compar-
   atively little calcium; muscles and tendons have a bit more, ligaments more still, with bones having the most.
6. The body shifts calcium around throughout your life. This is why
   babies' bones are still very soft, children get "green stick" frac-
   tures (where the bone splits rather than breaks), and the elderly
   get extra calcium deposits. It supports and protects against the
   wear and tear occurring during life. But too much sedimentation
   can cause various forms of arthritis.
7. Too much flexibility in a joint causes the body to buttress it with
   extra bone outside as the softer cartilage inside wears, causing
   osteoarthritis. Too little calcium, and the bone softens and crum-
   bles and may cause early gum and tooth decay, and in later life, it
   may cause osteoporosis.

OSSIFICATION AGES

Although bones are the spacers that give the body shape, they grow and
harden at different rates. In general, long bones such as the shinbone
(tibia) are formed in several parts (a shaft and end parts, with a growing
plate between). The parts join up and harden fully at puberty.

Because they are soft while growing, their final shape may be depen-
dent upon the pull of the muscles attached to them. For example, a boy
who plays too much football at too young an age will overdevelop his
thigh muscles, which are attached to the growing point of the shin bone
just below the knee, and pull them out of shape (Osgood Schlatters disease), giving rise to mirth in "knobbly knees" competitions.

Most bones are not solid. They have a hard outer shell, but a honey-
comb interior that is arranged along the weight or stress lines of the
bone. The collarbone is visible on x-ray at birth because it contains
enough calcium. The wristbones are not visible but can be seen gradually as they gain more calcium. By the age of seven or eight years all
the wrist bones are visible. In the fingers, the cartilage parts only fully
join up to form three bones by the age of twenty. The forearm bone on
the thumb side can be seen at the age of five and on the little finger side
at ten.

The upper arm formative bones become one at age fourteen, and all arm bones join fully into whole bones by twenty. The shoulder blades and rib parts join fully between the ages of fifteen and twenty, so front ribs may get squashed in by holding the violin/viola too low on the chest. This can also have the effect of squashing the left lung and affecting blood and nerve supply to the left hand.

The breastbone parts may not join fully until age twenty-five. It is not uncommon for the lowest part of the breastbone to remain cartilaginous for life and it can be bent by leaning on a cello. Bones still have considerable plasticity and a tough flexibility but vulnerability at the time most children start to learn an instrument. This means the bones can be pulled out of shape if the instrument is too large too soon. Most children copy the posture and movement patterns of their parents or significant other adult such as their instrumental teacher, whether or not the adult's build and physique is the same as theirs. The plasticity of their young bones means they are thus very vulnerable especially if they start to play very young. This fact is well known in the sports and dance worlds but seems to have escaped the music world entirely. Posture and "use" in the Alexander sense are extremely important for health in later life.

JOINTS

Between the bones are joints of different types this s. *Fibrous and cartilaginous* joints provide pliability but only microscopically small movement. There are fibrous joints in the skull, between the forearm bones, and in your jaw, which hold in your teeth. There are cartilaginous joints in the growing plates of bones between the first ribs and the breastbone, and there are discs of fibrous cartilage between each vertebra. These joints move minimally, having very little space in the joint that allows movement.

All the other main joints have cavities, thus there is more room and more movement. There are gliding movements between all the wristbones, the breastbone, and collarbones and between the collarbones and shoulder blades. The elbows and fingers exemplify hinge joints, allowing large angular movement. The two forearm bones form a pivot joint just below the elbow, allowing you to turn your hand palm up or palm down. The big ball-and-socket joint in the hip transmits the entire upper body weight, but in the shoulders, mobility takes precedence over weight bearing, and the socket is as small and flat as the bowl of a tea-spoon.

The thumb has a saddle joint that allows both freedom of movement to play scales on a keyboard, and allows for a powerful grip. The jaw joint has two cavities, which allows both opening/closing and forward/back-ward movements, enabling controlled holding of mouthpieces or letting out Wagnerian arias.

These cavity joints contain a tough dislocation-resistant outer capsule and antifriction fluid. The knees, jaw, and collar/breastbone joints also contain extra cartilages, which act as shock absorbers. Specialized nerve endings within and around the joint prevent damage by telling the brain where the joint is, both in space and in relation to other joints.

Each joint has an optimum range of movement, and damage occurs when it is constantly pushed beyond normal ranges, as in poor posture or faulty instrumental technique. Since many musicians have above-average flexibility in their joints, it would be useful to know the normal range of motion (according to Hoppenfeld) (see the following chart):

Neck	Flexion	45°
	Extension	90°
	Lateral bending	45° +45°
	Rotation	90° +90°
Shoulder	Abduction	180°
	Adduction	45°
	Flexion	90°
	Extension	45°
	Internal rotation	55°
	External rotation	40–45°
Elbow	Flexion	135–150°
	Extension	0–5°
	Supination	90°
	Pronation	90°
Wrist	Flexion	80°
	Extension	70°

	Ulnar deviation	30°
	Radial deviation	20°
Fingers	Flexion	90°
	Extension	30–40°
	Abduction	20°
	Adduction	0°
Thumb	Palmar abduction	70°
	Dorsal adduction	0°
	Flexion	45°
	Extension	45°

Girls tend to mature before boys. It's obvious that most women have larger hips than most men and that most men have broader shoulders than most women. However, there are other minor differences, not usually mentioned, which can have a bearing on playing an instrument. Women have narrower wrists and are therefore more prone to wrist problems such as repetitive strain injury (RSI or OOS). Men have less flexible elbows and cannot usually put both palms and elbows together when the arms are stretched straight out. This means they are more liable to tennis and golfer's elbow due to the twist so often required to play.

Other minor anomalies can also cause problems. Within the hand, the ligaments binding the fingers together are variable. The pattern and degree is frequently hereditary. The well-known binding of the little and ring fingers together means that the ring finger cannot be lifted very far without also raising the little finger. Schumann tried to rectify this with disastrous results. There are other less well-known patterns such as that which occurs when the thumb is bent, the last joint of the index finger also bends slightly. Extending or flexing the wrist to its maximum brings the finger ends closer together, restricting stretch. This is more marked in some people than in others. Certainly coordination will be easier for those who have a "square" hand with fingers of nearly similar length than for those with a more pointed hand shape. The brain has to make more calculations subconsciously to get good coordination with the more uneven finger lengths.

And what moves the joints? Muscles!

MUSCLES

Muscles need demystification for musicians (see figures 2.1 through 2.5). They use those muscles like sportsmen, and although their performing lives last much longer, they have less of an idea how muscles work than most serious sports people. Let us go through the salient facts.

Muscles are large (antigravitational) and small (for flexibility, dexterity, and fine movement). Latin names are logical, describing the muscles shape (trapezius), its function (flexor), and its place: radialis, that is, it is found running from the wristbones along the bone on the thumb (radial) side of the forearm, so flexor carpi radialis flexes the wristbones on the thumb side against the forearm. Size gives clues, too—the term "medius" (middle sized) means there will also be a "maximus" and a "minimus."

Muscles are formed from multiple fiber bundles, wrapped in retaining tissues like sausage skins. The ends of these "sausage skin" tissues fuse, forming tendons that attach the muscle to bone. Muscles contract actively and relax passively like a ratchet in your car handbrake. Their main electrochemical fuel is a combination of a sugar derivative and oxygen, which are supplied by the blood (and which also clears the waste products). The only difference between your muscles and those of an Olympic athlete is not the number of muscle fibers but the throughput—the speed of food supply and clearance of waste products.

Muscles of similar function are arranged in groups: for instance, those that straighten the elbow are on the back of the arm and those that flex it are attached to the front. Their "origin" is found on the bone you wish to keep still. And the other end—the "insertion"—is attached to the bone you wish to move by contracting the muscle like a lever.

Several sorts of nerve endings are embedded within muscles, giving the brain feedback by measuring their length, the amount of contraction against gravity, the speed of contraction, and relative position in space.

Muscles never work alone. Other similar functioning or synergistic muscles work to back up, counterbalance, and stabilize the bone to which the main muscle you intend to use is attached. For example, the deltoid muscle stabilizes the upper arm so that the biceps can bend and also stabilize the elbow; the wrist and fingers can then reach the keyboard to play.

Because each muscle has only one function—to contract—it needs

Anterior Muscles

Superficial Muscles   *Deep Muscles*

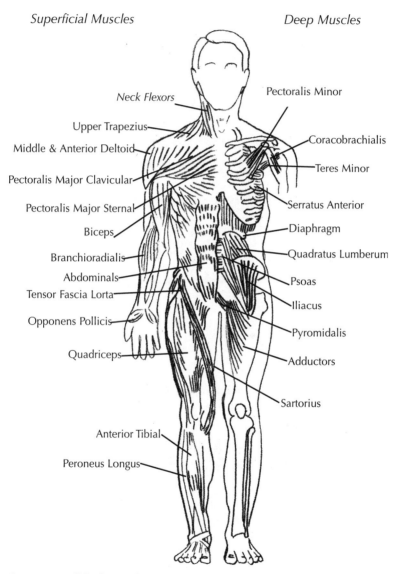

Neck Flexors

Upper Trapezius

Middle & Anterior Deltoid

Pectoralis Major Clavicular

Pectoralis Major Sternal

Biceps

Branchioradialis

Abdominals

Tensor Fascia Lorta

Opponens Pollicis

Quadriceps

Anterior Tibial

Peroneus Longus

Pectoralis Minor

Coracobrachialis

Teres Minor

Serratus Anterior

Diaphragm

Quadratus Lumberum

Psoas

Iliacus

Pyromidalis

Adductors

Sartorius

Figure 2.1   Full body muscles.

Posterior Muscles

Superficial Muscles   *Deep Muscles*

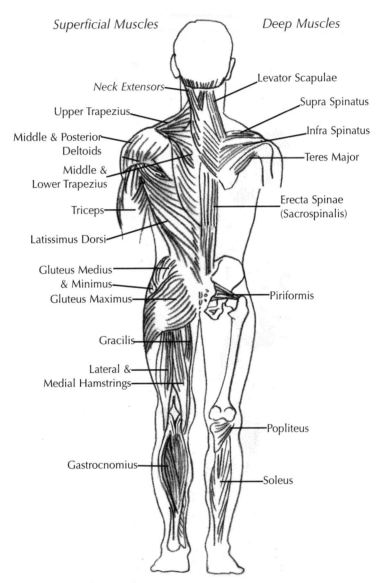

Neck Extensors

Upper Trapezius

Middle & Posterior
Deltoids

Middle &
Lower Trapezius

Triceps

Latissimus Dorsi

Gluteus Medius
& Minimus
Gluteus Maximus

Gracilis

Lateral &
Medial Hamstrings

Gastrocnomius

Levator Scapulae

Supra Spinatus

Infra Spinatus

Teres Major

Erecta Spinae
(Sacrospinalis)

Piriformis

Popliteus

Soleus

Figure 2.2   Posterior muscles.

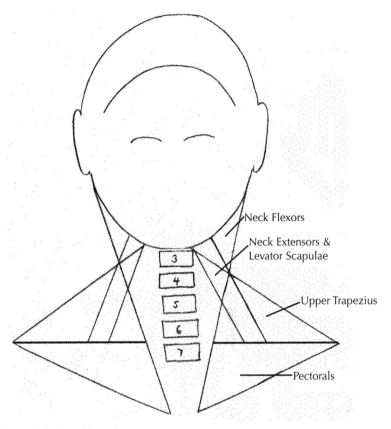

Figure 2.3   Head muscle ring.

an antagonist to pull against it, inhibiting the original muscle contraction and causing passive relaxation. The balance and coordination between all these muscles are vital and their primary function. Acting as levers to pull on bones is secondary to these, because without coordination, you would have no balance to stand up against gravity.

So what is the ideal muscle tone? Certainly not no tone! It is the balance between power and coordination, relaxation and contraction that is most efficient, economic, and appropriate to the task at hand, and contraction is released when no longer needed.

In the body as a whole, there should not be a feeling of rigid support,

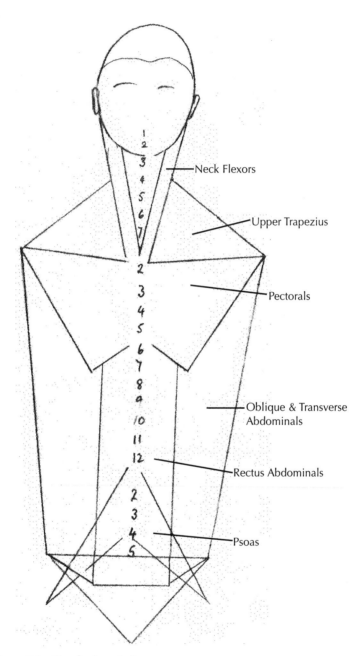

Figure 2.4 Muscle rig. anterior.

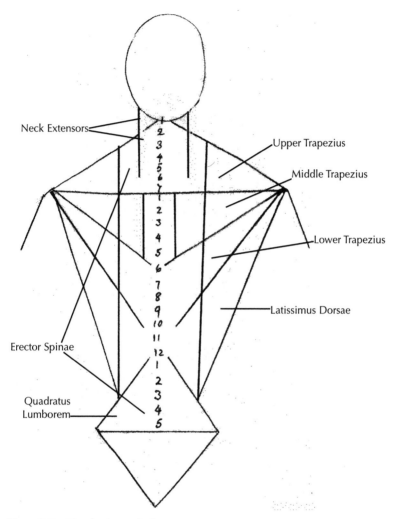

Figure 2.5   Muscle rig. posterior.

but a dynamic center of balance supporting and giving freedom of movement in any direction—the "centered" feeling as described in martial arts. Sway of the whole body may be legitimate as a follow-through after a strong action, but it should never be "stuck on" to produce theatrical effect. A common misuse of sway in violinists is to move the body and instrument together instead of moving the bow. This keeps the body dynamic but seems rather uneconomic!

Each muscle has its natural range of contraction and relaxation. It may refuse to function for many reasons. It may feel weak because it cannot pull against antagonists that are not letting go, or because it is taxed beyond its strength. It may also be slack because it is starved of blood and nerve supply due to impingement by poor posture or spinal misalignments. No amount of weightlifting will strengthen a muscle that has "switched off" protectively any more than a car will start if you have plenty of fuel but no battery.

Muscles also respond to anxiety (see chapter 10). Unresolved emotional problems result in defensive posture such as hunched shoulders and clenched buttocks. This is also true for the muscles used in breathing.

BREATHING

You can live for a month without food, three or so days without water, but no more than a few minutes without air. Because it is essential to life, normal breathing is done almost as a reflex by muscles. They expand the chest space by lowering the diaphragm, by widening the spaces between ribs, and by raising the breastbone and upper ribs. This lowers the pressure inside, causing fresh air to rush into the lungs— inhalation. To contract the chest space, the muscles relax, mainly with gravity, which causes exhalation, pushing the stale air out.

Wind and brass players and singers are taught about breathing, but other instrumentalists are not. Since it is associated with emotion, many string players and pianists hold on with everything including their breathing when stressed by playing a difficult passage, because it gives a seeming sense of security. Worse, upper strings frequently grip their instrument as it sags, clamping the shoulder rest against the upper chest, squashing down and in, affecting the left lung and blood and nerve supply to the left arm and hand. Cellists and bass players also have this problem when leaning over their instrument to play in high positions. The problem is not that this happens, so much as that normal positions are not reassumed after the difficult passage is over, so such a position gradually becomes the norm.

Exploration 1

1. Breathe out, sag, hollow your chest, and round your shoulders. Imagine it is the end of the day of very long and exceedingly boring rehearsals. Keeping this position, take a deep breath and note how much air you can take in. Sit back up and breathe normally.

2. Now place your hands on your abdomen and breathe out, squashing in with your hands. When you now breathe in, note how your hands are pushed outward as the diaphragm lowers in the abdominal cavity. Do this and register the relationship between "breathe in" and "tummy out." (Note Bene: So often in a crowded space people are asked to breathe in to make more room, when what is meant is pull your tummy in!) Now breathe normally.

3. Place your hands on the sides of your ribs. Breathe out and push your ribs in. As you breathe in again, note how your hands are pushed out sideways and backward. The ribs work like a series of bucket handles, fixed at both ends but able to rise and fall at the middle of the arc.

4. Now place your hands on your breastbone at the base of your throat. Press down as you breathe out. Breathe in and note how it rises up. There is far less movement here than in the ribs or abdomen.

5. At no point in all of this should your shoulders rise and fall as you breathe. If they do, then you are using the emergency auxiliary breathing muscles used when the normal ones are restricted in some way as by people with respiratory disease such as emphysema. Normal breathing is not an effortful activity!

6. Now sit in a good relaxed but alert position and breathe out all the air you can. In swift succession, breathe in from the abdomen, ribs, and breastbone areas. Notice how you can now take in at least twice as much air as when you sagged. This is not the way you breathe normally, but it does enlarge your ideas about your capacity and how you can interfere with it out of sheer tiredness

at the end of the day without even realizing it.

Often with stress your breathing can become fast and shallow. When associated with playing over many hours a day, this shallow breathing may become the normal mode of breathing for you. Alexander technique, yoga, and Pilates will all help to reeducate you, so that your brain is not starved of oxygen when it most needs it in performance, but you really need to put breathing marks in when studying new repertoire too (see chapter 3). Proceed gently. If you suddenly and repeatedly breathe too much oxygen in, it upsets the balance with carbon dioxide in the brain and may cause hyperventilation symptoms (giddiness and tingling in the fingers). If this happens, grab a small paper bag, fit it around your mouth so no air escapes and breathe in and out several times to restore normal oxygen levels. If you have a tendency toward asthma, breathing through a straw helps control diaphragm spasm.

Breathing Misconceptions

Wind players and singers work with breath all the time and will know when their breathing is not working well, but some possible causes of malfunction may not be obvious to them. They too may have acquired breathing habits that may not be the best for their well-being as a whole. They will have received all sorts of advice, some of it good, some perhaps not so good, which they interpret according to their own conceptions of what is being asked of them. A simple, but common example is the instruction to "take a deep breath." Most people assume that if you are going to talk about improving breathing, then you need to focus on breathing in. They also assume that breathing in requires effort, and when they deliberately breathe deeply, they will stiffen the neck, pull the head back, raise the shoulders and puff out the chest, tighten the low back and legs before breathing in, then suck air in with an audible gasping sound. All this tightening actually hampers the attempt to increase the internal volume of the chest cavity and the lungs.

Good breathing happens when the conditions are right. It is a reflex process depending on good posture of the body, on the absence of inappropriate tension, and on a mental attitude that includes calm, clear understanding of what is required and what is not. Breathing in is often not the problem, so much as the collapsing or stiffening and bracing when breathing out. If we can avoid or at least reduce the amount of disturbance to our posture and balance when we breathe out, breathing in will take care of itself.

Exploration 2

Lie on the floor, eyes open, with two to three paperback books under your head and your knees up (in the Alexander position). Allow the floor to support you, neither pressing into it nor lifting away from it. Throughout this exploration, monitor that you do not stiffen your neck or back (concentrate on keeping them soft and free to move in any direction). Become aware of the airflow through your nostrils. Feel it coming and going, but in this exploration, do not get involved in whether your ribs are moving; just be aware that if you fix them, you prevent them from moving.

Decide that in a moment you are going to make an out-breath a little bit longer. Wait a little before you do it, however, and without interfering with the natural breathing that is already taking place, remind yourself and make sure that your neck is free and your torso is long and wide and all of you is supported on the floor. Then make that slightly long out-breath, and if you don't prevent it, air will come back into your lungs spontaneously and a little more deeply than before. If that happens, you have learned two things: Breathing happens by itself (if it is not interfered with) and how much air you take in depends on how much you breathed out, and your body "use" (an Alexander term).

If you are a wind player, you may be thinking, "That's all very well, but if I am going to play a long phrase, I've got to take a lot of air in, and that must require effort." Alexander teachers find it fascinating to watch wind players' growing appreciation of how, when they can maintain the free poise of head, neck, and spine before and during playing, more air seems to be available. It is a gradual process and takes time and experience to acquire the spontaneous rapid recoil of inspiration needed in short breaks between phrases.

If you play an instrument that does not have to be blown, the subject of breathing may never have arisen in your studies. You may be unaware that you hold your breath; and if you do, it will reflect inappropriate postural tension. Becoming aware of your breathing habits and learning to reduce tension will go hand in hand.

Chapter 2

NERVOUS SYSTEM DEVELOPMENT
AND REFLEXES

The human newborn does not have a fully developed nervous system. As the embryo develops, neural connections are laid down that evoke reflex or automatic responses. In the beginning, these are not differentiated according to specific conditions or purposes; they just happen. Some are already linked to specific stimuli such as skin contact (for example, if the side of the face of a baby is stimulated, the head will turn to that side). The processes for laying down the "wiring" for all the responses necessary for all the skills of movement and speech are not complete until the end of the third year of life. How these processes happen throws light on how movement skills are acquired, and for this reason, some understanding of them is important in instrument teaching.

Out of the melee of random reflexes displayed by the newborn, combinations of movement satisfy specific needs (e.g., to reach out and grasp an object). For this to happen, all the inappropriate movements have to be inhibited—that is, all the signals firing unwanted muscular contractions have to be switched off, leaving appropriate activity that results in the arm being extended. Note that muscular activity was already present. It is a matter of deselecting what is not useful. The movement now gradually becomes a skilled response stimulated by intention. The baby's eyes become interested in the object, the head turns to help vision, and as the head turns, the arm extends. Now the baby needs to get the object into the mouth for further exploration, so more inhibitory control has to be developed to allow the arm to bend while the head is turned toward it. When this new reflex comes into play, it involves inhibition of the previous one without removing the choice, since ultimately both responses must be available.

There are four main points here:

1. Learning a skill is mostly a question of what *not* to do, refinement, and memory.
2. In nature, learning arises from a need to explore the environment.
3. In the reflexes of posture, it seems possible to refine the nerve circuits even after maturity.
4. There are frequently minor hiccups in the process of infant devel-

opment. Each successive phase of development involves the satisfactory completion of the preceding stage, but complete or not, nature moves on. If there are residual responses in the system still uninhibited from the previous phase, further development continues but there may now be conflict in the nervous system that may not show up unless there is a significant cluster of such problems. A residual reflex is a possible source of tension conflict. For example, in a violinist, if there is still a slight tendency for the arm to straighten when you turn your head to the left, you have to exert extra effort to overcome this and perform the many bent arm movements so necessary for the left arm in violin playing.

Development of mature movement patterns depends on the integration where automatic (reflex) responses comply appropriately and economically with conscious decision making. How well they do this seems to depend on a variety of factors. Perhaps up to 50 percent of this developmental potential is genetically determined. Childhood environmental influences could include bonding with parents and permission and opportunity to explore. However, lack of these, an accident at birth, or too early an encouragement to sit or walk can interfere with this development.

Unsatisfactory integration of reflexes causes interference with movement learning. Babies who miss out the creeping stage and go from shuffling on their bottoms to walking perform poorly in situations that challenge balance. Emotional states have a constant influence over learning. A hostile negative critical environment makes us afraid to explore, for fear of getting it wrong. If our self-esteem is eroded by criticism, we are likely to be tense, with stiffened joints, a restricted breathing rhythm, and clumsy movements. The internal messages are "Go, but don't go in case it's wrong." Posturally we will be out of balance, and movement learning and performance will suffer. The child presenting for music lessons will exhibit the sum total of all such influences and experiences, and the ability to learn the complex movement patterns and fine control of instrumental playing will be either helped or hindered by them. Alexander technique, Feldenkreis work, martial arts, and other therapies whether psychologically or physiologically orientated certainly support this view.

THE AXES OF MOVEMENT

There are three main axes around which the body moves. The X-axis is exemplified by facing front and side bending. The Y-axis is rotation of the upper part of the body against the stable lower part, and the Z-axis is the forward and backward movement as shown by bending at the knees, hips, waist, or head.

Most damage happens to the spine when we combine X- or Z-axes with Y, when carrying a heavy weight. The amount the spine can turn in any one area depends on the shape of the vertebrae and how fixed they are by proximity to other body structures. The head restricts the movement of the top of the neck. The spine in the upper back area is partly held by the ribs, and the bottom of the spine is held by the pelvis. This means that the midneck is the most flexible area of all, followed by the mid–lower back. It also means these areas have the smallest support facets or flanges on the vertebrae and are the most vulnerable. The large low back vertebrae are built for bearing the weight of the whole upper body and for forward and backward flexibility rather than twisting, so each lumbar vertebra has extra facets for strength that stop twisting but allow a small amount of side bending. This is why twisting and lifting at the same time so often causes grief.

Playing a "one-sided" instrument (violin, flute) that exaggerates the Y-axis, sitting with more weight on one side than the other (piano, cello), which exaggerates the X-axis, or standing to play wearing high heels or sitting on a sloping backed chair (Z-axis) are common causes of continuous unequal muscle tension, upsetting the coordination of all the others that work with it in an integrated way. Remember, the body tries to compensate by using other muscles to help, and when these complain, using others even further afield. Acute tension can be undone by doing mirror image stretches (see the section "Cool Down" in chapter 3), but left to itself, compensation easily becomes a chronic uneconomic habit needing Alexander technique lessons to unlearn.

It is worth remembering that just as with your body, every instrument also has three axes around which it can be moved. We are taught how to "hold" our instrument and many of us never cease doing so, especially if it is valuable; we hold on for dear life! The relationship between you and your instrument should be dynamic and supporting, moving or changing slightly according to the needs of playing at that moment. Yet when we have a difficult passage to play, that is when we grip tightly, trying hard with every part of our being and getting horribly in our own way. It is utterly appropriate to temporally turn the instrument slightly to accommodate a long passage on the highest or lowest string. You are then effectively making the instrument fit you, rather than twisting and damaging yourself to fit the instrument.

FOUR TYPES OF POSTURE

When people think of good posture, they frequently think in terms of figure 2.6, and they stand in what they imagine is a quasi-military, stiff posture with "chin up and shoulders back."

However, human beings were born to move! Posture is a lifelong sport with gravity and your instrument. Within the parameters of reflexes, balance, equilibrium, voluntary and involuntary muscle use, and posture described earlier, when speaking of instrumental playing, you might also say there are four types of posture:

1. *General posture,* which includes how you bend down to lift toddlers, how you talk to or teach people shorter than you, and how you get off of a sofa and cope with car, train, and plane seating. It also includes equalizing and balancing the one-sided way you stand, when you catch yourself standing with more weight on one leg than the other in the supermarket line, when you shave in a mirror that's too low, when you vacuum the floor, rake the lawn, or when you put the groceries in the car trunk.

2. *Environmental posture* is dictated by your chair when you perform, the sloping stage, your desk partner in the orchestra, the conductor's visibility, and your high heels (if you wear them to perform).

3. *Instrumental posture,* which you mostly only adopt when playing, is dictated by the shape and size of the instrument relative to your body proportions. Playing a one-sided instrument (violin, flute) and sitting with more weight on one buttock than the other (piano, cello) or with one foot up on a stool (guitar) distorts sitting posture, made worse by sitting on a sloping back chair. Standing posture can be distorted by playing or singing wearing high-heeled

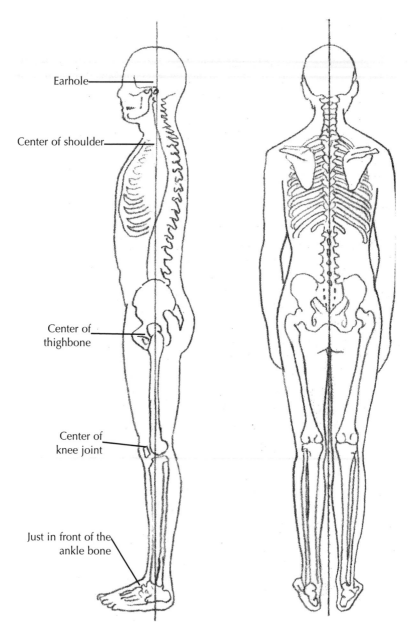

Earhole

Center of shoulder

Center of thighbone

Center of knee joint

Just in front of the ankle bone

Figure 2.6   Plumbline posture.

shoes or constantly standing with more weight on one leg than the other. In each case, there is continuous unequal muscle tension, upsetting the coordination of all the other muscles that work with it. The body tries to compensate by using other muscles to help, and when these complain, by using others yet further afield to help. This compensation easily becomes a chronic uneconomic habit that needs Alexander lessons to become aware of the pattern and unlearn it. The healing process is often not unlike un-peeling an onion; the last involved muscle is the one complained of first and heals first as it is sorted out. The previous one then shouts for attention, and as it is given attention, then the one before that shows up, until the basic cause of imbalance or misuse is sorted out.

4. *Specific technique posture* is where you may be continuously reaching for a wide stretch in a piece of music you are practising, as in fingered octaves, playing at the top of a string or large chords. This kind of unusual posture requires equal and opposite cool-down stretching as soon as you can when you have finished, to return the muscles to their normal state (see chapter 3).

EQUILIBRIUM

Although posture is in itself a lifelong sport, we take equilibrium for granted. It is so inherent in our activity that we do not notice it until it is threatened, by the fear of falling, by emotional anxieties, or by mental struggle. But the problems posed by that gigantic evolutionary step, in which we came to balance a vertical spine on two legs, are always with us. The most basic problem is to support ourselves against the constant influence of gravity, and yet be free to move, which potentially threatens our stability. If the support mechanism is not working well, we stiffen to make up for it, and movement with compressed joints and shortened muscles ultimately leads to wear and tear.

We have sophisticated systems to maintain balance. You can get an impression of their activity by making it difficult for such systems to function.

Exploration 3

Try standing on a cushion. It's a little tricky, but no great problem. Now try standing on one leg on the cushion. More difficult? Now clasp your hands behind your back, shut your eyes, and tilt your head to one side. This is probably threatening your balance quite seriously! Why?

First, by depriving your feet of the firm resistance of the floor, you have partially disabled some of the nerve receptors in the muscles, tendons, joints, and skin, which sense gravity as weight and pressure and which rely on a firm surface to function properly. Similar effects happen when you deprive your "seat bones" of the firm resistance they need for balancing when you sit in a soft, so-called easy chair.

Second, by closing your eyes you cut out the strong involvement of the visual system in sensing the positioning in space. When our eyes are engaged for long periods, peering at music or a screen, our other balancing systems need to work extremely well to compensate. If they don't we will inevitably stiffen or slump. Indeed the very way in which we habitually use our eyes may, over the years, have come to involve a good deal of stiffening in the neck and facial muscles and probably elsewhere.

Third, tilting your head confuses the vestibular, or inner ear, balancing system. With eyes shut and head tilted, your brain doesn't have a clear idea where horizontal and vertical are, and it needs that information to keep you from falling.

Fourth, by clasping your hands behind your back you stopped your arms from coming to the rescue as a backup for the balancing operation. It is a fundamental consideration for instrumentalists that our arms have several different functions. They can act as supports when needed (try the exploration again, but have the cushion where you can reach out and touch a wall with your fingers), or they can be used as counterweights. If the body is not well-balanced, the arms will try to help out with balance. (In the exploration, what do your arms want to do if you don't clasp them behind your back?) If your balance is not good when playing, the arms may be wanting to help, but because they cannot be released from their job with the instrument, a conflict arises, the arms tend to stiffen, and you lose the freedom and flexibility needed for playing well. Another problem with the arms arises because the position of the arms for playing an instrument does itself threaten balance.

THE BODY SUPPORT SYSTEM

The mechanical process of equilibrium involves the complex interactions of the skeletal structure, the muscles, and connective tissue (tendons, ligaments, and fascia). The center of activity is the spine and the deep muscles lying close to it, which as we shall see, work reflexively. The spine behaves as a sort of spring, and some impression of what this means can be gained from the following exploration.

Exploration 4

Take a fairly long thin piece of dowelling, garden cane, or any flexible rod. Rest one end on a surface and push on the other end to create a single curve. You will feel a certain amount of elasticity, but not much resistance to your attempts to bend it further. If you bend it too much the stick will begin to lose its elasticity, and perhaps eventually break.

Now manipulate the stick (you may need help) so that there is a double curve. It will now be far more resistant, although it still absorbs some of the stress you are putting on it by bending more when you increase the pressure. At the same time it pushes up against your hand, trying to straighten. So long as you prevent it from uncurving completely, but don't on the other hand bend it too much (so as to weaken the spring effect), it will remain a sort of energy store, able to absorb shock by yielding, but also to give a powerful resistance to a certain amount of downward force.

This model illustrates the two opposing forces, one downward, one upward, which are fundamental in human equilibrium. Downward force is a combination of gravity and of activity of those muscles that tend to pull the head toward the feet. There is also elastic resistance from connective tissue to the upward components. (Connective tissues are elastic supporting tissues within the body such as surrounding and separating one muscle from another or around and anchoring internal organs.) The upward force is a combination of up-thrust from the ground, the multiple curvature of the spine storing energy, and the activity of those muscles that tend to raise the spine and straighten the joints, taking the head away from the feet.

The up-thrust from the ground is the result of gravity pulling us against the ground. According to Newtonian laws of motion, "Every action has an equal and opposite reaction," and it seems reasonable to suggest that when your weight is conveyed through the bones of your feet to the ground (or, if you are sitting, through your "seat bones" to the chair), there is a corresponding up-thrust, sometimes referred to as a support force, acting upward through the bones. The more effectively you can "stack" the rest of your skeleton vertically above the feet (or seat bones), the more you can make use of this up-thrust to reduce muscular effort and strain on joints, tendons, and ligaments.

The multiple curves of the spine act to increase the up-thrust effect as the spine continually tries to un-curve but is restrained by muscles and connective tissue, just as the curves of the stick were maintained by your hand in the above exploration. The mechanisms of posture are designed to maintain this dynamic "energy-store" effect. When they are working well, there is a balance between the downward and upward forces described.

To control and maintain equilibrium, there must be some continual monitoring to inform the brain how we are doing. In the exploration with the cushion, we noticed the function of the eyes, of the sensory equipment in the joints, muscles and tendons, and of the inner-ear balancing equipment.

The information gathered by all this marvelous equipment is processed by the nervous system, which works constantly to maintain balance, anticipating any threat to it or correcting it if it has already been threatened. All this information gathering and processing is largely unconscious; we are aware of only a little of it until it goes wrong.

WHY IT GOES WRONG

The mechanisms of balance and support in human beings are delicate and easily interfered with. This interference may have any one or a combination of the following causes:

1. Poor habits of general "use." This refers to a concept in the Alexander technique. It includes all the processes, mental and physical, which make up the way in which we habitually manage our balance and poise in any activity.
2. Emotional states.

3. External factors—poor or unsuitable furniture; bad working conditions.
4. Tiredness, illness, or poor nutrition.

Although we cannot be conscious of the mechanisms of balance, we can become aware of how we react to these influences, and in doing so give ourselves the possibility of changing either the circumstance or our reaction to it. We can't do much about the effects of illness, of course, but it is possible to cope better with poor chairs. Poor habits of use can be changed, although slowly and with the investment of a lot of attention. This is an area in which the Alexander technique works best. Emotional states are often difficult to cope with, but we can become skillful in this area, through talking or reading, or perhaps with the help of a therapist or counselor to discover the cause of the emotional state.

It is in the nature of these sorts of habit that we have no awareness of them. We suffer, Alexander suggested, from "unreliable sensory appreciation," which means that we don't have an accurate register of feeling of what we are doing. Posture may slowly deteriorate, for example, but feel quite normal and "natural" to us because we have become used to it. Becoming aware of our habits of "misuse" is the starting point for working at changing them.

It is certain that the more we continue with unsatisfactory habits of equilibrium, the more effort and compensatory muscle tension we will apply, with the resultant threat to our health—the state of our joints, breathing, circulation, digestion, and mental equilibrium, too. Mind and body influence each other, as more and more experts in various fields are beginning to realize. Alexander even considered the separation of mind and body to be a false distinction. Instead, he saw it as a continuum in which too much focus on one area threatens the integrated working of the whole. We like to think that we can train "the body" or concentrate "the mind," but if our mental attitude is wrong, physical training can be detrimental. If we indulge in excessive mental activity in a state of physical collapse or imbalance, our general health will be impaired, threatening our ability to continue to work.

Ultimately the only person who can change this state of affairs is one's self. It is not a responsibility that can be handed over to someone else. The expert may be able to help in the process of becoming aware, and to teach techniques for change. Beyond that, it is up to the individual to work away at it!

Postural Reflexes

What do we mean by "posture"? The word is colored by popular misconception. It has strayed from physiology into areas of moral rectitude and discipline. To most of us it carries overtones of stiff, puppetlike behavior, conjuring up inner parental voices barking out preremptory commands: "Sit up straight," "Pull yourself together," "Head up and shoulders back," "Stand straight when I am talking to you." In other words do it "right," but according to *them* rather than you. Many of us have, on the one hand, an idea that having good posture or a straight back is probably good for us, and on the other hand, some part of us perhaps rebels against being controlled by inner voices and the external authorities they represent.

Perhaps we decide every now and then to turn over a new leaf, to improve our posture and so put an end to all that slumping about. But how? All we have to fall back on are those inner voices. What they tell us is that we have to do something: "Make an effort, try your hardest!" So we set about it and after a few minutes, shoulders and back tire and begin to ache. Perhaps we persist, thinking that enduring discomfort is part of it, and must, at least, be morally admirable. Sooner or later we give up. With a sigh of relief, and a promise to try again some other time, we slump down, probably even worse than before.

Perhaps it's because our muscles are not strong enough: better sign on at a gym to "get fit." But fit for what? Which muscles need strength to support us? However much fitness training, jogging, or other exercise a person may undergo, it will not affect his or her ability to sit well in a chair or stand well, whether playing a musical instrument or waiting for a train. This is because there will be a well-established habitual pattern for these activities, and it is these patterns that must be addressed if there is to be improvement.

Two Sorts of Muscle Function

The average muscle chart or popular books about the human body usually only show the superficial muscles of the body, or at best two layers.

These outer layers are, largely speaking, the muscles of movement. They move one part of the body relative to another, or move the body in space. The deeper muscle layers that lie close to the spine are not often shown. These are the muscles of posture and they have certain characteristics:

- We don't feel them because they are so deep.
- We cannot command them directly.
- We have no direct feedback as to how well they're functioning.

Now compare these to the muscles of movement. Providing there is no damage, I can lift my arm, deciding exactly when and how far I shall move it, and I can feel with excellent accuracy whether I have done what I intended. This is voluntary action. It's immediate and it's fast, but it tires more quickly than postural muscles.

So when I take myself "in hand" and decide to "improve my posture" by using voluntary muscles, my attempts to sit up straight give me immediate sensory reward. I know I have done something, and I assume—as with my arm—that it was what I intended. But the problem is that I have used muscles of movement for the purpose of holding myself up, not the postural muscles, and muscles of movement fatigue quickly, and my admirable intentions are eroded.

Most of us want to get quick results and to know for certain that we have succeeded, yet when it comes to posture these desires are worse than useless because the sensory feedback is very different from that which follows movement. It is elusive and unclear, a kind of deep awareness only appreciated with experience, when the desire for quick achievement is withheld.

Instrumental teachers commonly assert that posture is of great importance. A few will attempt more than a superficial definition of good posture and then leave the students to make sense of the instructions and carry them out as best they can to proceed on a trial-and-error basis, but with no means of knowing which is error and which is not. Most of us are in need of far more help.

Whether engaged in the normal activities of daily living or executing the complex and highly refined skills of instrumental playing, our bodies must be supported with equilibrium or be centered as in martial arts, maintaining a constant readiness for movement. How with a flexible, multijointed, highly moveable structure do we maintain stability against gravity? Falling over is bad news! Stability and equilibrium must give rise to movement, in the wake of which, equilibrium must be reestablished. These dynamic mechanisms of support must be seen to be primary, and those of movement, only secondary.

Voluntary and Involuntary Pathways from the Brain to the Muscles

The description of the distinct layers of muscle—one for movement and one for support—is a bit oversimplified. In fact, some groups of muscles have both functions, depending on how they receive information from the brain and nervous system.

Imagine there are two sorts of pathway from the brain to muscles. First, the processes of support and balance are dealt with by the old brain, the innate or evolutionary ancient, lower sections of the brain or brain stem, where activity happens below conscious levels of awareness. There are connections to the more conscious parts, but these old brain pathways are not activated by the kind of voluntary decisions that result in what we might refer to as "doing" These pathways are in charge of reflexes and self-righting mechanisms of deep postural musculature. Second, there is the voluntary pathway (we used the example of lifting the arm). This comes from the cortex in the brain (the newer part, highly developed in humans where conscious, learned [educated] processes take place) and goes to the spinal cord and from there out to the rest of the body. However, in reality it is not quite that simple; posture and movement, voluntary and involuntary, are not entirely polarized functions. In reality each flows imperceptibly into each other.

If you look at an illustration of the muscles of the upper arm (in chapter 6) you get an impression of how support of the arm must rely on the head, neck, and spine. But with a musician's intense work on the specialized voluntary movement of arms, hands, and fingers, the support mechanisms are easily overruled and neglected, with consequent strain on the upper back, shoulders, and arms that have to overwork to compensate for the loss of postural support.

The arms, indeed, have a dual function to perform. They must execute the voluntary components of playing (voluntary pathway), and they must be supported in space according to the ever-changing demands of playing. Such support must meet the demands of equilibrium, counter-balancing the body and maybe also the instrument at the same time, while maintaining constant readiness for further adjustment (old brain pathway).

What are the optimum working conditions for the old brain pathway? What, in practical terms, can any of us do about posture?

Prerequisites for Fine Motor Control

To move freely and accurately, postural equilibrium must be maintained (remembering also that stiffening strategies do not work). Responses that are largely automatic will work when conditions are right and will not work or only work poorly when they are unsatisfactory. There is continual interchange between the voluntary and old brain pathways such that it is more appropriate to talk of semiautomatic responses. Even the reflex processes themselves are influenced by attitudes, under-standing, ideas, and emotion. It is probably for this reason that the kind of conscious attention employed in Alexander technique, martial arts, and the like can be very effective in raising the efficiency of the postural mechanisms. In practice, they depend on the following factors:

1. Absence of inappropriate tension, causing bracing, shrinking, or breathing restriction
2. Free poise of the head and absence of neck tension
3. Support of a firm resistant surface against weight-bearing areas (bones of the feet, seat bones)
4. Eyes engaged, interested, mobile
5. An alert, interested "open-minded" mental attitude (with an absence of excessive concentration as in trying too hard)
6. Calmness (with a minimum of anxiety)
7. Attention to overall intentions, regarding balance and direction of movement, rather than detail of movement or how it feels

Exploration 5—Standing

Stand on a firm floor. Allow time for the mind to quiet. Cease striving and wanting to get everything right. Allow your eyes to see the color and movement before you, letting them move from one object of interest to another in a normal, everyday way. Pay attention (without trying to make something happen) to your feet on the floor. You are supported through three weight-bearing points in each foot: the heel, the ball of the big toe, and the ball of the little toe, as if on a tripod. Distribute the weight between these three points, with a little more on the heels (without leaning back). Allow breathing to continue quietly and naturally. Don't brace the knees back; it may be necessary to allow them to bend minimally. Consider the idea that your weight is transmitted through the whole structure to the ground and that there is a corresponding "equal and opposite" force of support coming from the ground and operating upward through your whole structure, continuing on up through the crown of your head and beyond. Just think about it; don't try to make it happen.

Now raise your arms into playing position. (Keyboard players, cellists, and sitting bass players do it, even though you don't stand to play—a corresponding sitting experiment follows.)

Did this alter your balance? What happened? Raising your arms in front of you must alter your balance, unless you stiffen quite strongly in the ankle, knee, and hip joints. This is because you are throwing the weight of your arms out beyond the center of balance in the base provided by your feet. Your body must compensate somehow to counterbalance this extra weight. The question is how. Do you: (a) move back freely on adjusting ankles and hip joints using the whole body as a lever? or (b) bend in the middle of your back, which focuses the load on the low back, and if you do this, do you find that the neck and shoulders drop forward, too? The second version is a common habit among violin and viola players, resulting in excessive low back tension, compensatory tension in the head and neck, and stiffening in the legs. And all this must affect the freedom of the arms, hands, and fingers! Using your instrument and its weight will probably intensify the effect of throwing you off balance.

Some of the questions raised in such practical explorations of your own posture may be difficult to answer and you may need an objective and preferably experienced observer to spot what is happening. You can use a camcorder, but best of all is an Alexander teacher who also plays your instrument. He or she will at least have inspected the same set of conundrums! It is in the nature of habit that we don't feel what's happening. The pattern has become so familiar, you have learned the movement patterns so thoroughly over many years practice, that your sensory feedback systems don't comment on it, so you are unaware on a conscious level. This is normal!

The more you lift the lid on these habits and allow your conscious brain to explore them, the more awareness you will gain and the more options you will have about changing them if you so wish. Not all habits are bad—playing an instrument requires complex sets of movement skills to be in place, and unless they become habitual, you cannot bring your creative musical talents into play. On the other hand, fixed strategies can limit choice and creativity, and unless you are aware of them, you are limited by them.

Exploration 6—Sitting

Sit on a firm chair. If you are average height or above, many chairs are too low. You need your hip joints (which are at the level of the groin creases) to be a little higher than your knees. If the hip joints are lower than the knees, it is mechanically difficult to maintain upright balance for the spine without excessive muscle effort in the buttocks and lumbar areas.

Sit as near the front of the chair as you can without feeling unsafe (and given the room available), so that the chair is not cutting into your thigh muscles. Short people and children may need to put their feet on a solid cushion, stool, or small box. Keep your eyes focused and interested. Can you feel the two bones that bear your weight? Sitting on your hands for a moment may make you feel the bones more clearly. As you take your hands out again, allow the seat bones to lower fully on to the chair. Think of your weight being conveyed through your spine, via the seat bones into the chair, neither slumping your torso, nor stiffening it. Pay attention to the contact between seat bones and chair, and keep your eyes focused. You should by now have a feeling that you are "centered" in the martial arts sense and can move in any direction or not as you choose.

In the earth's gravitational field, wherever an object rests on the earth's surface, the earth pushes up against it with an equal and opposite force. If you stack objects up, be they bricks or vertebrae, each one pushes up against the one above it. Let us call this effect "support force." The contact of the chair against your seat bones is an example of this support force. Pay attention to it. Think of it rising up through your spine like water in a pipe. Each vertebra rests its weight on the bone below, and the bone below provides an upward support to match.

Keep your back soft, making sure you don't arch it as you think of the upward component. Arching lifts your seat bones and causes your weight to be held on the tensed muscles of the thighs. Check as far as you can that you are not also raising your chest, stiffening your neck, or locking your head into a fixed position. It should be possible to sit upright without strain and without needing a backrest, but it may take a lot of attention at first. Until the deep supporting mechanisms are working to their best potential, it may be difficult to maintain for any length of time, especially if you have a sloping back chair (see later for ways to cope with this).

How does it change when you raise your arms and change again when you bring your instrument into position? What is the effect of playing a simple phrase very loudly or very softly?

You may find it helpful to tape these instructions somewhere where you can easily see them so you can explore the activity without referring to the text. You may also find it helpful to be filmed with a camcorder when you play, so that you can spot the exact moment when you tense voluntary muscles unnecessarily. A written text cannot provide all the information and advice each individual needs for this kind of exploration. It is a slow, ongoing process. Understanding will change as progress is made. Guidance should preferably be sought from someone experienced in this sphere because of the habit patterns that have been formed over years.

Sensory information about balance and equilibrium is gathered by the nervous system prior to movement, and is the foundation for organization of the movement itself. (You cannot go from London to Glasgow unless you know where London is!) Yet in reality, most of us are in such a hurry to do the job that we rarely give the moments of preparation any attention. Creating the "prerequisites for fine motor control" referred to earlier is the first step.

CHAIRS—ARE YOU SITTING COMFORTABLY?

A chair is usually seen by manufacturers as a design feature, for relaxing in, or for easy stacking. They are not usually good for working on, let alone playing a musical instrument. The ideal chair is right for *you*, not Mr. Average. Specialist chairs are available but expensive and not usually easily portable. Yet a good chair is essential for posture for excellent work. Let's summarize a few simple, useful rules:

1. When you sit, remember the rule that the creases at the top of your legs in the groin area (where your hip joints are) should be about 1 inch (2–3 cm) higher than the top of your knee joints when your shins are vertical. Your vertebrae will now be stacked easily one on top of the other. You will then have the correct sacral angle and there will be no stress on the lower back, so it will be no effort to sit up straight. In this position you should not need to use a back-rest. If you sit in a seat that slopes back, as you lean back to let the chair support you, and by using the lumbar support, you may have to stretch to reach the keyboard. Your head pokes forward to counterbalance the backward lean, so you may also get neck ache. Even if you perch on the front of the seat to bring your head and arms into correct alignment, your internal low back muscles still have to fight to hold you up against the back slope gravity, and this will cause fatigue and eventual low back pain.

2. If you constantly use one chair that is flat or slopes back, it is worth getting a wedge cushion or putting blocks under the back legs of your chair to reproduce the conditions described in 1. in this list.

3. If you frequently change chairs and they vary considerably, use a hand towel or bubble wrap (a piece 1 to 1.5 square meters, small bubble size, is usually sufficient). Fold it or roll it and place it on the back half of the seat only, to take up the adverse slope, or place it in the middle to fill out a sagging seat. Available from stationers and garden centers, bubble wrap is very light, cheap, and easily renewable (no, the bubbles won't pop when you sit on it!) and can be folded in many different ways, whereas a wedge cushion only fits one slope, is bulky to carry about, and is expensive to replace if forgotten. The same solutions apply to car, train, bus, and plane seats.

4. If your feet do not reach the floor, use a solid cushion or a small box under your feet to restore conditions described in 1. in this list, otherwise there will be undue pressure behind your knees as

your feet dangle. If you are a cellist and the chair edge cuts into the back of your thighs, put a thin strip of bubble wrap over the edge.

5. When using a PC, your forearms should be horizontal and the keyboard near you so your fingers fall easily on to the keys. Your eye height should be level with the middle of the music (or screen): too low and you will slump and get midback ache; too high and you will get neck ache. Your feet should face toward the music (or screen). Try never to twist your back or neck when sitting with a music stand or working at a PC. Use your feet to turn you to face your work. If you share a music stand, you will have to compromise, but negotiate to change places with your desk partner occasionally. In the office, if you have to hold a phone between chin and shoulder or type in a manuscript placed on one side of the keyboard, vary its position from side to side to balance muscle use, and get a head set for the phone.

6. On stage, use the intervals between movements to wiggle gently and unobtrusively. In the office, every hour get up, walk about, stretch your arms up and wide to give your lungs room and take deep breaths to refresh yourself. Write the alphabet in the air with your nose to relax your neck muscles and look at distant objects to change your focal length, resting your eyes. If the atmosphere is centrally heated, warm, and dry, have a drink of water rather than coffee or alcohol.

REFERENCES

Gray, H. *Osteology, Development (Anatomy, Descriptive and Surgical),* 15th ed. Bounty Books, 1901.

Hoppenfeld, S. *Physical Examination of the Spine and Extremities.* New York: Appleton-Century-Crofts, Prentice-Hall Inc., 1976.

Smith, D. *Paganini's Hand. Arthritis and Rheumatism* 25, no. 11 (1982): 1385–1386.

Szende, O., and M. Nemessuri. *The Physiology of Violin Playing.* London: Collet, 1970.

Wale, J. (Ed.). *Tidy's Massage and Remedial Exercises in Medical and Surgical Conditions,* 11th ed. Bristol: John Wright and Sons Ltd., 1987.

3

Best Practice

BEST PRACTICE ONE WARM-UP

First you need to warm up. Cold muscles are slow and more prone to injury. The purpose of warming up is to increase blood flow, nerve conduction, muscle flexibility, accuracy, and feel. Begin with a good all-round stretch.

Stretching without Tears

The purpose of stretching is to wake muscles up gently and to remind them of their full range of movement. This is particularly important when we use a specific group of muscles professionally, only within certain less-than-full parameters. To stretch properly, you must wear clothing that is loose, and free of restrictions, absorbent, and warm even when damp from sweat.

When you are doing a stretch, the temptation is to bounce, because muscles are elastic. However, this simply activates the recoil mechanism and doesn't stretch muscles usefully. Safe stretching happens when you reach out as far as you can gently, until you feel a slight stretch as you breathe out. Hold it there for a few seconds breathing normally. This resets the proprioceptors (nerve endings that measure stretch in a muscle) and the stretch feeling will go. Now you can reach a little further; you can repeat this "reach and hold" process up to three times, gaining more each time. After this you will gain nothing more but pain and microtear damage, so stop. I repeat, never bounce—you may easily tear muscle fibers, especially if they are cold. This is not the Stretch Olympics but preparation for playing! You don't need to stretch every muscle separately; work in groups. When you finish, your body should not feel wrung out and exhausted, but ready, eager, and alert, in prime condition for playing. While the following stretches are safe for someone in good health, do not attempt these stretches if you have any kind of back or neck problems without full consultation with your therapist. Neither I nor the publishers will take responsibility if you misuse or overdo these exercises. Your health is your responsibility, not ours.

1. The main areas to stretch are postural muscles in a general stretch, followed by specific muscles for all musicians. Those specific to your instrument you will do as part of your instrumental warm-up. You can do isometric muscle work in a car as a last resort if you are stuck in a traffic jam, but such work doesn't stretch the whole range of movement.

2. Low back. Curl up with knees on your chest and hug them to you as you breathe out. You can do this before getting out of bed as a wake-up exercise. If you want to loosen up the pelvis, do this on a hard surface and gently rock back and forth, side to side, for a minute or so. If you get stiff sitting, try the following: Lie face up, knees together and bent at 90°, feet on the floor. Pretend you have a balloon with a string held between your knees so it won't fly away. Bounce it with your abdomenal muscles. Let it go and then polish the floor under you with your bottom, going side to side and both clockwise and counter-clockwise. Now draw huge letters of the alphabet with each knee in turn. Finally stand up, hands on hips, and pretend you have a hula-hoop or do belly dancing. These will loosen the lower back and pelvic joints and could improve your sex life!

3. (a) Full twist. With feet shoulder-width apart and hands on hips, twist as far as possible one way without moving your feet. Twist the other way. (b) Half twist. Sit or hold the hips facing front, while you twist the shoulders as far around one way as you can. Now twist the other way.

4. (a) Side stretch. Place feet shoulder-width apart. With right hand on hip, left hand over the head, bend to the right as far as possible while still facing front. Swap hands and sides.

    (b) Low abdomen. Stand with one leg forward and one back as far apart as it is comfortable, feet facing forward. Hands on hips. Keep the back leg straight, lean back as you bend the front leg. Swap legs.
5. Thigh stretch. Stand on one leg, lean back and grab the other ankle. Straighten your back and keep it vertical as you pull your ankle up behind your buttocks. Do not lean forward; it negates the stretch. Do the other thigh.
6. Hamstring stretch. With hands on waist, cross one straight leg over the other. Bend forward from the hip joint (not the waist) to stretch the back leg. Swap legs.
7. Foot stretch. Walk about on tiptoe, then on your heels, then on the outsides and then the insides of your feet. Wriggle your toes. If you haven't got room to do that in your shoes, they are too tight, and will give you neck weakness.
8. Arm stretch. Lift straight arms up and back behind the head, then down and back up behind your back, then lift them to shoulder height and cross them in front, then behind as far as possible. Finally twist the arms palm in and palm out as far as you can.
9. Neck stretch. Drop the head on to the chest and hold, then look up and as far back as you can and hold that. Next get your ear as near your shoulder as possible without raising your shoulders. Do the other side; next, look over each shoulder as far as you can. Now rest your head in its normal position.

More Specific Flexibility Exercises and Stretches

1. Shoulder joint. Place hands on shoulders. Write your whole name in capital letters as large as possible with the point of one elbow (or do both together if you like). You can write what you like, the letters will give you every possible range of motion.
2. Wrist stretch. With fingers vertical, stretch your wrist and flex it up and down as far as possible, ten seconds each way. You can do both hands together. Put palms together at chest height and, lowering both hands, turn the hands so that the backs are

together at waist height. Raise them up to chest height. (Abilities will vary enormously here.)

STOP if you have any pain, tingling, or loss of feeling and turn to advice on carpal tunnel syndrome that follows later.

Next, put the forearm and hand on a flat surface and stretch the little finger side by bending the hand and wrist toward the thumb, and the thumb side by bending the hand sideways toward the little finger. Finally, keeping the forearm flat, lift first the thumb side away, then the little finger side away. In all these there will be only a small amount of movement, except in the forward and backward stretches.

3. Now complete the wrist flexibility by holding the forearm and (by way of a change) write half the alphabet in lowercase letters as large as possible with your right knuckles and the other half with your left.

4. Hand, finger, and thumb sideways stretch. First stretch the fingers as far apart as you can. Then using the righthand thumb and middle finger, hold the stretch for ten seconds between the left thumb to index, thumb to middle, thumb to ring, and thumb to little fingers. Next stretch and hold the index to middle, index to ring, and index to little fingers. Continue with middle to ring and middle to little fingers and finally ring to little fingers. Now swap hands.

5. Hand, finger, and thumb front to back stretch. Use the wrist of one hand between the fingers of the other successively to gently push and stretch one finger back and the other forward. End with a stretch of the thumb across the palm to the base of the little finger.

6. Finger and thumb flexibility. Hold the right wrist still with the left hand to prevent it helping. Keeping tip-to-tip contact between thumb and each finger of the right hand, successively do some more alphabet writing, and then swap hands. It's not as easy as it seems!

7. I'll bet by now that you have forgotten all about breathing! It is important for everyone to keep the breathing muscles stretched, not just those of you who use wind instruments. Start sitting hunched up and bent forward with elbows crossed and down between your legs. Fill your "stomach" with air and let it push

your arms out of the way. Unfold your body enough so that your hands can go to the side of your ribs. Fill with air and push your ribs out against your hands.

Next, use your hands to fight the breastbone as it rises as you fill up with air. Finally, fling your arms up, out and back, and as wide as you can, to take in the last scrap of air that you can, and then relax before you either levitate or explode! (This exercise takes far more time to explain than to do.)

8. Face stretch. Singers, wind, and brass players will each have their own version of this. However, in general, begin by puffing out the cheeks and then sucking them in, next protrude the lips to whistle, next bring the lower jaw as far forward and back as possible, then yawn, and finally smile as wide as you can.
9. For facial flexibility, mouth the letters of the alphabet, and if you are singing in a foreign language, do it in that language, too.
10. Don't forget the eye exercises listed in chapter 5.

More hand and whole body stretching and exercises relevant to musicians can be found in Schneider (1994) and Anderson (1980). Both are excellent books. We also recommend keeping fit, Pilates, line dancing, and running for general good health and fun.

Quick Version before Going on Stage

Start with whole body stretches. Go for forward and backward stretches, then stretch your sides by bending both ways, and finally twist your upper body against your lower body. Next, gently twist sitting down. Next stretch your arms across the body. Then stretch up your back, down behind your neck, and do shoulder circles or the alphabet exercise (see chapter 11, on rehabilitation). Move on to elbows, wrists, and fingers in the same way. Wake the body up, shaking and kneading the middle part of each muscle. A bit of massaging, especially between the fingers, gets the blood flow going. Work on each side while you breathe deeply.

Now do an instrumental warm-up—scales, studies, tone control, and so on. If your instrument represents all the agony of mistakes and fear of playing and you hate opening the case, make a decision. Can you practice for just ten minutes? If not, don't. If you can, read on and enroll yourself in the idea of fun with some new tools.

BEST PRACTICE 2 FOCUSED PRACTICE

Superefficient practice works! A new piece is pristine on the page and pristine in your mind. Your approach is vital. Be clear what you want from the piece, then focus your thoughts. Read it through and bracket the difficult bits in pencil. They amount usually only to 20 percent of the piece. The rest (80 percent) will be easy or a repeat of what has gone before. Don't waste any more time playing through it until the entire piece is problem-free. See the brackets as interim goals full of possibilities and opportunities. Break down each bracket into chunks of one problem each. Write in the goal (speed, leaps, tone, bowing, coordination, control, etc.) immediately above the passage on the page. Taken to pieces like this, you can solve each problem chunk in ten minutes. List them in a logbook as a practice plan, in the form of a patchwork of ten-minute slots, so that you vary between hands and techniques needing work. This keeps you fresh, stops boredom, and prevents muscle overuse.

Inspire yourself! Mark in breathing places (especially if you are a pianist or a string player!), and breathe there whether you need to or not—you will in performance! Forget breathing places now and you will forget them when performing because you have associated that passage with not breathing.

Especially when beginning study, spend 80 percent of the time thinking about a passage away from your instrument, hearing it through in your head, seeing it in your mind's eye, and feeling it in your fingers. Then you will only need 20 percent of the time with your instrument. Until it is crystal clear in your head without any vague edges, precise instructions can't get through to your arms and hands properly. Fluffy brain means fluffy fingers!

Pick the *hardest* bracket—anything else you tackle after this will be easier. Choose one aspect of your interim goal to practice (speed, tone, style, character, etc.). Hear in your head the required result; focus and conquer it in ten minutes. Add aspects you have conquered together (e.g., speed and tone). Put the bit that used to be a problem back into context by adding the bar before and also the bar after it. Pick the "problem" nearest the end of the piece, and solve it. Then when you play it through in performance, the nearer you get to the end of the piece, the more you are on home ground, rather than running out of steam and into the less-practiced bits at the same time.

Any bit you can't solve usually contains more than one "problem," so break it down further technically. If you need advice, define the problem as precisely as you can in your logbook and ASK. Ask your teacher/professor/colleague. Keeping a logbook helps you to work on one thing at a time. It gives a sense of purpose to what you work at today, because you can see it in relation to the whole piece of music. Students using this method teach themselves and have initiative and motivation, but also recognize when they need help, thus making far better use of the teacher as a resource. Both student and teacher can see the progress as they tick off one bit after another and they can look back on their list of successes when they get depressed.

An example of student lead practice might be to vary the means of tackling speed problems by making a fun game of:

1. starting slowly and putting the metronome up a notch every third repetition, or
2. doubling up speed at each repetition, or
3. imaginative use of different rhythms (not forgetting to return to the original rhythm afterwards).

Remember, never repeat a passage so fast that it continually falls to bits—that way you practice making mistakes, which reappear under stress. Take it back a notch until you are very sure of it at that speed before continuing.

Program your mind for success with what's right, not what's wrong! Go for excellence not perfection, but always end each session on a good example (even if it's still a little slow).

Your mind remembers best the first and last things you do. Don't expect to pick up exactly where you left off, but if need be, start next time at a slightly easier pace than you stopped and you will quickly get up to speed. Aim finally for 120 percent of the speed or length of breath control you need. This will give you ease at the right speed under performance conditions. Above all, practice the fun, not the fear. Stop before you are worn out—you will make fewer mistakes and be eager to restart!

BEST PRACTICE 3 MEMORY

Always practice from memory (frequently visualizing the perfect example) rather than staring at the notes; it's your mind that has to learn, not your eyes. Memorizing makes the piece "your own," allowing far more direct authenticity of communication. Anyone can memorize a passage short enough to contain the few notes encompassing only one problem.

Learn which sort of memory is strongest for you. Don't assume that because you are a musician that it must be aural, and that what you remember first is the sound. It may be that your visual memory is best—you can read it off the page in your mind's eye. Kinesthetic memory is memorizing by feel. Can you finger the whole piece through in your head? Perhaps you excel at analytical memory, where you remember the form and architecture of the piece. Most people have a good mixture of at least two sorts of memory. Learn by your best first, and back it up with the others. Use your memory to be absolutely clear about each technical trick as it flashes by so that there are no fuzzy edges in your mind. Then you will have enough brain power left for the music itself to speak, and it plays itself.

How many repetitions should you do? There are some useful memory rules.

1. Never try to learn when you are tired or stressed. Memorizing is a holistic process, not just fingering and expression marks. It involves your whole body. Staring at the music as you learn technically becomes a crutch that is hard to drop when you then try to commit a passage to memory. Remember it's how, not how many!

2. You remember funny, ridiculous, rude, and traumatic things most easily. Invent games of tone, volume, bow, finger or lip pressure, vibrato width, and the like, or make up words, rhymes, and stories around the passage. They widen your technique and add interest and local color. Make memorizing part of the fun, not a drudge!

3. For most people, there are four memory stages. Ultra-short is used in sight-reading. Short-term memory occurs where a short passage is repeated three times, and you can play or sing it back immediately, as in aural tests. This memory only lasts about ten minutes (or less if there is intervening input of other material). It fades quickly unless there are more repetitions, and it will now last about an hour before fading again. A few more repetitions after an hour has passed, and it will last a day. Repetitions will be needed after a day, a week, a month, six months, and a year as it changes from medium-term to long-term memory.

4. Each repetition increases the memory connections in the brain. Adding other short passages you have meanwhile been working on gives it a context in terms of the whole piece. In the later stages you remember things best in chunks rather than small bits. Remember, *memory repetitions don't have to be played.* Thinking the passage through may be enough.

Finally, build stamina by putting together a whole passage, then half a movement, then the other half, go for a whole movement, then the whole work. Here you are concentrating on joining up your "study brackets," working on your architectural and stylistic conception of the whole, and hearing the entire accompaniment in your head.

BEST PRACTICE 4 COOL-DOWN

Musicians pay great attention to cleaning, packing up, and putting away their instrument after practicing but ignore their poor bodies. You need to put your body away in the same way you put your instrument away.

Cool down by mirror-image stretching, using all the opposite directions of movement to those required to play. Stretch the bent fingers, wrists, and arms back, untwist and unbend the neck and hips. Throw your arms wide and look up to the ceiling to open out your squashed chest. Breathe deeply. Put your fists in your low back and stretch back if you have been sitting.

If you are a wind player, don't forget the face muscles and tongue. Pout and smile, open your mouth wide to stretch the jaw joints, blow out and suck in your cheeks. Stick out your tongue, stretching it right

left, up, down, and trill. Lift your ribs up and out from underneath to
relax the diaphragm. Write the alphabet with your nose to free your
neck. Do the same with your right thumb if it carries the weight of your
instrument.

Your eyes are moved and focused by muscles, too; blink lots and look
at distant objects (your focus has been fixed between narrow limits if
you have been reading music).

You need only ten seconds for each stretch to bring your body back
to its center of balance and equilibrium. The principle to work from is:

1. Work from joint to joint—stretching where it was bent and bend-
    ing where it was stretched. Twist the opposite way you do when
    you play.
2. Work from small to large areas to reverse your warm-up.
3. Don't forget to stretch the muscles that hold your instrument and
    your arms so they can put your fingers in the right place to play.
4. Remember to reverse the environmental position caused by the
    chair, stage, conductor, and so on.

Erase the brackets on the music as you complete them. Don't forget
to congratulate yourself! Make a note of your successes (in your logbook) and decide what is next to conquer. Avoid coercive words like
"try," "ought," "should," "but," "don't" (they tend to mean a lot of
resentful effort without implying success). Just focus and trust yourself
to do your best. Watch your way of thinking in daily life as well.
Replace "try" with "do"; "ought and should" (which mean someone
else has told you to, therefore, you do it to please them) with "I want
to". Replace "but" with "and," and don't use the word "don't"—it
holds you back. Find something positive to "do"! Look for interesting
and fun ways to practice. This greatly improves response-ability. You
are now in the driving seat with your playing, not a victim in its thrall.

Use all these methods to clean up and "debug" old repertoire. Never
play a technical "to do" list when performing; it becomes tedious very
quickly. If you have practiced the fun, then sharing your success in performance will be fun and you have the power to rise to the magic of the
moment and really communicate.

Your body is your business, and your best investment. Look after it!

Plan in recreation time. Life is not all work. You actually absorb more when you are not practicing than when you are, if you have prepared yourself well. There is definitely some truth in putting what you want to learn under your pillow before you go to sleep!

So, to summarize, before you nod off, "Best Practice" is about warm up, focused practice and good memory, cool down, and keeping healthy!

Good practicing needs:

1. Planning your ten-minutes slots.
2. Warming up your body.
3. Warming up with your instrument
4. Completing your ten-minute slots, varying techniques to be practiced as you go.
5. Cooling down.
6. Cleaning your instrument.
7. Crossing off your completed slots. Congratulating yourself.
8. Noting questions to ask.
9. Planning your next session.

KEEP FIT

You don't need to go to a gym or use weights to exercise your chest and shoulder muscles; they get exercised every time you play. The rest of your body, however, probably gets ignored.

Boost your general fitness between practicing with a sport that exercises the muscles not used in playing by walking, running, doing aerobics, salsa and line dancing, yoga, and Pilates, tai chi, or backstroke swimming. It's healthy practice!

Many talented musicians were actively discouraged from sports at school because they might damage their hands, or because their gentler nature hated combat and contact sports. Taken sensibly, with proper precautions, sports are no more dangerous than cutting bread with a sharp bread knife, or crossing the road. However, little or no sport means that musicians mostly live in their heads except when playing their instrument, are bodily very unaware, and often become short in team spirit, which can cause problems in orchestras. Musicians are also

short of spare time, sit about a lot, and use some muscles disproportion-
ately more than others. They are well coordinated and well motivated
in the muscles they use and lazy about the rest because of mental and
emotional fatigue. A three-hour rehearsal is said to have a similar
energy output to a rugby match. This unbalanced unfitness is not specific to musicians. Many sports professionals are just as unfit and unbalanced! Doing something to keep fit generally is, therefore, very much
more important than most people realize.

1. General fitness actually improves your playing, your feeling of
   well-being, and your ability to cope with stress of all types.
2. It redresses overuse imbalance.
3. It keeps your spine straight.
4. It improves your coordination.
5. It releases endorphins in the brain, helping you feel positive about
   life.
6. It keeps your weight nearer to normal.
7. It balances the meridians.

As a musician, your inclination, patience, and times are likely to be
in short supply, so you are probably reduced to three options:

1. Do ten minutes of Keep Fit a day in a graded way until you reach
   optimum fitness for your age, maintaining it thereafter with sessions three times a week This is good if you are shy, or are embarrassed about your slothful body. However, it needs a lot of
   discipline to keep it up.
2. You might find it easier to have a personal coach, who will supply
   you with motive and drive, but will cost you quite a bit.
3. Or you can join a gym or a club and do dance aerobics, or go
   swimming (especially backstroke), do some form of yoga or
   Pilates, or learn tai chi. All will get you meeting people who are
   not musicians. Swimming, Pilates, yoga, and tai chi are more
   "portable" when touring, but will lose you fewer calories. All of
   these activities provide properly balanced body use, but golf, tennis, and other racquet sports are one-sided and may actually compound an existing problem due to the occupational hazards of the
   instrument you play.

For burning calories fastest and making your leaner, the top three exercises are jogging (can be hard on the knees), dance aerobics, and fast walking (cheapest and best). For undoing a squashed chest, swimming is good, but usually won't use so many calories. Indoor bikes and ski machines are surprisingly only slightly better at burning calories, no matter what their sales people say.

When you get home after a hard day, it's often pleasant to have an Epsom salts soak. Not a couple of tablespoons of scented bath salts, but as much as three cups or one pound (half a kilo) of dissolved Epsom salts. *Don't drink the water!* This is an old rugby players' remedy for easing out aches and stiffness.

CARRYING

Carrying instruments, music, stands, and suitcases is part of a musician's life. There are a few golden rules for avoiding injury:

1. Never reach to lift anything. Keep the load near your body and near your center of balance.
2. Keep your feet in line with the object you are lifting and then use YOUR FEET to turn your body and the load. Never twist.
3. Bend your knees, never your back.
4. If you are in a slow-moving line with a heavy weight such as a suitcase, get a trolly or skateboard and kick your case along; don't keep lifting it to move it a few inches forward.
5. Fix castors on your instrument case if it is large, or get a backpack case if you can, even for a cello; it is less stress on the body.
6. Other loads (music, shopping)—if you can divide the load between your hands, do it. Two smaller bags are always better than one large box. Use your feet in two journeys rather than damaging your back in one.
7. If you have a strap, put it over one shoulder and across the body so the weight is pulling inward toward the body's center of balance rather than away from it.

Predisposition to back pain arises in those who break these rules and play a very one-sided instrument such as a violin, viola, or flute; or play a one-sided sport such as golf or tennis; or already have neck, shoulder, or back problems. Do as little lifting as you can get away with; a tip to a porter is much cheaper than medical treatment!

When you are lifting, if you feel a sudden pain,

STOP IMMEDIATELY!!

Use a strong mirror-image stretch (see the Cool Down section in this chapter) and take four drops of Rescue Remedy, Arnica 6x, or Rhus Tox 6x immediately and then two every two hours. If the pain continues for more than twenty-four hours, see a chiropractor or osteopath. Don't just hope it goes away! The faster you get it treated, the less the compensation your body has to make and the faster the cure.

AIRLINE AND CAR STRETCHES

While on the subject of travel, and remembering the recent well-publicized scare about deep vein thrombosis, a few stretches easily done in confined spaces are worth noting. We move frequently throughout our lives even when asleep. Only when stuck in a car (especially if someone else is driving) or on a plane, sitting at a desk or watching TV do we remain still for more than an hour. If we don't move, blood pools in our legs, stressing the valves in the veins and can cause life-threatening deep vein thrombosis. As children, we were often told to "sit still and behave," but what all adults need to do is wriggle! Good wriggle times are during TV advertisements, at traffic lights, and in traffic jams. However, this doesn't apply to planes, where your only recourse is to sit in an aisle seat, so you have to get up frequently. In all cases, do the following:

1. Your legs are bent when you sit, so stretch them out (in the aisle) several times. Walk about and stretch back to relieve your hip joints at least once every hour.
2. Write the letters of the alphabet in the air with your toes, ankles, bottom/low back, shoulders, and nose. Explain why to your neighbor if you get odd looks!

REFERENCES

Anderson, R. *Stretching: Exercises for Everyday Fitness for 25 Sports.* London: Penguin, 1980.

Balck, R. *Getting Things Done,* ed. Michael Joseph. New York: Penguin, 1981.

Blanchard K. et al. *The One Minute Manager Series.* New York: Fontana, Harper Collins, 1983–1986.

Downing, G. *The Massage Book.* London: Wildwood House Ltd., 1972.

Fry, H. Overuse Syndrome in Musicians: Prevention and Management in Occupational Health. *The Lancet* (September 27, 1986): 728–731.

Gelb, H. *Killing Pain without Prescription.* New York: Thorsons, Harper Collins, 1983.

Orlick, T. *Coach's Training Manual to Psyching for Sport.* Champaign, Ill.: Leisure Press, 1986.

Proto, L. *Take Charge of Your Life—How Not to Be A Victim.* New York: Thorsons, Harper Collins, 1988.

Prudden, B. *Pain Erasure the Bonnie Prudden Way.* New York: Ballentine Books, 1977.

Read, M. *Sports Injuries. A Unique Guide to Self-Diagnosis and Rehabilitation.* London: Breslich and Foss, 1984.

Royal Canadian Airforce. *Physical Fitness 5BX 11 Minute-a-Day Plan for Men, XBX 12 Minute-a-Day Plan for Women. Two Series of Exercises Developed by the Royal Canadian Air Force.* New York: Penguin, 1953.

Schneider, M. *The Handbook of Self-Healing.* New York: Penguin Arkana, 1994.

Skynner, R., and J. Cleese. *Families and How to Survive Them.* London: Methuen, 1989.

4

Testing What's Wrong

INTRODUCTION TO THE CONCEPT
OF MUSCLE TESTING

Pain and muscle tension are the principal reasons for you to be reading this and ensuing chapters. Pain is most often suffered in the left hand by string and guitar players, in the right hand by woodwind and keyboard players, in the fingertips by pianists, in the forearms by string and keyboard players, and in the upper arm and shoulders by all who hold up an instrument or a bow. Wide finger stretches may also cause problems for pianists, string players, bass guitar, and bassoon players. As well as using these techniques, consider the possibility that the cause of your pain may be a fault in your instrumental technique. There may be nothing wrong with the method you have been taught, but how you have interpreted it and the habits that have crept in since it was first explained to you are another matter!

The methods presented in the ensuing chapters are both preventive and restorative. They are about muscle management for musicians. This is where you find out if you are an instrumentalist first or a musician first. The techniques aim to catch stresses, strains, and potential weaknesses before they become serious problems and before accidents happen. These methods often work when nothing else will, and are especially good when there is still a remaining hesitancy in performance following the best of modern medicine and physiotherapy. They are simple to use, are safe, and do not conflict with conventional medicine or instrumental practice according to any specific "method" of playing. Mainly they are common sense. Despite their apparent simplicity, they have been welcomed by those medics who have had the courage to try them. You need no specialist knowledge, just a willing pair of hands.

The techniques were developed almost thirty-five years ago by an American chiropractor, George Goodheart, from techniques and lore drawn from chiropractic, osteopathy, cranial work, dentistry, homeopathy, herbalism, nutrition, acupuncture, and conventional medicine. He formulated the International College of Applied Kinesiology (ICAK), which continues research and correlation between disciplines. An associate of his, John Thie, DC, made the basic technique available to a wider readership through his book *Touch for Health* (see chapter 1). *No claims of originality are made here other than the translation into musical terms.*

Muscle testing is a form of functional neurology. It deals with the quality of reaction within level 5 (or possibly 4) on the medical model scale, which means the muscle reaction is potentially normal and is not grossly weakened as it might be after a complete tear or surgery. In applied kinesiology (AK) circles, it is common parlance to use the terms "weak" or "strong." However, these terms are neither accurately descriptive of a dynamic process nor precisely appropriate. What is assessed is not gross strength or quantity of response so much as quality. Better terms suggested have been "inhibited," "normal," and "overfacilitated."

There are over fifty reasons why muscles become "weak." They can roughly be divided into a triangle of mental, physical, and chemical causes. Few problems have only one cause; the other two sides of the triangle are almost always affected to some degree. With self-help, once you have found the right relief points to work on, the effect is instantaneous and very pleasantly surprising. It's very exciting to feel the strength and certainty return and know that you have done it yourself.

The relief points are often not at the site of pain, but nevertheless speed the healing process; they can be used before and after playing and even in the green room between appearances on stage. I have covered the most common relief points and a few advanced techniques, which together will deal with 80 percent of the niggling sort of problems that musicians encounter. The other 20 percent are way beyond the scope of this book, and for these you will need to see an applied kinesiologist approved by the ICAK. Don't be dismayed: What you can do is easy, fun, and safe, and will work wonders in most cases. I have updated the treatment points and meridian associations from *Touch for Health* and *Healthy Practice for Musicians* to fit with the most recent International College of Applied Kinesiology researches.

The subject of discussion here is why muscles "switch off" just when they are needed, and how old injuries can inhibit present performance (especially in areas of accuracy, speed of reaction, and coordination), even though you are not thinking consciously of the old injury.

The assumption is that you are basically healthy. You may want an outline of how you can get that extra coordination needed for really clean playing, or to find out about food sensitivities and vitamin deficiencies, as well as to understand better the causes of muscles feeling "weak, wobbly, and unsure." We can take a single example: Muscle pain leads to mental stress, which impinges on clear thinking. Fuzzy, negative thinking, causes "holding back" in a difficult passage, then worrying about it and having "butterflies in your stomach." This means poor digestion and causes poor assimilation of vitamins and minerals, and toxicity in the system from half-digested foods. Such chemical stress leads eventually to clogging of muscle fibers with waste products and muscle starvation, which means they function poorly and fatigue easily. Poor response is disappointing and leads to "trying too hard" (or too long), and this is when accidents and injuries occur, causing yet more pain. You are now part of a downward spiral that compounds itself as it goes.

Only when the whole body machine is working perfectly can smooth improvement be hoped for in terms of good coordination, injury avoidance, and the confidence to reach for success and full potential. With all these in place, the performer has the chance to satisfy his or her hunger for a really fine performance of pure musical communication.

How do you do it? First you have to realize that there is no such thing as a reachable state of "perfect health" where you can stay. Health is a continuous process, not an event. Optimum health is all you can aim for in a world where conditions are changing all the time. The body is in a constant state of repair and renewal. All you can do is find out what it needs to function optimally, given the conditions that exist right now, and do your best to provide that. The best way to find out what is needed is to ask the body itself by muscle testing.

HOW TO TEST MUSCLES

(Note Bene: Without reading this section most carefully, you will fail to get results. Be aware also of child safety laws. It may be simpler to work with the child's teacher, a nurse, or parent present as these techniques are essentially "hands on.")

Unfortunately you cannot remove a muscle, test it, and replace it like a spare part in a car! You will need two people to test muscles. (I will assume that you are the Tester, testing the injured musician—the Testee.) Nor can you ever really test one muscle at a time. There are bound to be other muscles helping, because there is almost always a back-up system of synergistic muscles. All you can do is make sure that the one muscle you think you are testing is doing the main work and that the synergists are put at a disadvantage by your positioning before testing. Frequently, if the main muscle is "weak," the Testee will twist to try to use one of these synergists. So precision positioning by you as Tester is essential to get the right muscle. Sloppy testing gets sloppy, unreliable results. Be precise in following the illustrations about positioning the Testee's limbs. Look at the picture, perhaps practice the position yourself, then look at the person you are testing and visualize the muscle within the body before placing the body for testing.

As often as possible, an alternative test position for each muscle is given so that you can either use the most comfortable one or test both to make sure your findings are correct. Do not test each muscle more than twice in close succession, or you will cause fatigue, causing the muscle to seem weak when it actually isn't. If you are still not sure, practice the positioning of the same muscle on the opposite side of the body and then revert to the original muscle you wished to test.

There are two types of muscle action important to the musician: (a) action—as when you leap off the ground, or push or lift (the brain is used because you decide to leap, push, or lift) and (b) reaction—such as when your muscles take up the shock when you land after your jump or play a keyboard staccato or a bowed spiccato (using the spine reflex pathway, which is instinctive).

The test position is the same; it's a matter of who initiates the test; the Tester (you) or the Testee (the injured party). Either action or reaction can be upset, so both need to be tested.

To test an action, place the limb accurately in the position described for the muscle concerned and ask your Testee to push gently against your hold first (so the muscle is engaged); then, one second later, you push in the opposite direction to feel the Testee's push. Beware of this becoming a contest. You are only *testing quality of reaction, not strength*.

To test reaction, place the limb accurately and ask the Testee to "hold the position" (often against gravity). Wait one to two seconds and then push against the hold. The Testee reacts instinctively to hold the limb in place.

Realize that this way of testing is not quite the same as the type of testing that is taught in hospitals and medical schools (although it does come under their definition of Grade 5 testing). Here we are not testing for gross strength or range of movement. Nor is it competitive testing. Nor is there a right- or left-handedness about it. You are testing too lightly for any of these to make any difference. You are simply discovering if the muscle "switches on" or locks when you ask it to by saying "Hold" before testing it.

You are looking for *quality of reaction, not quantity*. The test is done within a two- or three-second timeframe and between half an inch to a 2-inch depth of travel as you push, not more. As you push, ask yourself "How does it feel?" Is the locking reaction immediate, spongy, jagged, painful? Anything other than an immediate lock against the Tester's light pressure counts as "weak" or inhibited. In other words, you test slowly and lightly and deliberately but not too deeply. Using the same pressure each time, it's almost as if you were listening for the response.

If you are testing the many fibers of a large muscle, you then vary the starting angle slightly, but not the depth of testing. Beginners may find a little difficulty for the first few minutes, but as musicians we are used to varying our touch, and it's quite easy to attune yourself to the "feel" of your Testee's reaction. The more people you test the better you get, and the better you become at teaching others to test you.

Always compare right and left, not because they will be different (although your Testee will try to tell you they are), but because they should be the same at this level of input. Also, don't forget that a muscle must have a stable base to push against or the whole body will twist to give support, and that then gives you no idea of what you are testing. Support varies according to whether your Testee is standing, sitting, or lying down, because gravity and support change relative to body position. When you find a weak muscle, note it down, and go on to find any others. Then look and see if they have massage points or holding points (discussed later) in common. Treat those first and retest, because they may clear up the whole problem. Finally, when you have finished your treatment on the muscle, retest and make sure it is strong when in a playing position. If it's not, refix it in that position (or as near it as possible).

ASSESSING THE PROBLEM

How do you know which muscle to test? First, assess the problem by asking the "patient" or Testee what muscle or muscle group performs the action that causes the pain—questions in the following list will help. Write down the answers. They will be useful reference points to check back on later; they give useful clues about where to look and so how to solve the problem. Ask the questions again after working on the points twice a day for a week, and you will be surprised at the change in the answers.

1. Where is the pain? Does it feel deep or on the surface?
2. Does it have a defined size or border or is it vaguely in an undefined area? (This often indicates a referred pain.) Does it move about or stay in one place?
3. What kind of pain is it? Shooting, stabbing, radiating (often muscular or structural cause)? Searing, burning (often a chemical cause)? Throbbing, pounding (often to do with circulation)? An ache and stiffness (often a chronic or residual problem rather than acute)?
4. What caused it and when does it happen now? (Be precise about the body position of the Testee when it happens; it may be

necessary to test the muscle when playing, or in the bodily position in which the accident occurred.)

5. What makes it worse and what relieves it? Does it hurt without movement?
6. What precisely does it stop the Testee from doing?
7. Is it getting better or worse suddenly or gradually?
8. How long has it existed? Has it happened before, or has something like it happened before?
9. Has there been an operation with scar tissue there or nearby?
10. What type of warm-up/cool-down and stretching exercises are done? You may need to invent some relevant exercises (see the section Rehabilitation Ladders).
11. What are the flexibility and range of movement like on both sides of the body using this muscle(s)?
12. Is the Testee overpracticed or overperformed?
13. Is adequate endurance practice done? Is the Testee used to playing the whole work through with all its repeats and movements as in a performance?
14. Are the muscles generally used equally on both sides of the body, or does playing this specific instrument use one limb much more, or even exclude others from movement?
15. What is the general fitness level—what sports does the Testee do?
16. On a scale of zero to ten, if zero equals no pain and ten equals the worst pain imaginable, how bad is it now? At its best? At its worst? Give a score out of ten and make a careful note of it, because it is hard to remember how bad pain is when it's gone.

Which Muscle?

Now find the muscles to test by consulting figure 4.1 and identify which muscles most nearly approximate the same area as the pain. Don't forget that there may be several layers of muscles with fibers going in different directions. List them. Look up the information for each specific muscle. Test each muscle by copying the positioning in the accompanying illustration as closely as possible. The position given offers you access because it brings the two ends of the muscle as close as possible to each other, while at the same time putting other muscles with a similar action at a disadvantage. If the muscle is strong, reacts immediately and easily, and does not cause more pain, then test the others around it that have a similar action. Also test the ones that have the opposite or antagonistic action, which could be the cause of pain now because they are overfacilitated or "hyper." Remember, when a muscle is switched off and slack (to protect it from trauma), it causes imbalance with its opposite number (its antagonist). That muscle now has to take up the slack and may therefore have gone into spasm. Do not assume that if a muscle tests strong that it is working normally. It may be hypertense and unable to let go. The reverse can also happen; a muscle may be cramping through overwork and congestion with uncleared waste products and may be weak through no fault of its own. It has to work at half strength and, naturally, it complains by being painful.

It is also worth testing the same muscle on the opposite side of the body (i.e., test both right and left latissimus dorsi). Also test muscles with a similar action antigravity (i.e., abdominals and sacrospinalis). The presence of pain does not mean that you should not test, although of course you proceed with caution, rest between tests, and don't test repeatedly. Often the pain will disappear if the Tester or Testee touches the relief points at the same time as the muscle being tested. If this occurs, it means that the points are active and need working on, because they are directly related to the problem. Strengthen the muscles according to the relief points on the relevant page. To assist you to understand the information given in the following chapters, you may find it useful to photocopy the following list and use it as a bookmark for quick reference.

1. Test Position: It is vital that you copy this exactly. You may need to practice on the "good" side before testing the doubtful side, which may respond badly and painfully to repeated testing. Be clear in your mind what you are going to do first before testing.
2. Antagonist muscle: This is a muscle that has the opposite action to the muscle you intend to test. It may need work on it as well.
3. Massage points: These are shown as solid dots (figs. 4.1 and 4.2). These are areas of lymphatic congestion that feel puffy and engorged. Approach with caution. They can feel anything from ticklish or "a bit bruised" to "hit the roof" tender. In locating these points, we often mention ribs and rib spaces. The collarbone

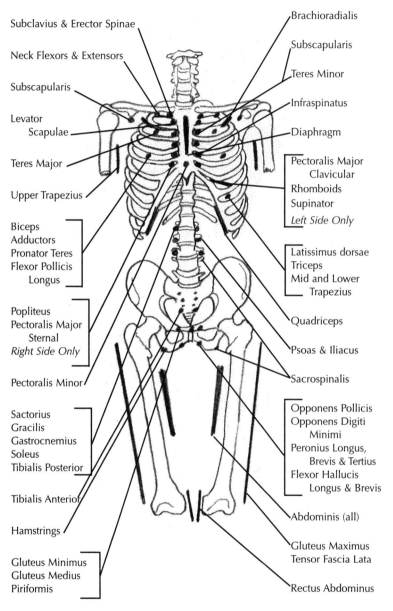

Subclavius & Erector Spinae

Neck Flexors & Extensors

Subscapularis

Levator Scapulae

Teres Major

Upper Trapezius

Biceps
Adductors
Pronator Teres
Flexor Pollicis
Longus

Popliteus
Pectoralis Major
Sternal
Right Side Only

Pectoralis Minor

Sactorius
Gracilis
Gastrocnemius
Soleus
Tibialis Posterior

Tibialis Anterior

Hamstrings

Gluteus Minimus
Gluteus Medius
Piriformis

Brachioradialis

Subscapularis

Teres Minor

Infraspinatus

Diaphragm

Pectoralis Major
Clavicular
Rhomboids
Supinator
Left Side Only

Latissimus dorsae
Triceps
Mid and Lower
Trapezius

Quadriceps

Psoas & Iliacus

Sacrospinalis

Opponens Pollicis
Opponens Digiti
Minimi
Peronius Longus,
Brevis & Tertius
Flexor Hallucis
Longus & Brevis

Abdominis (all)

Gluteus Maximus
Tensor Fascia Lata

Rectus Abdominus

Figure 4.1 Anterior Massage Points (Neurolymphatics).

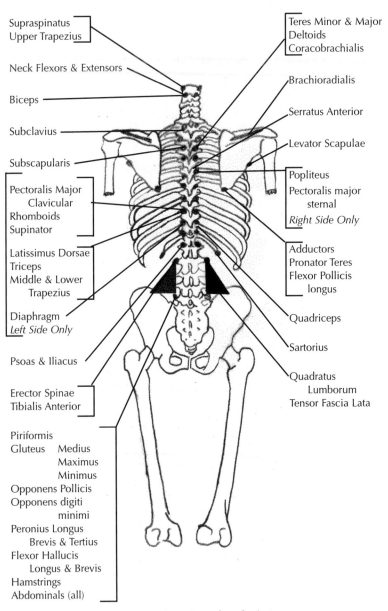

Supraspinatus
Upper Trapezius

Neck Flexors & Extensors

Biceps

Subclavius

Subscapularis

Pectoralis Major
    Clavicular
Rhomboids
Supinator

Latissimus Dorsae
Triceps
Middle & Lower
    Trapezius

Diaphragm
Left Side Only

Psoas & Iliacus

Erector Spinae
Tibialis Anterior

Piriformis
Gluteus   Medius
        Maximus
        Minimus
Opponens Pollicis
Opponens digiti
        minimi
Peronius Longus
    Brevis & Tertius
Flexor Hallucis
    Longus & Brevis
Hamstrings
Abdominals (all)

Teres Minor & Major
Deltoids
Coracobrachialis

Brachioradialis

Serratus Anterior

Levator Scapulae

Popliteus
Pectoralis major
    sternal
Right Side Only

Adductors
Pronator Teres
Flexor Pollicis
    longus

Quadriceps

Sartorius

Quadratus
    Lumborum
Tensor Fascia Lata

Figure 4.2   Posterior Massage Points (Neurolymphatics).

sits directly on top of the first rib in the front so count it as though it were such. Rib spaces are the dips between the ribs. The tenderness of the points will lessen if you do them twice daily, until they are no longer sore. More than thirty seconds will simply fatigue the points. However, be aware that lightly brushing the skin won't help at all and will actually make the muscle weaker, so work on them as deeply down to the underlying bone as pain will allow. Never massage over any broken skin, as you will only rub in infection. If the points stay tender for weeks rather than days, assist lymphatic drainage by avoiding all caffeine, alcohol, refined sugar, red meat, whole milk products, and processed foods. Instead, eat only fresh fruit and vegetables and drink two liters of water a day. If you can, fast one day a week and take a sauna twice a week. Begin breathing exercises and ask advice from a herbalist.

Holding points

These are shown as open circles (fig. 4.3). These are neurovascular and acupuncture points that should be very lightly held, perhaps with a slight skin stretch, but never massaged. You may or may not feel a pulse: If you do feel a pulse, wait until it is slow and even. Hold these points for at least thirty seconds. You do not need to have an acupuncturist's pin-point accuracy on the acupoints; three finger pads over the area will do. If you feel a pulse, you can narrow it down to one finger over that spot. However, do not worry if you feel nothing; just wait a couple of minutes anyway, you can do no harm. (Note Bene: When you hold points, make sure you hold the same hand as foot [i.e., right hand and right foot]. Do not mix them.) Occasionally there are two sets of holding points included. This is because different authorities ascribe the muscle concerned to different acupuncture meridians. Where there are two sets, try both to see which strengthens best. The holding points are tonification acupuncture points and are for strengthening only. Although extremely useful to trained AK and acupuncturist professionals, sedation points are not included.

To see whether a muscle needs the massage point or holding point first, have the Testee place his or her hands over each of the points in turn while you retest the muscle (not forgetting to rest the muscle between tests). Work most on the points that strengthen the weak

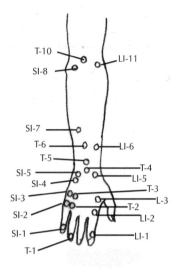

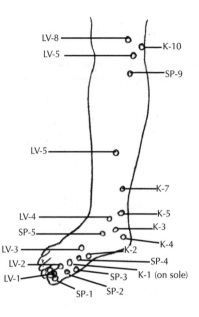

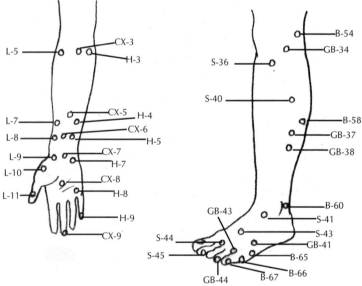

Figure 4.3   Holding Points (Neurovasculars).

muscle best and then back it up with the other points. Continue until all the muscle points that are needed are done.

Now reassess the pain level (out of ten) and retest, but do not try out the muscle in full playing action yet. Be content with immediate pain reduction and greater strength. Healing takes time, so let it settle and, if necessary, work on it again tomorrow. If there is still a problem, then go to the sections on advanced techniques in chapters 10 and 11. If there is no pain, then the muscle doesn't work by itself; the whole body has to rebalance itself in the light of the newfound strength (as any dancer will tell you). (Note Bene: Pain is there as a warning and should never be "worked through." That only stores up trouble for later.)

NUTRITION

Mostly it is suggested that you increase the intake of the food substance suggested rather than take pills. This avoids most possibilities of overdose. Since you are not medically trained, you cannot and must not prescribe. However, there is nothing to stop you choosing to eat that food yourself.

The list that follows will enable you to increase certain nutrients in your diet as part of the healing process, using the substance's natural sources rather than taking pills and supplements. If you can, eat organically grown food that is as fresh as possible.

Vitamins

Foods first in the list generally have the highest content of that nutrient.

- A: Fish oil, milk, butter, eggs, liver, carrots, yellow and dark green fruits and vegetables, tomato, melon. Deficiency can cause night blindness, kidney stones, and skin complaints.
- B1 Thiamin: Brewer's yeast, whole grains and brown rice, black strap molasses, offal (organ meats), egg yolk, soy beans, sunflower seeds. Deficiency can be caused by pregnancy, too many high-sugar foods, alcohol, stress, and habitual use of antacids, and deficiency can cause loss of mental alertness, depression, muscle

weakness, respiratory problems, water retention, and subsequent heart damage.

- B2 (G) Riboflavin: Brewer's yeast, whole grains, peas and beans, organ meats, black strap molasses, mushrooms, spinach. Deficiency can cause tired, gritty, bloodshot eyes, cracks and sores around the mouth, dizziness, insomnia, and slow learning, and is exacerbated by alcohol, tobacco, and some contraceptive pills.
- B3 Niacin: Brewer's yeast, lean meats, poultry and fish, peanuts, almonds, mushrooms, and brown rice.
- B5 Pantothenic acid and B6 Pyridoxine: Same as for B3 plus wheatgerm and soy. Deficiency can cause anemia, premenstrual tension, nettle rash, and asthma.
- B9 Folic acid: Dark green leafy vegetables and root vegetables, organ meats, oysters, salmon, and milk.
- B12: Organ meats, fish, pork, lamb, eggs, milk and cheese, bananas, kelp, and peanuts. Deficiency can cause a sore tongue, nerve deterioration and tremors, menstrual problems, and anemia.
- C: Acerola cherry juice, cabbage, bean sprouts, broccoli and cauliflower, all the citrus fruits, chilis, peppers and tomatoes, melon, asparagus, strawberries, and mango. Deficiency can cause lassitude, muscle and joint pain, bleeding gums, increased allergic sensitivity, and decreased resistance to colds and flu.
- Bioflavinoids: Citrus zest and pulp (especially lemon), apricots, black currants, broccoli, buckwheat, cherries, grapes, capsicums, tomatoes. Deficiency can cause easy bruising and tiny skin hemorrhages.
- D: Cod-liver oil, salmon, sardines, herring, tuna, milk, egg yolk, sprouts. Deficiency can cause rickets and osteomalacia (bone softening), brittle bones, and muscle spasm or weakness.
- E: Cod-liver oil, wheat germ, cold-pressed plant oils, organ meats, eggs, parsley, peas and kale, molasses, shrimps, soy, sweet potatoes, nuts and peanuts. Deficiency can cause irritability, water retention, anemia, lethargy and apathy, loss of libido, poor concentration, and muscle weakness.

Be careful that your sources of vitamins A, D, and E are not rancid.

Minerals

- Calcium: Almonds, apricots, bananas, cabbage, cauliflower, milk and cheese, egg yolks, figs, lemon zest, lettuce, onions, parsnips, prunes, radishes, spinach, watercress, and whole wheat. Deficiency can cause gum and bone disease and poor circulation.
- Iron: Almonds, apples, asparagus, apricots, beetroot, carrots, dates, egg-yolks, figs, lettuce, leeks, all meats, peas, potato skins, prunes and raisins, radishes, spinach, tomatoes, walnuts, and whole wheat. Deficiency can cause anemia, low vitality, and poor disease resistance.
- Magnesium: Almonds, bananas, beetroot, brewer's yeast, whole barley, cabbage, chestnuts, coconut, corn on the cob, egg yolks, dates, figs, lettuce, lemons and oranges, milk, peas, prunes, seafood, soy, tomatoes, and walnuts. Deficiency can cause acidosis, insomnia, and nervous ailments.
- Manganese: Almonds, whole barley, beetroot, chestnuts, citrus, egg yolks, endive, kelp, mint, pineapple, walnuts, watercress. Deficiency may cause hysteria, nerve problems, and poor memory and may be present in diabetes, muscle wasting, and arthritis.
- Phosphorus: Almonds, apples, asparagus, bananas, beans, brewer's yeast, cabbage family, celery, milk and cheese, egg yolks, canned fish, nuts, oats, cucumber, prunes, radishes, soy, spinach, walnuts, watercress, and whole wheat. Deficiency can cause brain tiredness, poor bone development, and hair loss.
- Potassium: Almonds, apricots, runner beans, cabbage and cauliflower, celery, coconut, figs, fish, citrus, milk, molasses, oats, parsnips, potato skins, soya, tomatoes, turnips, watercress. Deficiency can cause constipation, liver disorders, and skin eruptions.
- Zinc: Beans, brewer's yeast, canned fish, eggs, green-leaf vegetables, hard cheese, liver, meat, oysters, shellfish, potatoes, rice, wholemeal bread. Deficiency can cause poor libido, poor appetite, poor sense of taste.

Excess sodium (salt) can cause water retention and metabolite disturbance and make high blood pressure worse. Avoid apples, asparagus, runner beans, beetroot, cabbage, carrots cheese, coconut, cucumber, eggs, endive, figs, fizzy drinks, processed cereals and other salted foods, sea salt, leeks, lettuce, milk, oats, prunes, raisins, spinach, strawberries, turnips, and watermelon.

Excess iodine can cause thyroid problems, weight loss, hyperactivity and irritability, finger- and toenail discoloration and malformation. Avoid asparagus, artichokes, bananas, beetroots, cabbage, carrots, garlic, kelp, lettuce, onions, potato skins, seafood, strawberries, tomatoes, and watercress. Deficiency of iodine can cause goiter, obesity, toxemia, and low vitality.

The preceding list contains but a tiny selection to show you how you can help yourself by eating appropriately.

Sensitivity

Where they occur under this heading, there may be allergy or hypersensitivity to the substances named. It is best to avoid them until the problem is solved.

EMOTION

Relevant words are added for making affirmations. These are not the only causative emotions but they are the most likely ones. You may need to look for similar words. What matters is the meaning to the Testee, not the dictionary meaning. Together with most of the nutritional suggestions, they have been researched by John Barton, DC. The fact that there are many repetitions only goes to show how destructive the negative emotions can be. More than one pair may be relevant. (See also chapter 10 on stress and emotions.)

Bach Flower Remedies

Those given are the main ones for the relevant acupuncture meridian, but are not the only ones that can be used for the prevailing negative emotion.

THERAPY LOCALIZATION POINTS
(TOUCH POINTS)

Touching this point while you test an otherwise "strong"/normal indicator muscle (SIM) will cause it to weaken and become a "weak"/inhibited indicator muscle (WIM) if there is a problem of whatever kind at this point. It does not indicate specifically what is wrong, or whether it is surface or deep.

Where any of this information is omitted under the instructions for a particular muscle, either it has not been researched, is unknown to the author, or is not thought suitable for self-help treatment. It is worth repeating that if you are not sure about your testing, work on the relevant massage point and holding point anyway. You will do no harm. Then seek out your nearest applied kinesiology practitioner.

General Use

Use the relief points given for each muscle as a preventative measure to keep you fit longer as part of the "cool down" routine after a practice session to help the body clear away the excess waste products of your work in the muscles. This will pay handsome dividends in reduced stiffness and aches, as well as improving posture, balance, muscle strength, and general physical fitness.

If, after trying even the extra points in the advanced techniques, there is still a high level of pain, then you should go to see a doctor, chiropractor, or osteopath. The muscle may have been more damaged than you realize. Safety first! These techniques do not replace injury treatment; they are simple aids to rehabilitation, injury prevention, and muscle improvement.

The Pitfalls to Avoid

"What happens if I do it wrong?" Very little! If you mistakenly weaken a normally strong muscle by mistreating the points, the body will quickly put it right. The worst you can do, if you follow the directions given earlier, is to cause bruising by massaging too hard. Be aware some people bruise very easily. If in doubt, show them where the points are and have them do the rubbing (or their parents if they are present).

This is a useful solution in a music lesson situation. Avoidable pitfalls occur in two areas: Tester faults and Testee faults.

The most common *Tester faults* are:

1. Poor positioning of the Tester or Testee. Both must be as comfortable as possible. An awkward or unbalanced Tester can't do a good test. Think about your position and hand-holds before picking up the limb to be tested. Don't have more than one joint between your testing hand and the muscle you intend to test, because then you will be testing joints, not muscles. Above all, do not put your stabilizing hand on, or squeeze, the muscle you are attempting to test!

2. Too heavy, too long, or too deep testing, and too may repetitions, will tire a muscle already under stress. Be clear about what you are doing and feeling and do it efficiently. Twice is enough without a rest period in between.

3. Making the Testee hold the test position for a long time, while you make up your mind how to test, leads to needless fatigue and poor results. Work it out first, then test. Leave one second after asking the Testee to hold before applying pressure. He or she needs time to hear and understand your request and then react.

4. Squeezing the part of the limb you are holding will cause pain, and the muscle will "weaken" as a reaction. Watch out for rings and bangles digging in also.

5. You treat the wrong muscle, or your own muscle is weak and your Testee acts as a surrogate for you (see chapter 11 for this).

6. Your testing is not objective. Because you so want to find the weak muscle, they all test weak, or you so want a muscle to be strong that your willpower alters the test result. If you suspect either might be happening, get someone else to check you, or deliberately think about something else or count out loud as you test. You should have no vested interest in the result of the test. The mark of a good tester is that they are frequently surprised by the result. Make no assumptions!

7. Asking the Testee to "try to hold" or "try it again" instead of just saying "hold" or "hold up/down/in/out" as appropriate. Asking someone to try implies that they may not succeed. It is a mixed message and confuses the brain by asking for effort, but not for

success in a specific action. The muscle will invariably test weak, and the harder you try, the weaker it will be, no matter how much energy and effort is expended (Teachers, please note!).

The most common *Testee faults* are:

1. The Testee will use a synergist to help. This is unconscious cheating. The first priority of a human being is survival. Knowing at an unconscious level that the muscle is weak, the Testee will "survive" by using other muscles to do the job, by moving or twisting slightly, or bending another part of the body to use the synergist muscle back-up system provided by nature. Watch out for this. Other muscle "recruiting" can be quite subtle. In particular, be careful when the Testee starts to learn the test position. He or she will helpfully hold the limb up, but of course it will be in the strongest position and not the best test position, so it is important that the Tester places the limb, not the Testee.
2. The Testee will hold his or her breath while you test. This can change the result of the test. If in doubt, make him or her talk or count out loud as you test.
3. The Testee will hook one limb or joint round another or around the edge of the testing table to give support. Unhook the limb and retest.
4. The Testee will forget to concentrate. Too often they will say "I do not understand what you want me to do." They mean they instinctively know they can't do it, so they don't understand physically. Frequently too they will lift the head to see what you are doing, or close the eyes to concentrate better. Do not allow this as results can be altered. Physically show them what is wanted by patting the part and say "Push/hold here." That also avoids any confusion over left and right.
5. Subconsciously the Testee knows what will strengthen his or her body and will frequently instinctively place his or her hands over the relief points for that muscle. Watch especially for crossing the hands on the chest or putting them behind the head. Remove them to either side of the body and not touching it, then retest.
6. Most people can't wait to get back to normal playing, but just occasionally the Testee may be so worried about a muscle that he

or she "quits" on the test. Show the test first on the opposite (strong) side of the body, then go back and test the first muscle while you make them talk about something else like " What are you doing for the holidays?" This problem is rare and usually means either that they have no incentive to get back to playing or are more damaged than you realize. If this does happen, look at chapter 11 on psychological reversal.

As you can see from these lists, it pays to be a bit persnickety at first, until you get the hang of it. Ideally find someone who can already muscle test to show you, or go to a "Touch for Health" class. Above all, don't dive in and test without first asking permission. You risk a charge of common assault! Make sure, too, that there is no known reason why you should not test muscles, such as a pinned joint, plate or replacement hip, or other such problem. Do not assume such things will be obvious; they won't be. People don't usually advertise such things, or volunteer information, so always ask.

Indicator muscles

Just as you have been testing a weak muscle to see if it is now strong, you can also test a muscle known to be strong/normal and use it as an indicator of what causes the Testee's body to go weak. This is useful in testing for emotional upset (chapter 10) and food sensitivity. In these cases, it matters not which muscle is used, provided it is strong first and will weaken when you deliberately switch it off (see chapter 11). All you are looking for in this case is a change in strength as a direct result of the thought of the emotive thing or situation (or contact with the substance). The only time a strong muscle will not respond normally like this is when it is overfacilitated or hypertense. (See chapter 10.)

The muscles in succeeding chapters are arranged in groups according to location and action, and the relevance of each muscle to the musician is explained, with instructions and illustrations on how to position the Testee and in which direction the testing should be done. This is followed by the relief points to work on, specific to that muscle, together with dietary and allergy advice, and finally emotional connections for use with affirmations (see chapter 10).

Surrogate Testing

There are times when you would like to, but cannot, test muscles. Such times are when the musician is exhausted, in a wheel chair, cannot get into a convenient testing position, or cannot understand what you say because of a language barrier. It might also be of use where there is too much pain to test a specific muscle or where the parent does not wish you to touch the child physically. Under such circumstances, you might use a surrogate—someone else preferably of the same family and same sex. This person is muscle tested while touching the musician. Obviously the surrogate's muscles must test strong first! Proceed as follows:

1. Test the surrogate and correct any muscle weaknesses.
2. Retest the surrogate while he or she is in physical contact with the musician, checking relevant holding and massage points by placing the surrogate's hands on the relevant places on the musician's body. The surrogate then breaks contact with the musician.
3. Work on the helpful points you have found on the musician's body using their hands under yours. This also teaches the musician where the points are for future self-treatment.
4. Retest the surrogate who is now in contact with the musician again. If you have done the corrections well, the surrogate's muscles should test strong again, which means the musician's muscles are now strong. Dramatic changes have been known to occur in the space of a few minutes with this method.

REFERENCES

Airola, P. *How to Get Well.* Phoenix, Ariz.: Health Plus Publishers, 1974.

Berkow, R., and A. Fletcher (Eds.). *The Merck Manual.* Whitehouse Station, NJ: Merck and Co Inc., 1992.

British National Formulary. London: British Medical Association and Royal Pharmaceutical Society of Great Britain, 1993– .

Caillet, R. *Hand Pain and Impairment.* Philadelphia: F.A. Davis, 1982.

———. *Neck and Arm Pain.* Philadelphia: F.A. Davis, 1991.

Hay, L. *Heal Your Body—The Mental Causes for Physical Illness, and the Metaphysical Way to Overcome Them.* New York: Author, 1976.

Hoppenfeld, S. *Physical Examination of the Spine and Extremities.* New York: Appleton-Century-Crofts, Prentice Hall, 1976.

Kendall, F., and E. McCreary. *Muscles Testing and Function*, 3rd ed. Baltimore, Md.: Williams and Wilkins, 1983.

Netter, F. *Atlas of Human Anatomy*. Basle, Switzerland: Ciba Geigy Ltd., 1989.

Ramsak, I., and W. Gerz. *AK Muscle Tests at a Glance*. Translated by T. Gates. Munchen/Mainberg, Germany: AKSE, 2000.

Sobel D., and A. Klein. *Arthritis: What Exercises Really Work*. London: Robinson Pub. Ltd., 1996.

Walther, D. "Applied Kinesiology Synopsis." In *Meridian Therapy*, 234–240. Pueblo, Colo.: Systems DC, 1980.

———. *Applied Kinesiology Vol. 2 Head, Neck and Jaw Pain and Dysfunction— The Stomatognathic System*. Pueblo, Colo.: Systems DC, 1983.

———. *ICAK-E Presentation and Applied Kinesiology*, Vols. 1 & 2. Pueblo, Colo.: Systems DC, 1989.

Weiss, S. *The Anatomy Book for Musicians, Muscle Dynamics*. Glenview, Ill.: Author, 1996.

5

Mucsles of the Head

In this chapter we examine how to test and assist the muscles of eyes, ears, facial expression, cheek and jaw, and neck. We shall not deal with all the muscles of the face, but the important ones for instrumental musicians. The information available on these muscles is not as full as for the muscles of the rest of the body, as less research has been done on their connection with acupuncture meridians, massage points, and nutrition. Many of them are also so small that strengthening techniques are limited to working on the muscle itself (see chapter 10). Against that, they are being exercised every time we speak, so they are strong for their size. This means that the main tendency of these muscles is to cramp through overuse rather than to be weak. They can also, with the exception of the neck and jaw muscles, be tested by you when you are alone.

When testing, pull the appropriate "face" and observe yourself in the mirror to see if both sides are contracting equally. If not, work on the longer muscle to shorten it by pushing the two ends together, and on the shorter ones to stretch it by pulling the two ends of that muscle apart till they are balanced. Do the holding points where given; construct affirmations around the relevant emotions mentioned, and work also on all the other nearby muscles. Then observe how you play and whether that upsets the muscle balance, the habits of your embouchure, or whether other unnecessary tensions might have crept in. It's possible you may even need a jaw adjustment from an applied kinesiologist rather than a dentist. The face muscles are not affected by the position of your head and neck in a way you can work on yourself, because the cranial nerves that supply them leave the brain stem via the skull, not the spine.

The consequence of this is that any misalignments and torsions on the skull bones, through which these muscles have, affect their function together with that of the ears, eyes, nose, throat, and tongue. Such problems might occur following a bang to the head, heavy dental work or plates, bridges, and false teeth, or due to embouchure changes. The therapist you then need is a cranial osteopath or kinesiologist, who may be able to help you considerably, even before possible referral to an ear, nose, and throat specialist (to whom the doctor may send you).

THE EYES

Although you don't need your eyes to play your instrument, you do need them to read music, sight-read, and drive, so I make no excuse for including them here. You will also notice that Alexander teachers often ask you to keep your focus "soft." The eye is moved by six pairs of external muscles attached round its vertical "equator": two for up and down, two for right and left, and two to swivel. The inside of the eye also has muscles: those that control the size of the pupil, affecting how much light comes in; and those that control the thickness of the lens for focus. The internal muscles move more than 100,000 times a day to react to light and focus.

Eye muscles, whether internal or external, are like any other muscles and need to be fully used or they deteriorate. They will also tire if you stare, holding one focus and level of contraction for a length of time. Weak external eye muscles will not hold the shape of the eyeball properly and it becomes horizontally egg-shaped. Overtense external eye muscles will cause it to go egg-shaped vertically. Astigmatism occurs where there is an uneven pull on the eyeball. All of these conditions can be helped by exercise as set out in the early 1900s by Bates Hauser (Hauser, *Better Eyes Without Glasses*). Modern exercises can be found in J. Goodrich's *Natural Vision Improvement*.

In their natural state, the internal eye muscles controlling the lens are

set for distance vision (a survival mechanism, so you can see any preda-
tor on the horizon and have time to run away). However, if instead of
using the full range, you constantly use only a small part of the range
for near vision, their action becomes unbalanced and they "forget" that
the whole range is available and gradually lose that ability and you are
told you need spectacles. In fact (eye)glasses and contact lenses are
often crutches that simply hasten the process of disuse of the full range
and you gradually need stronger and more pairs—reading, music, driving, and distance—or put up with awful combinations such as bifocals
or varifocals. What you need for healthy eyes is not glasses but a regular eye workout. Such an activity has only one real disadvantage, you
may have to get another weaker prescription pair of glasses, which, if
you persist in your exercises, you may eventually have to throw away.

Bates Exercises and Nutrition

1. Rest your elbows on the table and cup your chin in your hands.
   Without moving your head, let your eyes trace/write huge letters
   of the alphabet. Use capital letters or lower case; it doesn't matter.
   Write them as large as your eyes will let you so you use as full a
   range of movement as possible, but do it without strain! This exercise will give you all ranges of movement but is not so boring as
   fifty circles right, fifty circles left. You may need to start with half
   an alphabet if it makes your eye muscles ache. If you get bored
   with that, another option is to trace around the edges of everything
   you can see without moving your head.
2. Remove your glasses. Hold your arm out in front of you at shoulder height. Stick your thumb up. Look at your elbow crease, your
   thumb, and a distant object in line with them in quick succession
   and back, but no faster than you can focus on each as clearly as
   possible. Make friends with your blur and watch it disappear as
   your eye muscles get stronger.
3. Keep your head and eyes facing front and spread your arms wide
   at shoulder height until you can no longer see your fingers (wiggle
   them to be sure). Now take them over your head and wiggle again.
   You should be able to see almost 180° in all directions except
   across your nose. A wide range of vision is essential for chamber
   music as well as for driving safety.

4. "Palm" by covering your eyes with your palms pressed against your eye sockets, not your eyes. Shut out all the light. Total darkness is very therapeutic for your eyes. Just closing your eyes is not dark enough! Breathe deeply and relax for five minutes. Then do exercise 1 from this list with your eyes closed under your palms. Finish with another five minutes' deep-eye relaxation.

5. Buy or borrow a copy of Goodrich's *Natural Vision Improvement*. It's a great fun book for people of all ages. Good nutrition is as good for the eyes as anywhere else in the body—eat whole food and avoid junk food as much as possible. Eyes particularly need vitamins A, B, and complex.

Spotlights

The times when your near/far range of vision is restricted are when reading, when reading music, when driving, and when, if you sit in a permanent seat in an orchestra, you do a lot of work always looking at the same angle (to and from your music and the conductor). Sitting on a platform, you may be beset by glaring spotlights, as often as not, just behind the conductor, which cause you to screw up your eyes tensely. You may also end up with poorly written copy with uneven ledger-lines and again have to screw up your eyes to decipher it all. This is followed by a long highway or night drive home before your poor eyes can rest for the night. If you can't lose the light behind the conductor, ask if it can at least be shielded. Often theatre lighting is done by stage engineers who think it more important that the audience sees you than you the conductor. Orchestral playing is not primarily a visual spectacle! If the worst comes to the worst, wear dark glasses, play with your section leader, and don't look at the conductor—but don't let the conductor know that!

Poor copy is a legitimate cause for complaint. It means that someone has written the part out themselves instead of employing a professional copyist. They deserve any wrong notes they get.

Driving

Highway driving, day or night, causes you to keep a steady high speed. This means that you (a) probably fix or lock your neck muscles, and may hold them more tensely still if visibility is poor, and (b) your eyes have a fixed focal length like a stare, which they find extremely tiring and conducive to falling asleep at the wheel. Try these exercises while driving; they won't compromise safety. Take advantage of traffic lights or sitting in a traffic jam, when it is safe to do so:

1. Without taking your eyes off the road, gently turn your head 45° each way right and left, then tip it toward each shoulder in turn, and finally raise and lower your head. This will softly exercise and free up both neck and eye muscles.
2. Talk to a companion, or if you are alone sing loudly to break down neck and facial tension.
3. Keeping your head looking forward, safely but randomly flick your eyes to one side or the other, and see what you notice of the roadside flora and fauna. There are some beautiful mini-nature reserves to be seen—but stay safe!
4. Blink a lot.
5. Focus on your car hood, then let your vision slide out to the horizon and back.
6. Where possible, avoid driving for miles on roads with evenly spaced trees (e.g., in France) in bright sunlight. The constantly flickering light is known to trigger epileptic fits and that might disqualify you from driving in the future.
7. Stop at least five minutes for every hour you drive and do some palming (see earlier exercise). Remember the world lost a wonderful horn player in Dennis Brain who fell asleep at the wheel and drove into a tree.

Night driving, when both you and your eyes are tired, and you have probably had coffee to keep you awake, is definitely not good news for your eyes. They are probably feeling grainy from your evening's work, especially if there were spotlights or strip lighting. The coffee might keep your brain alert but will cause constriction of the arteries, and although the caffeine will temporarily help your hypoglycemic state if all you ate was junk food five hours earlier, it is far better to keep an apple in the car to nibble. Sugar and glucose tablets are quick-energy release agents but assimilating them will drain the body of vitamins A and B, both of which are needed for good night driving. If you have to drive for longer than one hour to an out-of-town gig, try to share the driving with someone else.

While on the subject of driving, be aware that it's an unfortunate biological fact that (a) one in eight people is color blind in total or in part and may well see red as green (this inherited tendency is ten times less likely in women) and (b) people of either gender may be unaware that they are slightly night blind. Because they have always been like that, they assume it is the same for everyone. It isn't, so allow for it.

Clean your windshield on arrival while it is still light and you can see what rubbish you have collected. You will be too tired later to bother and that simply adds to the hazard of poor vision night driving. If oncoming headlights are painful or have halos, you need to see an optician.

THE EARS

There's a tradition among advertisers that spectacles are more than respectable; they give you an air of erudition and make you an authority on the object being advertised. It's a curious thing that there is no stigma attached to a visual artist wearing spectacles, but a musician wearing a hearing aid is immediately suspect. Thank goodness Evelyn Glennie is changing all that. People with poor vision have a choice over the direction of their gaze, but those who are hard of hearing have no control over the source of sound. The populous forgets that poor hearing is not the same as low IQ and poor understanding, but can cause it.

Ears contain tiny muscles. Pitch definition is not the same as range or volume definition. Women and children hear in a higher range than men, but this should not be confused with an ability to differentiate between two sounds that are only one or two vibrations apart (e.g., 440 vibrations or 442 for A). Neither of these has anything to do with volume. Unfortunately we know of no muscle-related techniques for improving hearing. All we can do is beg you to take good care of your ears by keeping the volume down where possible, wearing cans or using screens when recording and investigating, and using new ear shields and ear plugs as they improve via the Musicians Union. As a result of continuous high volume, high-pitch sounds are lost first, making speech sound like a series of moanings. This means the most dangerous sounds are loud, high-pitched sounds as you might find in a disco. Just as the eyes react with temporary blindness when dazzled by a bright light, so the ears react with temporary deafness, which with repetition becomes progressive. Many pop stars become deaf, but it's not common knowledge, and often deliberately hidden. By the time hearing defects are discovered, they have made their money or have gone off the charts. Loud low-pitched sounds are much safer, allowing the ear more time to react with an eardrum tightening reflex, but still very bad, especially if they are continuous. According to Anthony McColl, "Virtually all executant musicians have had their hearing capacity reduced to some degree over the years by the mere fact of playing an instrument."

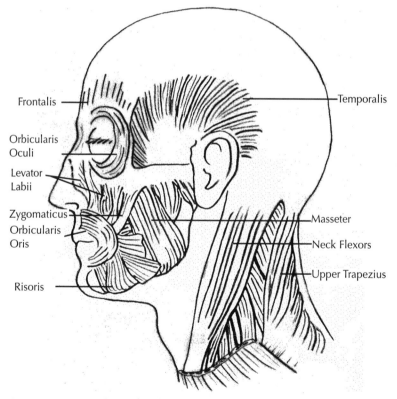

Figure 5.1 Face and Neck Muscles.

MUSCLES OF FACIAL EXPRESSION

1. Muscles that raise the upper lip (levator anguli oris, levator labii superioris)
2. Muscles that straighten the lips (risoris, zygomaticus)
3. Sphincter (orbicularis oris)
4. Muscles that lower the mouth/lower lip and tense the neck skin (mentalis, depressor anguli oris, depressor labii inferior, and platysma)

Levator Anguli Oris

This muscle is found on each side of the upper lip just on the nose side of the corner of the mouth. When both are used together, they form part of the embouchure, particularly in brass playing.

Test position: Draw one side of the angle of the upper lip as if to smile on one side and show one canine tooth. Look for matched contractions each side. Can also be tested by therapy localization (or touchpoint) (see chapter 4).

Antagonist muscle: Depressor anguli oris.

Risoris

This muscle is found on each side at the corners of the mouth in a straight line with the lips, and is important to oboists, bassoonists, flautists, and brass players.

Test position: Draw the angle of the mouth back toward the earlobe.

Meridian: Stomach.

Holding points: S-41 and SI-5. S-41 is found on the top of the foot in the center of the ankle crease. Hold it with SI-5, which is on the little finger side of the wrist, at the end of the forearm bone.

Emotion: Nervous/restful or upset/calm.

Bach flower: Willow.

Zygomaticus

This muscle, one each side, runs from the corners of the mouth to the cheekbone. It is important to all wind and brass players and anyone who likes smiling! Malfunction can cause speech difficulties and tender cheeks. It may also be an indicator of jaw-joint problems.

Test position: Draw the angle of the mouth upward and outward as in smiling and touch muscle while testing an indicator muscle. You may find it helpful to strengthen it by massaging from below the cheekbone under the corner of the eye to the corner of the mouth.

Emotion: Nervous/restful or upset/calm.

Bach flower: Willow.

Orbicularis Oris

This is the circular muscle found all around the lips. It is used in whistling, and (in part or entirety) in all woodwind and brass playing. Because of its meridian association, weakness is often associated with flatulence and tight abdominal muscles. It can also indicate jaw-joint problems.

Test position: Close lips and protrude them as for whistling or sucking a straw.

Antagonist muscles: All muscles that open the mouth wide.

Meridian: Small intestine.

Holding points: SI-3 and GB-41. SI-3 is on the back of the hand, halfway between the knuckles and wrist and between ring and little finger. Hold this with GB-41, which is similarly placed between the base of the fourth and fifth toes and the ankle crease on the top of the foot.

Emotion: Confused/confident or withholding/cooperative.

Bach flower: Star of Bethlehem.

Depressor Anguli Oris

This muscle is found between the corners of the mouth and the chin and is used by brass players to make the lower notes in conjunction with the muscles that drop the jaw a little.

Test position: Draw the angles of the mouth down.

Antagonist muscle: Levator anguli oris (which raises and protrudes upper lip).

Mentalis

This muscle is found between the lower lip and chin. It is most used by flautists. Weakness is sometimes associated with hemorrhoids because of the meridian association.

Test position: Contract chin skin against the jaw and protrude lower lip.

Meridian: Large intestine.

Holding points: LI-11 and S-36. LI-11 is found on the outside of the elbow (thumb side) about 2 inches (5 cm) from the point of the elbow, and just below the elbow crease. Hold it with S-36, which is below the knee in a little dip about 2 inches (5 cm) out on the fibula (little shin bone on the outside of the lower leg).

Nutrition: Magnesium.

Emotion: Unwilling/willing, separated/united.

Bach flower: Pine.

Platysma

This muscle is found under the skin over the front neck area and is contracted in conjunction with the use of depressor labii inferioris, which draws the angles of the mouth down. It is mostly used as part of the general contraction required to reach enough pressure for the highest notes in brass playing. Weakness often occurs at the same time as a dry, itchy throat or "frog in the throat," neck pain, frontal headaches, whiplash, and jaw-joint problems.

Test position: Draw angles of the mouth down and tense the neck skin.

Meridian: Stomach.

Holding points: Same as risoris.

Nutrition: Calcium

Emotion: Confused/confident, overbearing/submissive, grief for others/companionship.

Bach flower: Willow.

MUSCLES OF THE CHEEK AND JAW

1. Buccinator
2. Pterygoids

3. Masseter
4. Temporalis
5. Jaw joint

Buccinator

This muscle is found on each cheek and runs between the jaws and the angle of the mouth. It is vital to all brass and wind playing, particularly in so called "circular breathing." Weakness causes biting the cheek, speech problems, jaw-joint problems, and "hat-band" headaches.

Test position: Press the cheeks firmly against the side teeth, and pull back the angle of the mouth.

Nutrition: Vitamin B complex.

Emotion: Self-centered/kind, unobservant/observant.

Sensitivity: Foam rubber.

Pterygoids

These small, very strong muscles are vital to the jaw joint. They are found at the very back of the mouth on each side, behind the wisdom teeth. This means that they are vital to jaw alignment and embouchure of all sorts. Weakness causes clicking jaw, malocclusion and toothache, neck pain, cranial faults, and runny nose. The inside muscle clenches the teeth, the outside muscle protrudes the lower jaw and both are involved with chewing.

Test position: Protrude lower jaw.

Therapy localization: Inside mouth pointing directly back behind molar teeth.

Meridian: Stomach and liver.

Holding points: Same as risoris.

Nutrition: Vitamin B, potassium, orange peel.

Emotion: Confused/confident, imposed on/accepted, nervous/restful, unwilling/willing, empty/fulfilled, irresponsible/responsible, restless/calm.

Bach flower: Willow and Agrimony.

Masseter

This muscle is found on the outside of the cheek between the cheek-bones and the angles of the jaw. It is involved in holding onto a chin rest in upper strings. Malfunction causes restricted opening and other jaw-joint problems, difficulty chewing and holding the mouthpiece of a clarinet and saxophone, in brass and singing embouchures. Concurrently the incisor teeth may be painful, and there may be pain in the jaw or deep pain or ringing in the ear. There may also be a habit of teeth clenching under stress or teeth grinding at night.

Touch point: Bite firmly. You can feel the contraction easily by placing your fingers over the muscle near the back of the lower jaw.

Meridian: Pericardium (Cx).

Holding points: Cx-9 and Lv-1. Cx-9 is at the end of the middle finger pad, on the side nearest the index finger. Hold it with Lv-9, which is on the big toe, near the corner of the nailbed, on the side nearest the other toes.

Nutrition: Vitamin B3, magnesium, Brazil nuts, parsley.

Emotion: Unworthy/worthy, confused/confident, unfulfilled/fulfilled, useless/useful, unwilling/willing.

Bach flower: Holly.

Temporalis

This muscle is found in a fan shape above and behind the ear, and it runs down to the jaw, which it both closes and retracts. This means it is used greatly by all singers and wind and brass players for embouchure, for upper strings with the chin rest. It is involved in all jaw-joint problems, prolonged dental treatment, and teeth grinding. Clenching and spasm can cause headaches and cranial faults.

Meridian: Heart and lung.

Holding points: H-9 and Lv-1. H-9 is on the nailbed of the little finger. Hold it with Lv-1, which is on the corner of the nailbed of the big toe, on the side nearest the other toes.

Nutrition: Vitamins E and B6.

Emotion: Nervous/restful, unwilling/willing, depressed/cheerful, confused/confident, bitter/forgiving.

Bach flower: Hornbeam and water violet.

JAW JOINT

Temporo-mandibular joint (jaw joint) treatment is a wide field of particular interest to singers and wind and brass players. It should also be of interest to chiropractors and osteopaths treating musicians as well as to dentists, because it affects the body's balance and integrity. It is important to consider this joint as a whole as both sides work together. A muscle spasm or a tooth removed on one side affects the balance and integrity of both joints.

Test positions: First asses the jaw joint as a whole by comparing a line drawn through the levels of the ear lobes to a line drawn through the levels of the eyes. Ignore the fact that the head may not be held level. Eyes and ear lobes should be parallel. Ask about missing teeth. Find a strong indicator muscle and test:

1. Jaw opening. This should be done very slowly and any deviation or jerk to one side noted. When fully open, test the indicator muscle.
2. Jaw closing. Again do this very slowly and watch for wobbles. Test the indicator muscle as the teeth just touch.
3. Test jaw clenching and the indicator muscle.
4. Test chewing as if eating a raw carrot or a piece of gristle at the same time as testing the indicator muscle.
5. Push the lower jaw forward and test the indicator muscle.
6. Pull the lower jaw back and test the indicator muscle.
7. Keeping the head still, deviate or pull the jaw to one side and test the indicator muscle.
8. Test the indicator muscle pulling the jaw to the other side.

Corrections: In all the earlier cases, note which weakens the indicator muscle, return it to the position that caused the wobble or weakness, and treat in that position. Jaw open requires treatment on the pterygoids. Use the Testee's index finger to reach in behind the back teeth each side and poke the muscle six times strongly. It may be very tender. Jaw closed requires spindle cell treatment on the vertical temporalis fibers above the ear, masseter, and buccinator. Chewing requires treatment on the horizontal temporalis fibers behind the ear. Treat jaw deviation as follows: (a) The Tester takes the jaw to the side causing the indicator muscle to go weak and holds the head and jaw in that position as the Testee pulls the jaw back to the center against the Tester's resistance while breathing out. This is repeated three times. It stretches the horizontal temporalis fibers on one side and allows the other side to function correctly.

MUSCLES OF THE NECK

1. Neck flexors (sterno-cleido mastoid and scalenes)
2. Neck extensors (semispinalis and splenius) (figs. 5.2 and 5.3)
3. Hyoids (fig. 5.4)

Neck Flexors—Sterno-cleido Mastoid (SCM)

The SCM and scalenes together are called the "neck flexors." The SCM is the bar-shaped muscle that runs from just below and behind your ears, to the middle two ends of you collarbones. It becomes very prominent when you turn your head against resistance or lift your head against gravity when you are lying down. It is strongly assisted by the scalenes through which the nerves for the arm pass on their way from the spine. The scalenes are found at a deeper level and further back than SCM and are attached to the first and second ribs.

Apart from pulling the head and neck forward, these muscles are used as auxiliary breathing muscles when there are breathing problems (as in asthma, when the normal breathing muscles are in spasm) or when you need to breathe very deeply. They account for the high-chested and forward head position of may wind and string players because they can become overdeveloped or overcontracted through poor breathing habits and taking the head to the instrument rather than instrument to head in both wind and upper strings. It can also occur from holding a violin or viola too tightly or carrying a heavy instrument case on one shoulder. Chronic overcontraction causes neck pain, headaches, shoulder pain, and collarbone pain. There may also be sinus problems, tinnitus, vertigo or visual problems, heartburn, and constipation or diarrhea. These muscles are badly affected by any allergy or mental or physical stress, by a "crick in the neck" from sleeping on strange/ wrong pillows, or any kind of whiplash injury from even minor traffic accidents. Such problems are hazards for any freelance player who drives a lot, especially with the car window open, causing a draft on one side. Pain can also be "referred" to the neck from digestive or other

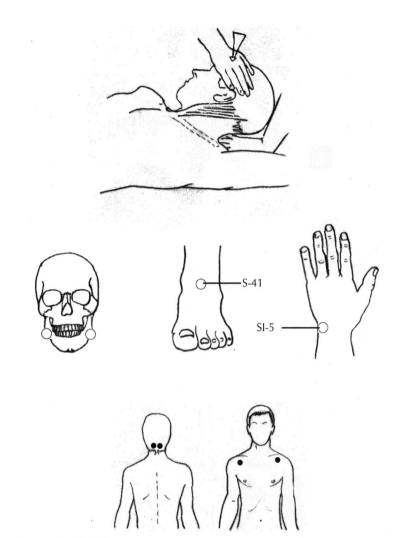

S-41

SI-5

Figure 5.2   Neck Flexors.

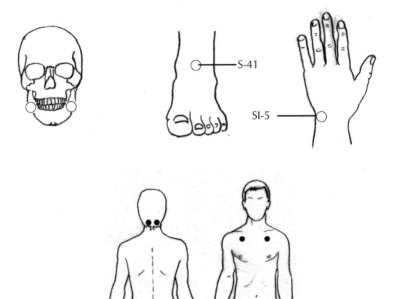

Figure 5.3   Neck extensors.

internal organ malfunction. One very surprising cause of neck-muscle weakness is overtight shoes, where the toes are pressed hard against the front of the shoe, or from high-heeled shoes, which have the same effect as far as the toes are concerned. Neck muscles are associated with the stomach meridian and crushing the second toes has a disempowering effect on the stomach meridian. Other symptoms might include slowness, tiredness, possible low blood-sugar, easy bruising, and cold hands.

Test position: Lie face up with the chin tucked in and the hands above the shoulders. The head is raised and pressure is placed on the forehead to push it back to the table. To test one side at a time, lift and turn the head at least 45°. Pressure is then applied to the uppermost temple to push the head directly back to the table. Watch that the Testee does not try to turn or twist the chin, to change the angle, to recruit other muscles. When pressing down, the Tester's other hand is placed under the head, not touching it. This is to break the fall if the muscle is weak, rather than allowing the head to bang down on the table. Extreme weakness means the Testee will be unable to hold the head up at all. To isolate the scalenes, turn the head 10° only, and test with pressure from the little finger side of the tester's hand on the forehead above the eye, straight back to the table (and not in line with the 10° turn). Watch that the Testee doesn't try to turn the head further to recruit extra SCM strength. If these muscles are weak, also test the pectorals and trapezius.

Antagonist muscles: Neck extensors.

Massage points: (a) The second space down from the collarbone between the ribs, directly above the nipples. (b) Either side of the spine at the very top of the neck (C2 lamina).

Meridian: Stomach.

Holding points: (a) On the side of the jaw directly under the outer corner of the eye. (b) Acupoints S-41 and SI-5. S-41 is on the top of the foot at the center of the ankle crease. Hold it at the same time as SI-5, which is on the side of the wrist, on the bump at the end of the forearm bone and below the little finger.

Nutrition: Since these muscles seem to have associations with the drainage for the head and sinuses, it is important to check for airborne or food sensitivities or allergies if there is constant muscle weakness. Eating seafood that contains iodine will help, but for general congestion problems, all the B vitamins are needed, especially B3 and B6. Yogurt may help, but otherwise cut down on all dairy products to lessen mucus formation generally. Increase nondairy sources of calcium, magnesium, manganese, iodine, and zinc; vitamin E face cream spread over the area is said to help.

Sensitivity: Mung bean, sprouts, and cinnamon.

Emotion: Unwilling/willing, irritated/tranquil, hard/adaptable, confused/confident, rebellious/accepting, defeated/successful, nervous/restful, insecure/secure.

Bach flower: Willow.

Neck Extensors—Semispinalis and Splenius

These muscles are the neck extensors, which hold the head up and back against gravity and are the upper part of the complicated system of cross-hatching of muscles that support the entire spine at the back. Semispinalis and splenius contract when you look up at the ceiling over your head and are involved in rotation of the head. In holding up the head, which is the heaviest part of your body and furthest from the ground, muscles in this group have to fight gravity and tire easily when you are constantly stretching them by looking down at a keyboard or holding a stringed instrument in a forward position. They are very strong and cramp when holding up the head (especially in small people) or looking upward at a conductor on a high rostrum or for a highly held wind or brass instrument, particularly in brass-band parades. They are susceptible to drafts down the neck and are often part of the cause of tension headaches. Good coordination between all the neck muscles is vital to your sense of balance, because it governs how you hold your head. Weakness may be accompanied by sinus and lymphatic problems in the head area. Chronic weakness can also be due to a problem in the area of the sacrum and low back; if this is so, seek help from a chiropractor.

Test position: The Testee lies face down with both arms above the head. The head is then raised off the table, and pressure is put on the back of the head to push it back down to the table. To test one side at a time, turn the head toward the side to be tested and put pressure on the head above the ear to push the head to the table. Watch for sideways bending to recruit other muscles, and with the neck flexors, it is kinder to place your hand between the head and the table. Other muscles to check if this is weak: pectoralis major clavicular (PMC) and upper trapezius.

Antagonist muscles: Neck flexors.
Massage point: Same as for neck flexors.
Meridian: Stomach.
Holding point: Same as for neck flexors.
Nutrition: Same as for neck flexors.
Sensitivity: Bay leaves.
Emotion and Bach flower: Same as for neck flexors.

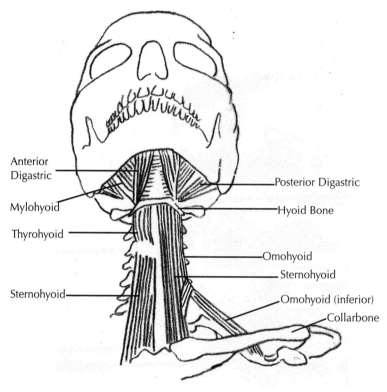

Anterior Digastric

Mylohyoid

Thyrohyoid

Sternohyoid

Posterior Digastric

Hyoid Bone

Omohyoid

Sternohyoid

Omohyoid (inferior)

Collarbone

Figure 5.4   Hyoids.

Hyoid

The hyoid is the one bone in the body not attached to any other bone. It is small, horseshoe-shaped, and is found in the throat, just above the Adam's apple. It is controlled by eight sets of muscles and is strongly involved in balance and head position. Suspect imbalance between the muscles if there is neurological disorganization such as dyslexia, emotional problems, poor balance, fatigue, or voice and breathing problems.

Test positions for specific muscle groups: Find a strong indicator muscle. Next, test the suprahyoid muscles, press and hold the hyoid toward the feet, and retest the indicator muscle. To test the infrahyoid muscles, pull and hold the hyoid toward the head. To test the muscles left and right, press and hold the hyoid to one side and test the indicator muscle; repeat, pulling the other side. To test the anterior muscles, gently push the hyoid toward the back of the head and test the indicator muscle. To test the posterior muscles, hold either side of the hyoid and pull it gently forward while testing the indicator muscle. A general test can be performed by rotating the hyoid one way and then the other, or by jiggling it about while testing the indicator muscle.

Corrections: Use spindle cell technique to pinch the belly of the muscles that are being stretched by the direction of pull. For example, to correct the suprahyoid muscles, vertically pinch together the belly of the muscles above the Adam's apple. Check for reactivity by asking the Testee to walk in a figure of eight several times before retesting. If the indicator muscle still goes weak, check gait (see chapter 10).

REFERENCES

Bunch, M. *Dynamics of the Singing Voice,* 3rd ed. New York: Springer Verlag, 1995.

Fitton, J. (Ed.). Acoustic Shields—A Practical Solution That May Be Provided by Managements to Help Players Endangered at Work. *Pan* 13, no. 2 (1995).

Goodrich, J. *Natural Vision Improvement.* Newton Abbot, Devon England: David and Charles Publishers, 1987.

Hauser, B. G. *Better Eyes Without Glasses.* London: Faber and Faber.

Lockie, A. *The Family Guide to Homeopathy—The Safe Form of Medicine for the Future.* London: Hamish Hamilton, Penguin Books Ltd., 1989.

McColl, A. Advances in Earplug Design—A Survey of the Options Available to the Practical Musician. *Pan* 3, no. 3 (1995a): 26–27.

———. Hearing Damage to the Musician—A Review of Audiometric Studies in Orchestras and Their Practical Conclusions. *Pan* 13, no. 3 (1995b): 24–25.

Porter, M. *Dental Problems in Wind Instrument Playing.* London: The British Dental Association, 1978.

Saunders, H. *Self-Help Manual for Your Neck.* Chaska, Minn.: The Saunders Group Inc., 1992, 32.

Skeath, J. Hard to Learn. *Music Teacher,* October 8–11, 1994.

Zimmers, P., and J. Gobetti. Head and Neck Lesions Commonly Found in Musicians. *JADA* 125 (November 1994): 1487–1496.

6

Muscles of the Shoulder, Upper Arm, and Elbow

MUSCLES OF THE SHOULDER

1. Muscles that raise the shoulders (upper trapezius and levator scapulae)
2. Muscles that rotate the shoulders (subscapularis, infraspinatus, teres major and teres minor)
3. Muscles that draw the shoulders down (lower trapezius) (Latissimus dorsi also performs this function. See under back muscles).
4. Muscles that draw the shoulders back and together (rhomboids and middle trapezius)

Upper Trapezius

This muscle is the upper division of the big, kite-shaped muscle on the back. It is attached to the nape of the neck and all the neck vertebrae (fig. 6.1). It goes out to the shoulder tip, is attached to the shoulder blades and the outer edge of the collarbone, and gives a slant to the top of the shoulder. It raises the shoulder girdle and bends the neck to one side, while turning the head to the other side, and rotates the shoulder blade. Right and left work against each other to hold the head and neck centrally between the shoulders.

By far the most common problem occurs when the shoulders are

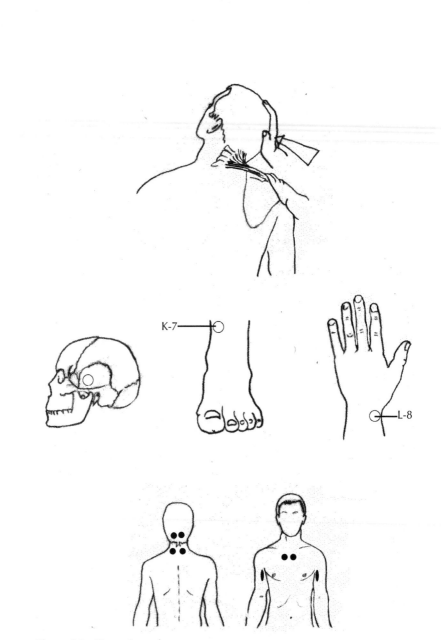

K-7

L-8

Figure 6.1　Upper trapezius.

raised because of stress. The pull of the upper trapezius on the back of the skull affects the balance of the ears, eyes, and hands in relation to the body and constricts some of the blood supply to the head, leading to blurred vision or ear problems and making it hard to think clearly. It is also often developed one-sidedly through holding upper-stringed instruments and flute, or always carrying the instrument case or handbag in one hand or on one shoulder. Weakness on both sides causes a hunched upper back and forward head position (as often occurs postmenopausally in women). This causes upper back pain and neck pain as the trapezius tries to compensate and hold the head up. It is common to find inner-ear disturbances such as tinnitus or loss of hearing with chronic weakness of this muscle.

Test position: The Testee sits and tilts the head to bring the back of the ear toward the shoulder. Pressure is put on the top of the shoulder and the side of the head to pry them apart. Other muscles to test if there is a weakness: levator scapulae, neck flexors and extensors, rhomboids, and pectorals. One-sided weakness may affect latissimus dorsi.

Antagonist muscle: The trapezius on the other shoulder.

Massage points: (a) The top 3 inches of the front/inner part of the upper arm in the groove between the muscles. (b) Up against the skull at the top center of the neck.

Meridian: Kidney (associated organs—ear and eye).

Holding points: (a) Halfway between the corner of the eye and the top of the ear. (b) Acupoints K-7 and L-8. K-7 can be located by measuring a spot one hand's width above the anklebone on the inside of the shin. Hold it at the same time as L-8, which is on the very end of the forearm bone under the thumb.

Nutrition: Increase intake of foods rich in vitamins A and B complex and essential fatty acids, calcium, and iron. Abstain from caffeinated drinks and food containing oxalic acid, such as rhubarb, purple fruits, and coffee and chocolate.

Sensitivity: Some grains and cooking oils, soy products and pineapple.

Emotion: Unwilling/willing, insecure/secure, doubtful/certain, guilty/innocent, irresponsible/responsible, irritable/agreeable.

Bach flower: Scleranthus.

Levator Scapulae

This muscle runs from the top four bones in the neck to the top inner corner of the shoulder blade (fig. 6.2). It lifts the shoulder blade and

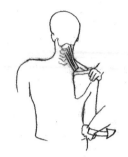

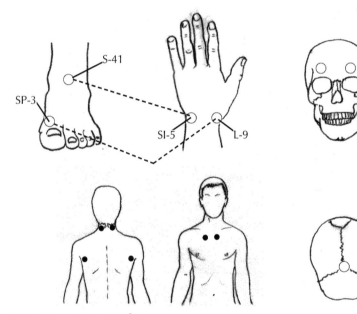

Figure 6.2   Levator scapulae.

draws it toward the spine and is therefore often used in holding upper
stringed instruments or flute/piccolo and telephone where the head
is turned to one side. It will also be affected by carrying heavy bags
on one side or falling asleep with the head bent too far forward and
twisted on long distance travel. It reacts badly to stress, being part of
the "shoulders-up-to-your-ears" syndrome, and weakness causes

headaches, the head feeling heavy, stiff neck, and sore shoulders. When it is very weak, the shoulder blade may wing out as it can't be drawn in toward the spine, so the upper trapezius has to take over and creates pain at the top of the shoulder. It is a common site for trigger points and knots in the muscle belly. Since the place of its attachment to the skull is frequently immediately over the nerves that go from there over the top of the head, tension in the muscle causes a headache that radiates from the back of the skull over the top of the head to behind the eye. Persistent weakness may need a chiropractic or osteopathic adjustment of the neck.

Test position: (a) The Testee is seated. The elbow is fully bent and pulled down (without bending the spine) until it is almost touching the top of the hip, slightly back from the center. The head should be held straight or slightly turned toward the side you are testing. Hold the top of the shoulder down toward the hip, while pulling the elbow away out to the side. Watch that the shoulder blade remains still. This position removes as much recruitment of the upper trapezius and rhomboids as possible. (b) Lie face down on the bench, side bend the head 45° and lift it on the side to be tested. The Tester supports the shoulder blade with one hand while pulling the head in an arc down and in to the bench. Other muscles to test if it's weak: rhomboids, trapezius, latissimus dorsi, pectoralis major clavicular, and neck muscles.

Antagonist muscles: Trapezius and neck extensors.

Massage points: (a) In the corner, just under where the collarbone and breastbone meet. (b) On the outer border of the shoulderblade, level with the armpit, when the arms are by the sides.

Meridian: Lung (parathyroid association).

Holding points: (a) Bregma—the spot one thumb's width back from the vertex of the head. (b) Acupoints use L-9 and Sp-3. L-9 is at the base of the thumb on the outside of the wrist cease. Hold it together with Sp-3, which is on the heel side of the big joint at the base of the big toe.

Nutrition: This muscle becomes weak if there is acid disturbance in the stomach or lack of ability to metabolize calcium. Avoid eating when stressed, and chew food very well. Avoid sugary foods as snacks just before a meal, and increase vitamin B intake.

Sensitivity: Sawdust and wood pulp products.

Emotion: Confused/confident, left out/included, unwilling/willing, irritated/tranquil, nervous/restful, haughty/meek, restless/calm, intolerant/understanding.

Bach flower: Mimulus.

Subclavius (No Illustration)

This is a small muscle found under the collarbone. It rotates the collarbone and raises its outer end. It is thus involved in controlling and stabilizing the collarbone and first rib relationships when the shoulder is rotated forward and the arm is raised. This means it is especially involved when playing at the tip of the bow. It is often involved with chronic raised shoulder and frozen shoulder problems and can refer pain to the upper arm and elbow mimicking tennis elbow.

Test position: The Testee sits with both straight arms raised next to the ears, palms forward. Keeping away from the wrists the Tester pulls the forearms apart, taking the arms away from the head. If tested singly, the Tester's free hand can feel for any slight movement of the collarbone, indicating weakness.

Massage points: (a) Under the joint where the collarbone meets the breastbone. (b) Either side of the prominent bone at the base of the back of the neck.

Meridians and Holding points: not known.

Nutrition: Magnesium.

Subscapularis

The name of this muscle means "under the shoulder blade," which is where it is (fig. 6.3). The nearest you can get to it is to feel the lower inner edge of the shoulder blade where it is attached. The other end is attached to the upper arm just below the shoulder joint. It pulls the upper arm in and down, when it is raised above the shoulder, and allows the shoulder blade to glide over the rib cage. It also helps to stabilize and hold the upper arm in to the shoulder joint. Symptoms that can be associated with its weakness are difficulty in raising the arm, difficulty combing your hair, and it often occurs with easy dislocation in very loose-jointed people (as musicians often are). It can cause shoulder pain (especially frozen shoulder), pain at the back of the shoulder when driving, and upper arm and chest pain that is relieved by raising the arm

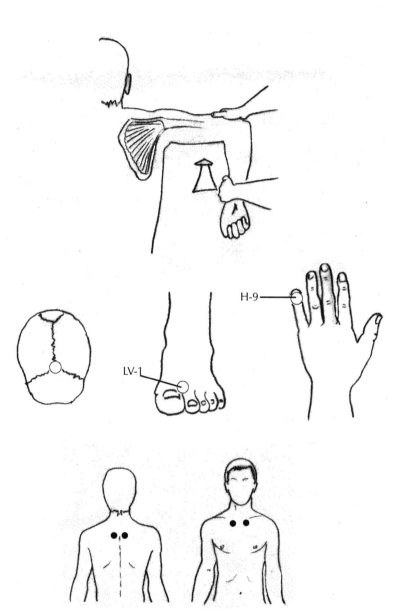

Figure 6.3   Subscapularis.

over the head, and it may be associated with palpitations, bleeding gums, dizziness, low blood-sugar, cold shivers and itchy, runny nose, tender shins, and hiatal hernia. It is involved in the "down bow" stroke of all string players, and especially cellists.

Test position: (a) The Testee sits, raises the arm to 90° out to the side, and the elbow is bent to 90°, so that the forearm hangs down, palm behind. The Tester stands behind the Testee and stabilizes the upper arm near but not on the elbow, while pushing the forearm straight-forward and up. (b) The Testee lies face down with the arm out to the side 90° and hanging off the edge of the table at the elbow. Stabilize the upper arm as you push the forearm away from the feet. Other muscles to test if it is weak: anterior serratus and middle trapezius.

Antagonist muscle: Infraspinatus

Massage points: (a) Between the second and third rib next to the breastbone. (b) Between the second and third ribs either side of the spine.

Meridian: Heart

Holding points: (a) Bregma, a spot one thumb's width back form the vertex of the head. (b) Acupoints Lv-1 and H-9. Lv-1 is found on the inside of the nailbed of the big toe. Hold it together with H-9, which is on the nailbed of the little finger.

Nutrition: Increase intake of calcium and vitamins E and B complex.

Emotion: Nervous/restful, irresponsible/responsible, unwilling/willing, confused/confident, unfulfilled/fulfilled, repulsive/acceptable, upset/calm.

Bach flower: Hornbeam.

Infraspinatus

This muscle is found on the back of the shoulder blade beneath its horizontal ridge (fig. 6.4). Like subscapularis, it is one of the four muscles that hold the upper arm into the shoulder joint. Very often it shares a common tendon with teres minor, to which it has a similar action. It is most active when the arm is raised above horizontal or when playing at the tip of the bow. It is partly used to hold the arm up. With coracobrachialis, it is used in order to produce the correct playing position for the upper strings and harp. It acts as an antagonist partner to subscapularis in the right arm for all string players and is often involved in

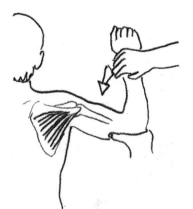

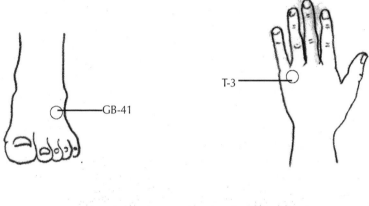

GB-41

T-3

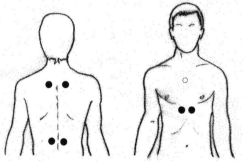

Figure 6.4 Infraspinatus.

"frozen shoulder" problems. Weakness may manifest as elbow, wrist, and shoulder difficulties in inability to reach over and touch the opposite ear, and as pain in the ring and little fingers. Digestive disturbance often accompanies weakness in this muscle, and because of its meridian association, it seems to be an indicator of thymus and thyroid function. When these are not in top form, there may be hyperactivity and irritability, weight change, unwarranted or uncontrolled crying, sweating, being out of breath, cold, chapped hands, redness around the eyes, dizziness, or a sluggish feeling that makes it hard to get out of bed in the morning. This muscle responds badly to heavy metal poisoning (e.g., from mercury from tooth amalgam) in the body.

Test position: The Testee sits with arm raised to 90° and the elbow bent at 90° with the forearm vertical and the hand upward. Stabilize the side of the elbow. Pressure is put on the back of the wrist to rotate the upper arm forward and downward toward the feet (and even beyond). If the shoulder blade moves, do the test lying down where the Testee's weight will prevent it from moving. Watch for any shoulder blade movement or attempt to move the arm in or out to recruit other muscles because of weakness. Other muscles to test if weak: teres minor, supraspinatus, upper and middle trapezius, and rhomboids.

Antagonist muscle: Supraspinatus.

Massage points: (a) Between the fifth and sixth ribs near the breastbone on the right chest wall. (b) Just above the lowest ribs on either side of the spine.

Meridian: Triple warmer.

Holding points: (a) The Angle of Louis, which is the ridge found about three fingers width down from the top of the breastbone. (b) Acupoints GB-41 and Tw-3: GB-41 is found on the top of the foot, about halfway between the ankle crease and the base of the fourth and fifth toes. Hold this with Tw-3, which is in a similar position on the back of the hand.

Nutrition: Vitamins A and C, zinc, and copper. This muscle also responds to foods high in natural iodine such as seafoods and seaweed. Poppyseed and tarragon are also beneficial. Avoid cheese, bananas, and oats and, if taking vitamin A for some other reason, check that you haven't overdone it.

Sensitivity: Soy products, cabbage, all peas and beans, and cedar products.

Emotion: Unwilling/willing, grouchy/agreeable, unjust/just, confused/confident, defensive/listening.

Bach flower: Mustard.

Teres Minor

This muscle runs from halfway up the outer edge of the shoulder blade to the back of the upper arm (fig. 6.5). It stabilizes and draws the arm in toward the body and turns the upper arm outward at the same time. It is often joined by a common tendon to infraspinatus and has a similar action. It also opposes subscapularis and is one of the muscles that holds the upper arm into the shoulder joint. It is most used by pianists playing at the extreme ends of the keyboard, by flautists (right hand), and by the "underhand" method of bowing used by some bass players. Tension in this muscle can cause deep pain at the back of the upper arm. Weakness can cause, or add to, shoulder, elbow, and wrist problems and can refer pain to the pelvic bones on which you sit. Its meridian connection with the triple warmer and thyroid mean that weakness may be accompanied by overwrought crying.

Test position: The Testee sits with arms by the side and elbows bent at 90°, palm forward. The Tester supports and stabilizes the elbow against the body while pushing the back of the forearm forward as though to cross the body in an arc. Watch that the Testee doesn't recruit biceps or triceps, retract the shoulder, pull it forward, or change the flexion of the elbow. Other muscles to test if weak: infraspinatus, trapezius, and rhomboids.

Antagonist muscle: Subscapularis.

Massage points: (a) Between the second and third ribs next to the breastbone. (b) Between the second and third ribs on the back, next to the spine, and level with the top of the shoulder blades.

Meridian: Triple warmer.

Holding points: (a) Just in the normal hairline, halfway between the corner of the eye and where the top of the ear meets the head. (b) Acupoints GB-41 and Tw-3. GB-41 is found on the top of the foot, halfway between the base of the fourth toe and the ankle. Hold it at the same time as Tw-3, which is on the back of the hand halfway between the base of the ring finger and the wrist.

Nutrition: This muscle can also be an indicator of thyroid function;

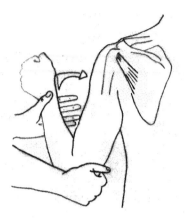

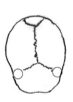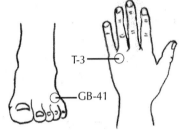

T-3

GB-41

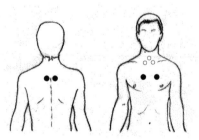

Figure 6.5   Teres minor.

therefore, eat foods containing organic iodine, such as seafood and seaweed and kelp. Use honey rather than sugar, and eat millet.

Emotion: Unwilling/willing, unworthy/worthy, confused/confident, lack of respect/respected.

Bach flower: Mustard.

Teres Major

This muscle runs from the bottom corner of the shoulder blade to the top front of the arm, so it draws the arm into the body, rotates the arm inward, and pulls it back slightly behind the body, near the shoulder blade (fig. 6.6). It is most often used by women doing up their bra strap behind their back and by horn players and bassoonists to position the lower hand, where it may cramp if the finger spread is too great, or the instrument is held too tightly or too close to the body. It is also very important in "frozen shoulder" syndromes. It may be the cause of shoulder blade pain.

Test position: (a) The Testee sits and places a fist on the back of the pelvis or low back, while pushing the elbow backward. The shoulder is stabilized, while the elbow is pushed from behind, outward, and forward by the Tester. (b) The Testee lies face down and the arm is bent back to place a closed fist on the back of the pelvis. Pressure is applied on the elbow to push it to the floor, while stabilizing the opposite shoulder to prevent body rock. In this position, both sides can be tested together. Take care not to overpower the Testee. Other muscles to test if weak: middle trapezius and rhomboids.

Antagonist muscle: Teres minor.

Massage points: (a) Between the second and third ribs, 2 inches (5 cm) from the breastbone. (b) Between the second and third ribs on the back, next to the spine and level with the top of the shoulder blades.

Holding points: (a) Just in the normal hairline, halfway between the corner of the eye and where the top of the ear meets the head. (b) Acupoints GB-41 and TW-3. GB-41 is found on the top of the foot, halfway between the base of the fourth toe and the ankle. Hold it at the same time as TW-3, which is on the back of the hand, halfway between the base of the ring finger and the wrist.

Nutrition: Same as for Teres minor. If food seems tasteless, add foods containing zinc and vitamin E to the diet rather than salt.

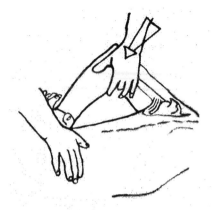

Figure 6.6   Teres major.

Emotion: Confused/confident, separated/united.
Bach flower: Mustard.

Middle and Lower Trapezius

There are also two lower divisions of the kite-shaped trapezius muscle found on the back (fig. 6.7). The middle division runs from the top five vertebrae of the back, out to the ridge in the middle of each shoulder blade. It holds the shoulder blade in to the center of the body and turns its outer end down. The lower division runs from the next six vertebrae down the back, out to the ridge in the middle of the shoulder blade, so that it rotates the shoulder blade, draws it in or stabilizes it, also keeping the midspine upright. These muscles are often involved in shoulder and arm problems in general, but most particularly in one-sided use, such as carrying heavy instruments on one shoulder, and midback problems, such as playing the cello, bass, bassoon, horn, and harp. They are also used in percussion and conducting. They will be stretched differently with unevenly developed shoulders in upper string players. Tension, especially unequal tension between sides, pulls the spine out of alignment, leading to a round-shouldered and/or slouched posture and caved-in upper chest, which compromises good breathing. This complaint is suffered by many musicians (especially upper strings, oboe, and any small manual keyboard player such as harpsichord) and anyone who has to sit for hours on a chair with a sloping back seat and on long drives to out-of-town gigs. If the muscles only test weak when standing, suspect and check for flat feet or tense pectoral muscles. Weakness in the trapezii is associated with poor spleen function, sore throats and hearing loss, anemia and other blood disorders, headache, or ache behind the eyes.

Test position: Middle trapezius. The Testee sits and raises the arm 90° to the side and level with the floor, with elbow straight and palm up. The same side shoulder or chest is stabilized while the upper arm is pulled forward. Lower trapezius: (a) The Testee sits with the arm raised to the side another 45° beyond horizontal, with palm in toward the head. The Tester stands behind the Testee, stabilizes the shoulder and pushes the upper arm forward. (b) The Testee is lying face down with the arm raised 45° away from the head, palm in, and the Tester stabilizes the opposite hip while pushing the upper arm to the floor. In all cases, the

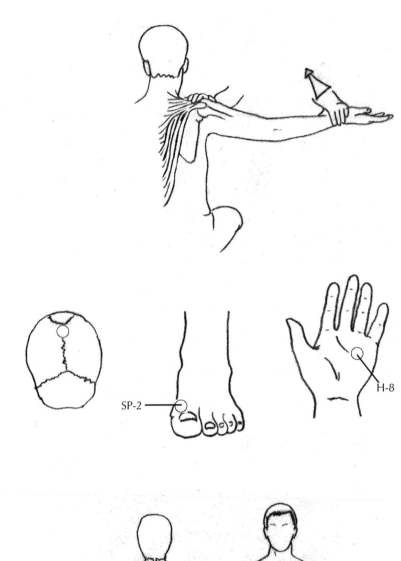

SP-2

H-8

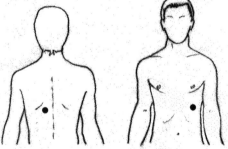

Figure 6.7   Middle and lower trapezius.

upper arm is being used as a lever via the shoulder blade, to test the muscle. Other muscles to test if either division is weak: anterior serratus, pectoralis major clavicular (PMC), upper trapezius, and levator scapulae.

Antagonist muscles: All three pectorals and latissimus dorsi.

Massage points: (a) Between the seventh and eighth ribs on the left, just below the level of the end of the breastbone (or for women, just under the bra cup wire). (b) On the back, on the left-hand side next to the spine between the seventh and eighth ribs, level with the bottom of the shoulder blades.

Meridian: Spleen.

Holding points: (a) At the midline of the head, directly above the back of the ears. (b) Acupoints Sp-2 and H-8. Sp-2 is found on the inside of the foot, on the nail side of the joint at the base of the big toe. Hold it together with H-8, which is on the palm of the hand, on the crease below the little and ring fingers, between the palm bones.

Nutrition: Buckwheat and foods high in vitamin C and calcium.

Emotion: Nervous/restful, hating/affectionate, unwilling/willing, tongue-tied/expressive.

Bach flower: Mimulus.

Rhomboids (Major and Minor)

These muscles are short, powerful, and so close together that they help each other (fig. 6.8). They join the inner edge of the shoulder blade to the spine in the upper back and draw the shoulder blades together. They also help counterbalance the weight of any instrument held in front of the body, keeping the player upright by stabilizing the back of the shoulder girdle, together with the trapezius. They help the posture of a pianist playing at both outer ends of the keyboard at once. Most problems occur with one-sided development (as in upper strings), having the effect of pulling the upper spine chronically to one side, causing one rhomboid to be flaccid and weak, and the other one to be tense and in spasm. This sort of tension causes and/or crunching noises along the spine side of the shoulder blade. Weakness generally causes pain between the shoulder blades and a sore lower neck. Other symptoms may include water retention and cold hands and feet.

Test position: The Testee sits, bends the elbow maximally so that the

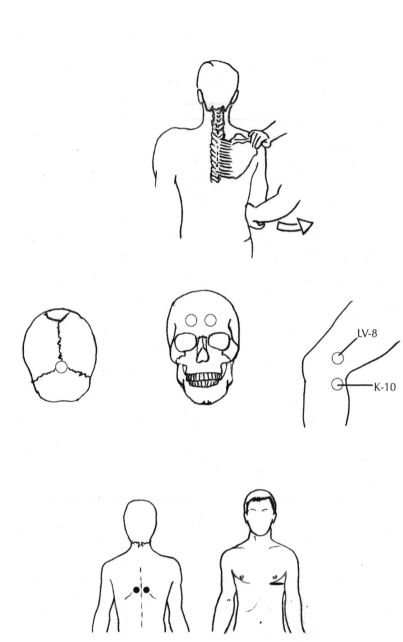

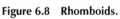

Figure 6.8   Rhomboids.

hand is at the shoulder, not on the chest wall (the other arm being raised above the shoulder to prevent recruitment). The shoulder is stabilized and the elbow is pulled away from the body to the side. Watch that the shoulders are level. If the rhomboid is weak, the shoulder blade will pull away or wing out from the spine as you test. Other muscles to test, if weak: the other rhomboid, upper trapezius, levator scapulae, anterior deltoid, latissimus dorsi, and the pectorals.

Antagonist muscles: Pectorals.

Massage points: (a) Between the fifth and sixth rib space on the chest wall, one rib space down from the nipple on the left side only. (b) Between the sixth and seventh rib space next to the spine on the left side only.

Meridian: Liver.

Holding points: (a) Frontal eminencies—above the center of each eye between the eyebrow and the hairline. (b) Acupoints Lv-8 and K-10. Lv-8 is found in between the lower, inner end of the thighbone and the hamstring tendon near the inner knee crease. K-10 is almost next door, at the innermost end of the knee crease when the knee is bent.

Nutrition: The association of the muscle is with the liver and the stomach, so avoid fizzy drinks, all forms of caffeine, and all foods that are rich, fatty, or fried. Increase intake of foods high in vitamins A and B complex, kelp and zinc, garlic, and parsley.

Emotion: Confused/confident, fearful/courageous, unwilling/willing, squeamish/settled, nervous/restful, unsociable/sociable, frustrated/satisfied, obligated/willing, unsupportive/supportive.

Bach flower: Agrimony.

MUSCLES OF THE UPPER ARM

1. Muscles that raise the upper arm (supraspinatus and deltoids)
2. Muscles that draw the upper arms forward and together (the three pectorals and coracobrachialis)

Supraspinatus

This is the last of the four muscles that hold the upper arm in the shoulder joint, which means this muscle is always slightly activated (fig. 6.9).

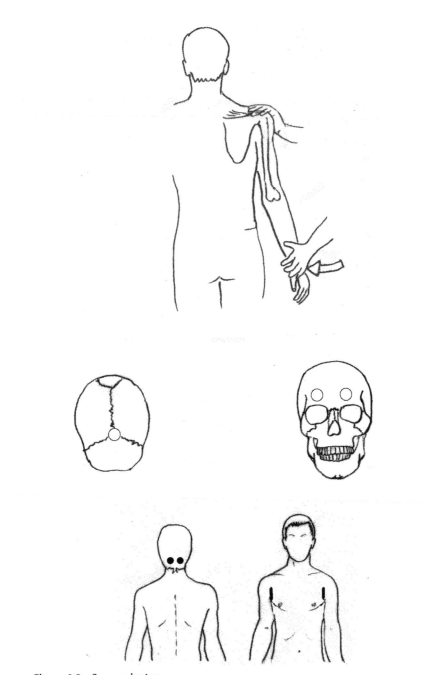

Figure 6.9   Supraspinatus.

It is found above the horizontal bar on the shoulder blade and therefore only has a mechanically weak lifting action on the arm from hanging by the side to about 15° away from the body. Any lifting of the arm beyond 15° is done by the deltoid group. Supraspinatus has no special significance on its own to musicians, other than the prevention of dislocation. However, weakness may accompany any shoulder problems such as frozen shoulder or dislocation and often causes shoulder pains. Because of its meridian association, hard mental work, driving, and emotional stress seem to fatigue it. It is often weak in children who are slow learners.

Test position: The Testee sits with head turned away from the muscle being tested to inactivate the trapezius as far as possible. The straight arm is taken out to the side and forward 15°, palm in and thumb forward. Pressure is put on the back of the forearm to push the arm back to the groin and upper thigh. Watch that the shoulder is not raised, nor the spine twisted to recruit other muscles. Other muscles to test if weak: deltoids, upper trapezius, and the pectorals.

Antagonist muscles: Teres major and coracobrachialis.

Massage points: (a) Under the outer end of the collarbone, just inside the shoulder joint and down along the chest wall for about 4 inches (10 cm). (b) As high as you can right up under the skull at the top of the neck either side of the spine.

Meridian: Central.

Holding points: Bregma, found one thumb's width back from the vertex of the head, with the two points over the center of each eye, halfway between the eyebrows and the hairline.

Nutrition: Foods high in lecithin and amino acids, such as soy products. Avoid high-fat, high-sugar foods, and over-the-counter drugs containing adrenaline and cortisol, unless prescribed by a doctor.

Emotion: Confused/confident, unsuccessful/successful, difficult/easy.

Deltoids—Middle, Anterior, and Posterior

The deltoids are the group of muscles that join the upper arm to the shoulder like a hinge (fig. 6.10). They spread all the way around the point of the shoulder like epaulettes. They are extremely strong, and because they wrap around the arm, they lift the arm forward and turn it

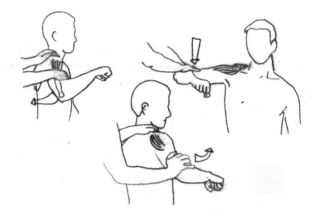

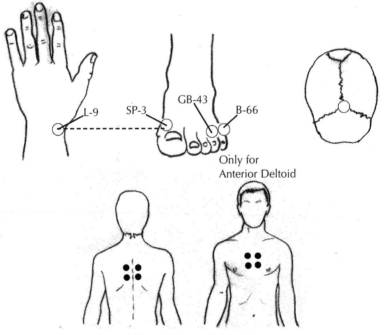

L-9   SP-3   GB-43   B-66

Only for
Anterior Deltoid

Figure 6.10   Deltoids (middle, anterior, and posterior).

slightly inward (anterior deltoid), sideways (middle deltoid), and backward and slightly outward (posterior deltoid). This means the front and back divisions work against each other when swinging the arms, but all three work together as a group for side lifts. In all instrumental playing, these muscles are used actively to raise the arms, or passively as upper arm stabilizers to allow lateral forearm movement, as when playing keyboards. Typical signs of weakness are: leaning away from the side being tested or trying to change the angle of elbow flexion; an inability to place your hand in your back pocket; upper arm or shoulder pain when you sleep or lie on it; and a rolling, unbalanced gait because there is no counterbalancing arm swing as the Testee walks. Because of meridian associations, weakness may be accompanied by chronic colon malfunction and pains, myopia and light-sensitivity, arthritis, or itchy palms. After injury or overuse, the three sections may be reactive to each other—especially posterior to anterior (see chapter 4).

Test position: The Testee sits or stands with the arm raised at 90° to the side and with the elbow bent 90° so the forearm is horizontal. Take care when stabilizing the shoulder. Hold it firmly near the neck, or stabilize the opposite shoulder, to stop body rotation and also avoid touching the muscle being tested. To test middle deltoid, the shoulder is stabilized and, while avoiding touching the elbow crease, the upper arm is pushed straight in toward the body. To test the anterior deltoid, the upper arm is brought forward 5° and the forearm is raised another 5°. The Tester stabilizes the shoulder near the neck while pulling the upper arm back and slightly down. To test the posterior deltoid, the upper arm is now retracted 5° and the forearm lowered 5°, the shoulder stabilized and pressure is applied to bring the upper arm forward and slightly down. If this muscle division is weak, check that there is no reactive pattern with hypertonic anterior deltoid or pectoral muscles.

Massage points: (a) Between the third and fourth ribs either side of the breastbone. (b) In between the shoulder blades against the spine (between third and fourth ribs).

Meridian: Lung.

Holding points: (a) Bregma, found one thumb's width from the vertex of the head. (b) Acupoints Sp-3 and L-9. Sp-3 is on the heel side of the big joint on the outside, at the base of the big toe. Hold it at the same time as L-9, which is on the outside of the wrist crease at the base of the thumb. You may also try (c) Acupoints B-66 and GB-43. B-66 is on the outside of the foot at the base of the little toe. Hold it together with GB-43, which is next door at the base of the fourth toe.

Nutrition: Vitamins C and water, figs and mushrooms, cayenne, garlic and parsley.

Sensitivity: Cotton.

Emotion: Unwilling/willing, shy/bold, nervous/restful, useless/useful, unsociable/sociable, incapable/capable, unresponsive/responsive, unfulfilled/fulfilled, confused/confident, hopeless/trusting, forsaken/accepted.

Bach flower: Water violet.

The Pectorals—Pectoralis Major Clavicular, Pectoralis Major Sternal, and Pectoralis Minor

These muscles are all found on the front of the chest in a fan shape on either side of the breastbone and just under the collarbone. They all bring the shoulder forward and are used to play every single musical instrument! Tension and too much contraction causes a round-shouldered position. Spasm frequently occurs when holding a violin or viola too tightly against the upper chest, squashing the nerve and blood supply to the arm and hand.

1. Pectoralis Major Clavicular (PMC)

This runs from the upper part of the breastbone and the collarbone, across the armpit, to the upper arm (fig. 6.11). It pulls the arm inward and up toward the opposite ear.

2. Pectoralis Major Sternal (PMS)

This runs from the breastbone below the PMC and joins it on to the upper arm (fig. 6.12). It pulls the arm in and down. The right PMC and PMS are therefore some of the main muscles used in moving the upper arm in bowing by all string players but particularly upper strings, and for crossing arms in all keyboard instruments.

3. Pectoralis Minor

This runs under the PMC and PMS in the opposite direction and joins a small extension of the shoulder blade (found just under the outer half of the collarbone) to the upper ribcage (fig. 6.13). Because it is a deep

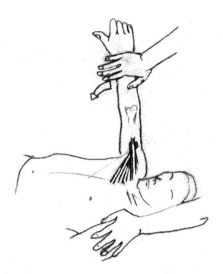

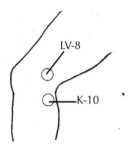

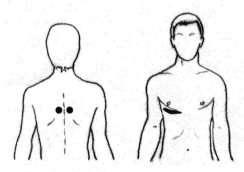

Figure 6.11 Pectoralis major clavicular.

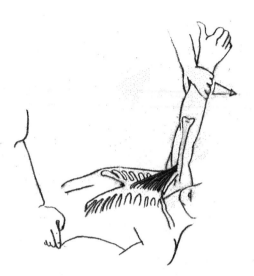

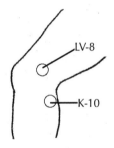

LV-8

K-10

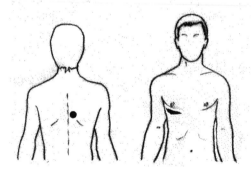

Figure 6.12   Pectoralis major sternal.

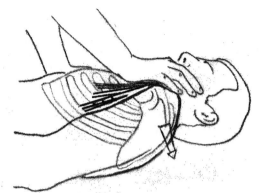

Figure 6.13   Pectoralis minor.

muscle, the nerves and blood vessels to the arm and the main body
lymph drainage systems are often affected by its malfunction. It is frequently compressed on the left side by holding the violin/viola or shoulder rest below the collarbone. A sure sign of congestion is if you often
wake with your arms above your head. This is your body's way of trying to clear the problem, but it can also cause pain on the shoulder
point. Because it is attached to the ribs, this muscle is also one of the
extra breathing muscles, used when there is a breathing problem such

as asthma, or when a sharp, hard intake of breath is required of a wind or brass player in a very long musical phrase.

All the pectorals are used to stabilize the shoulder and hold up the upper arms, which hold up all wind and brass instruments. Beware, also, that although pain in this area may be due to muscle tension, it could also be due to heart or lung problems. If you are in any doubt, go and see your general practitioner; better safe than sorry!

Test position: PMC, PMS—Testee sits or stands, the straight arm is raised 90° to the front, so that it is horizontal, and then the arm is turned so that the palm faces outward and the thumb points to the floor. The other shoulder is stabilized.

For PMC, the tester pushes the arm out and slightly down; for PMS the arm is pushed up and out. For pectoralis minor, the shoulder is pulled forward and the straight arm is held palm up, across the body toward the opposite knee. The opposite shoulder is stabilized, while the straight arm is pulled out and up toward the shoulder being tested. Alternatively, the Testee lies face up with the shoulder raised off the table and toward the opposite hip. The opposite shoulder is stabilized while the tester pushes the front of the shoulder back down to the table and slightly up toward the head, making sure the direction of push comes as if from the opposite hip. If this muscle is compressed, over-facilitated, or in spasm, it compromises lymph drainage capacity as it flows back into one of the main veins, causing congestion. Compression could also affect blood and nerve supply to the arm and hands, causing cold fingers or tingling in the fingers. Swimming backstroke or stretching the arms upward and outward is the best help for this condition. Other muscles to test if weak: middle trapezius, latissimus dorsi.

Antagonist muscles: Rhomboids and trapezius.

Massage points: PMC, PMS—(a) Under the left nipple, between the fifth and sixth ribs on the chest wall, left side only. (b) Either side of the spine at the level of the fifth to sixth ribs, level with halfway down the shoulder blade.

Pectoralis minor. At the lowest end of the breastbone, in the upturned V where it joins the ribs. There are no points on the back.

Meridian: PMC, stomach; PMS, liver.

Holding points: PMC—(a) Frontal eminences over the center of each eye, and midway between the eyebrows and the hairline. (b) Acupoints S-41 and SI-5. S-41 is on the top middle front of the ankle in a small dip. Hold it together with SI-5, which is on the side of the wrist below the little finger, on the end of the forearm bone (ulna nerve).

PMS—(a) In the hairline above the outer corner of each eye. (b) Acupoints Lv-8 and K-10. Lv-8 is in the dip on the inside of the knee joint between the extreme end of the thighbone and the hamstring tendon. Hold it with K-10, which is almost next door at the inside end of the knee crease, when the knee is bent.

Pectoralis minor—On the temple about 1 inch back from the outer corner of the eye.

Nutrition: PMC—This muscle reacts very badly to an upset stomach and mental stress. Don't eat when upset and don't drink caffeinated tea, coffee, or cola. Avoid sugar, the digestion of which will drain the body's store of B vitamins, so much needed to combat mental stress. Replace it with "slow release" carbohydrates such as whole grains. Increase intake of all foods that contain vitamin B complex, bicarbonate, garlic, and parsley. Avoid any food or drug that gives you a skin rash. Bilateral weakness is often a sign of too little stomach acid. If the muscle is found to be strong on each side if tested separately, but weak when both are tested together, it often indicates digestive disturbances or allergies as well as poor mineral metabolism, precipitating osteoporosis and periodontal disease.

PMS—Long-lasting headaches and photo phobia, spots in front of the eyes, "liverishness," and chronic immune system problems all contribute to a weak PMS, so avoid fatty and fried foods, fizzy drinks, caffeinated tea and coffee, and alcohol. Eating liver and foods high in vitamins A, B6, B12, and E, zinc, apple cider vinegar, and rosehip syrup will help.

Pectoralis minor—Foods rich in vitamin B complex, especially B3 and B6, lecithin, zinc and cayenne, water and lymphatic drainage massage on the muscle itself will help.

Emotion: PMC—Unwilling/willing, sour/agreeable, confused/confident, abandoned/included, nervous/restful, unappreciated/appreciated; PMS—Confused/confident, unloved/loved, abandoned/included; Pectoralis Minor—Unwilling/willing, fearful/courageous, intolerant/understanding, wrong/understood, nervous/restful, irritated/tranquil, unsuccessful/successful.

Bach flower: PMC—Willow; PMS—Agrimony.

Coracobrachialis

This muscle shares the same extension of the shoulder blade under the collarbone as pectoralis minor (fig. 6.14). The muscle runs from there to the front of the upper arm, so it draws the upper arm up and in. It comes into play when: (a) holding up the right arm near the violin or viola to play pizzicato; (b) to bow (at the heel of the bow, or in spiccato) on the lower strings of violin or viola or the upper cello strings; (c) in playing and tuning the top notes on a harp; and (d) holding up a smaller brass instrument. Weakness will cause shoulder pains, difficulty in putting the hand behind the head, combing the hair, or reaching to the opposite ear. There may be heaviness in the arms during eating, because the arms feel weak and tired. It is associated with insomnia, mouth sores, chronic cough, and exertion asthma. If both sides are weak there may be a problem with the hard palette inside the mouth, so wind and brass players should ask an applied kinesiologist for help.

Test position: The Testee sits, with elbow maximally bent and drawn in to the chest, the hand, palm up on top of the shoulder, or beyond. Support the back of the shoulder as the inner side of the upper arm is pushed down and back.

Antagonist muscle: Posterior deltoid.

Massage points: (a) Between the second, third, and fourth ribs, next to the breastbone. (b) Between the third and fourth ribs, either side of the spine between the shoulder blades.

Meridian: Lung.

Holding positions: (a) Bregma, one thumb's width back from the vertex of the head. (b) Acupoints Sp-3 and L-9. Sp-3 is on the heel side of the large joint at the base of the big toe. Hold it with L-9, which is at the base of the thumb, at the end of the wrist crease.

Nutrition: Vitamin C, water, Beta-carotene.

Emotion: Unwilling/willing, disorganized/organized, confused/confident, not needed/needed, upset/calm, nervous/peaceful, forlorn/hopeful.

Bach flower: Water Violet.

MUSCLES OF THE ELBOW

1. Muscles that bend the elbow (biceps brachii, brachialis, and brachioradialis)
2. Muscles that straighten the elbow (triceps and anconeus)

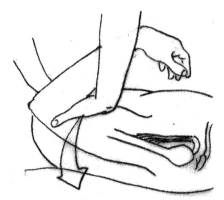

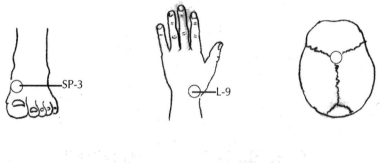

SP-3

L-9

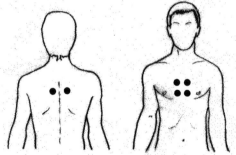

Figure 6.14   Coracobrachialis.

Biceps Brachii, Brachialis, and Brachioradialis

Biceps brachii and brachialis are both found on the front of the upper arm and have a similar action (fig. 6.15). Biceps brachii runs across two joints, the shoulder and elbow, attaching on the shoulder blade end with its long tendon and the upper arm with its short tendon and at the other end of the forearm on the thumb side (radius). Brachialis runs from the upper arm to the forearm on the little finger side (ulna). Both flex the elbow and, although not terribly well arranged mechanically for lifting, they have extra strength to make up for any inefficiency. All elbow flexors (together with brachioradialis) are used by musicians; however, overpracticing any one action repeatedly can tire these muscles and/or give you shoulder and elbow problems. Pain may radiate to the upper arm or down to the wrist, thumb, and index finger or when raising the arm above the head, which may be due to digestive (ileocaecal) problems. Check with an applied kinesiologist about this.

Brachioradialis is attached to the upper arm lower down than the other two and then runs down the forearm almost to the wrist on the thumb side (fig. 6.16). This means that it increases the strength of the upper arm muscles greatly. It is particularly active when quick bursts of energy are required (e.g., a fortissimo up-bow), although it normally only comes into play when you are lifting more than four pounds (two kilos). It can also assist supinator and pronator teres, turning the forearm palm up or palm down. Weakness will make it hard to put your hands up behind your back. There may also be a skin rash on the back of the forearm or itchy, scaly elbows.

Test position: For all three, the Testee sits with arm bent at 60° to 80°, elbow on to the side. For biceps brachii and brachialis, the palm should face the shoulder, and for brachioradialis it should be facing inward. In all three, the elbow is supported while pressure is put on the forearm to straighten the elbow. Other muscles to test if weak: rhomboids, teres major and minor, PMC, latissimus dorsi.

Antagonist muscles: Triceps and anconeus.

Massage points: (a) Between the fourth and fifth ribs 3 inches either side of the breastbone. (b) Either side of the very top of the spine, where it meets the skull. (c) Between the fifth and sixth ribs, either side of the spine—level with the middle of the shoulder blades. (d) Above the central ridge of the shoulder blade. Not all these areas might be tender; work on those that are.

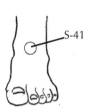

S-41

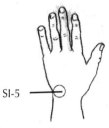

SI-5

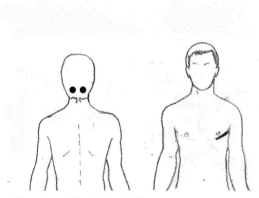

Figure 6.15   Biceps brachii and brachialis.

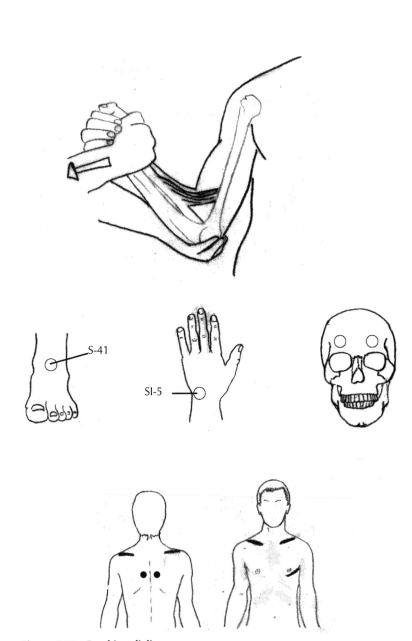

S-41

SI-5

Figure 6.16   Brachioradialis.

Meridian: Stomach.

Holding positions: (a) Frontal eminences—over the center of each eye, and halfway between the eyebrows and hairline. (b) Acupoints S-41 and SI-5. S-41 is found on the top of the foot, at the center of the ankle crease. Hold it with SI-5, which is found at the end of the forearm bone on the little finger side of the wrist.

Nutrition: These muscles are associated with stomach and intestinal disorders and gluten sensitivity, so go carefully in what you eat. Chew everything very well and avoid any food that makes you feel flushed, and all foods to which you are sensitive, especially white flour and white sugar. Increase intake of foods containing vitamin B complex, zinc, magnesium, iron, potassium, and calcium.

Sensitivity: Onions, polyester, and foam rubber.

Emotion: Self-centered/kind, reclusive/sociable, nervous/peaceful, forsaken/accepted, indignant/empathetic, apprehensive/secure, confused/confident, pressured/desirable, irritated/tranquil, defeated/success, forced/helpful, nauseated/comfortable.

Bach flower: Willow.

Triceps Brachii and Anconeus

These muscles are on the back of the upper arm, and work together to straighten the elbow (fig. 6.17). They are used by all musicians. Triceps brachii has three heads, two on the upper arm, and the long head that goes to the shoulder blade. The other end is attached to the back of the elbow (ulna).

Anconeus is much smaller and crosses on the outside of the elbow joint, but acts like a fourth division of triceps while stabilizing the joint. Because they work against the biceps group, they are in use as the antagonist "other half" of many of the same occupations for musicians, especially in bowing, wind instruments, and keyboard playing when holding the upper arm, so that the forearm and hands are appropriately placed for playing. Weakness of both can cause elbow and back of the shoulder problems, and triceps brachii is often blamed for tennis and golfer's elbow. In such situations, it is always worth checking latissimus dorsi, as weakness there causes triceps to overwork. Pain in the back of the arm can also be referred from the neck or wrist. Weakness in these muscles, especially in combination with a forward head

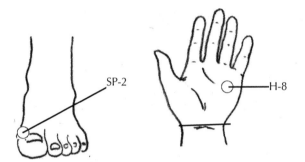

SP-2

H-8

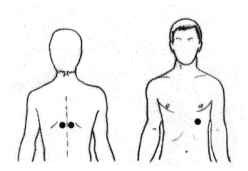

Figure 6.17   Triceps brachii and anconeus.

position, can be an indicator of low-neck disk herniation. If in doubt, ask an applied kinesiologist.

Test position: (a) These muscles are tested together as their action is similar. The Testee is seated, and the arm extended behind the shoulder. The elbow and upper arm are supported while the forearm is pushed to bend the elbow. (b) The Testee is seated, the elbow slightly flexed. The elbow is supported underneath, whole pressure is applied to the back of the wrist to flex the elbow more. Other muscles to test if weak: levator scapulae, rhomboids, and latissimus dorsi.

Antagonist muscles: Biceps group.

Massage points: (a) Between the seventh and eighth ribs on the left, more central than directly below the nipple. (b) Either side of the spine, between the seventh and eighth ribs, level with the bottom of the shoulder blades.

Meridian: Spleen/Pancreas.

Holding points: (a) On the head just above and behind the ears. (b) Acupoints Sp-2 and H-8. Sp-2 is found on the side of the foot at the nail end of the large joint at the base of the big toe. Hold it with H-8, which is on the palm of the hand in the crease just below the base of the ring finger.

Nutrition: Avoid sweets and refined sugars. Eat foods high in vitamin A, garlic and parsley, zinc, and kelp. Strawberry-leaf tea and herbal and homeopathic remedies to stimulate the pancreas may help.

Sensitivity: Aduki beans, buckwheat, citrus fruits.

Emotion: Nervous/peaceful or restful, sorrowful/joyful, pity/grateful, hard/adaptable, confused/confident, helpless/powerful, unwilling/willing, distressed/content, arrogant/listening, futile/assured.

Bach flower: Mimulus.

REFERENCES

Airola, P. *How to Get Well*. Phoenix, Ariz.: Health Plus Publishers, 1974.

Berkow, R., and A. Fletcher (Eds.). *The Merck Manual*. Whitehouse Station, NJ: Merck and Co Inc., 1992.

British National Formulary. London: British Medical Association and Royal Pharmaceutical Society of Great Britain, 1993– .

Caillet, R. *Hand Pain and Impairment*. Philadelphia: F.A. Davis, 1982.

———. *Neck and Arm Pain*. Philadelphia: F.A. Davis, 1991.

Hay, L. *Heal Your Body—The Mental Causes for Physical Illness, and the Metaphysical Way to Overcome Them.* New York: Author, 1976.

Hoppenfeld, S. *Physical Examination of the Spine and Extremities.* New York: Appleton-Century-Crofts, Prentice Hall, 1976.

Kendall, F., and E. McCreary. *Muscles Testing and Function,* 3rd ed. Baltimore, Md.: Williams and Wilkins, 1983.

Netter, F. *Atlas of Human Anatomy.* Basle, Switzerland: Ciba Geigy Ltd., 1989.

Ramsak, I., and W. Gerz. *AK Muscle Tests at a Glance.* Translated by Gates. Munchen/Mainberg, Germany: AKSE, 2000.

Sobel D., and A. Klein. *Arthritis: What Exercises Really Work.* London: Robinson Pub. Ltd., 1996.

Walther, D. Applied Kinesiology Synopsis. In *Meridian Therapy* (Chapter 7, pp 234–240). Pueblo, Colo.: Systems DC, 1980.

————. *Applied Kinesiology Vol. 2 Head, Neck and Jaw Pain and Dysfunction— The Stomatognathic System.* Pueblo, Colo.: Systems DC, 1983.

————. *ICAK-E Presentation and Applied Kinesiology,* Vols. 1 & 2. Pueblo, Colo.: Systems DC, 1989.

Weiss, S. *The Anatomy Book for Musicians, Muscle Dynamics.* Glenview, Ill.: Author, 1996.

7

Muscles of the Forearm, Wrist, and Hand

FOREARM MUSCLES

1. Supinator
2. Pronator teres and quadratus
3. Palmaris longus
4. Flexor carpi (radialis and ulnaris)
5. Extensor carpi radialis (longus and brevis) and extensor ulnaris

Supinator

This muscle turns the forearm from palm down to palm up (fig. 7.1). It is located at the elbow joint on the outside, like an extensor. It mostly lies between the upper arm bone and the forearm bone on the thumb side, but a little slip goes to the other forearm bone, too. Suspect weakness if the Testee becomes round-shouldered when extending the arm or suspect tension if there is pain on the outside of the elbow or in the webbing between thumb and index fingers. This muscle can also give rise to a nerve entrapment syndrome in the elbow area, causing symptoms from elbow to hand on the thumb side. The muscle is particularly used in the right arm by flautists, in the underhand method of bowing used by some bass players, by all upper-string players in the left arm, and in both arms by harmonica players. Spasm can also cause nerve entrapment and referred pain to wrist and shoulder.

147

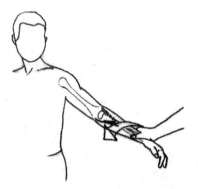

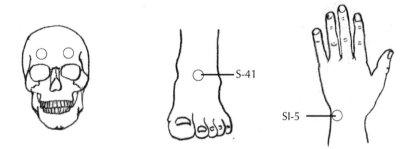

S-41

SI-5

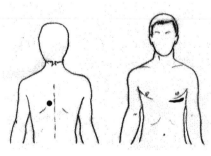

Figure 7.1   Supinator.

Test position: (a) The Testee sits or stands with the elbow bent and hand palm up. The upper arm is stabilized and the forearm is twisted into pronation (palm down). However, the biceps group is very active using this method. (b) Extend the straight arm behind the body, palm down. Stabilize the upper arm and twist the forearm palm up. In this position the biceps group is elongated and is at a disadvantage. Watch that the Testee does not twist the upper arm sideways. (c) The Testee bends the elbow and places it over the same shoulder, palm back. The elbow is stabilized and the forearm twisted palm front. Do this test gently or biceps will come into action and cramp. Other muscles to test if weak: triceps, biceps brachii.

Antagonist muscles: Pronator teres.

Massage points: (a) Between the fifth and sixth ribs on the left under the breast, near the breastbone. (b) Between the sixth and seventh ribs on the left side of the spine, one rib-space higher than the bottom of the shoulder blades.

Meridian: Stomach.

Holding points: (a) Frontal eminences, which are above the center of each eye and between the eyebrows and the hairline. (b) Acupoints S-41 and SI-4. S-41 is on top of the foot in the center of the ankle crease. Hold it with SI-4, which is on the little finger side of the wrist at the end of the forearm bone.

Nutrition: Eat extra foods that contain vitamins B complex and B2. May also need vitamins A and E, garlic, and parsley.

Emotion: Nervous/restful, compelled/eager.

Bach flower: Willow and Star of Bethlehem.

Pronator Teres and Quadratus

These are both muscles that turn the forearm bones so that the palm faces down toward the feet when the elbow is bent, or it turns the palm behind you if the arm is straight (fig. 7.2). Pronator teres is at the elbow and crosses the elbow joint on the inside (so it joins the elbow flexor group). It twists the swivel head of the radius against the ulna so the two forearm bones cross. Pronator quadratus has a similar though limited effect at the wrist. To twist as far as possible, both are needed. These muscles are used in most string playing when bowing, particularly at the tip, in pianists playing at extremes of the keyboard, by percussionists, and in the bassoonists' and guitarists' right forearm and

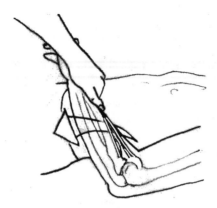

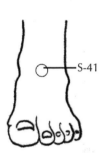

S-41

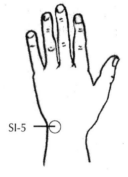

SI-5

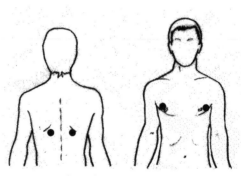

Figure 7.2 Pronator teres and quadratus.

hand. They can be overused in carpal tunnel syndrome, because pronator quadratus passes directly over the inside of the wrist. Any cramp
will restrict the space underneath, and can cause referred pain to the
elbow and shoulder as well as the wrist. Weak pronators can also cause
difficulty opening doors and jars, picking up a full cup, and itchy, swol-
len palms and fingers. They can also cause pain that is often mistaken
for tennis or golfer's elbow.

Test position: The Testee sits or stands. The elbow is bent less than
90° and the palm turned toward the feet. The upper arm is stabilized
and the forearm twisted to turn the palm up, away from the feet. To
isolate pronator quadratus, bend the elbow maximally and turn the palm
away from the body. The elbow is stabilized and the forearm twisted to
face the shoulder. Other muscle to test if weak: brachioradialis.

Antagonist muscle: Supinator.

Massage point: (a) Between the fourth and fifth ribs behind the nipples, gently! (b) Between the eighth and ninth ribs on the back, just
below the bottom of the shoulder blades.

Meridian: Stomach.

Holding points: (a) On the back of the head 2.5 inches (4 cm) diagonally up and out at 45° from the center of the top of the neck. (b) Acupoints as for supinator.

Nutrition: There is a meridian association with stomach function here
and both respond well to vitamins B2 and B6, with B complex and E.
Slippery elm is said to help. Check for zinc deficiency and possible
allergies.

Emotion: Unwilling/willing, unaccepted/accepted, nervous/restful,
disappointed/satisfied, confused/confident, insecure/secure.

Bach flower: Willow.

Palmaris Longus, Flexor Carpi Radialis, and Flexor Carpi Ulnaris

These are all muscles that bend the wrist and are all attached to the
common flexor tendon on the inside of the elbow. Palmaris longus pulls
the palm straight to the elbow and also crosses the elbow joint, helping
to bend that, too (fig. 7.3). Because it is attached to the fibrous band
across the inner wrist (the flexor retinaculum), it can be involved in carpal tunnel syndrome, causing pins and needles in the thumb and index
finger. Flexor carpi radialis flexes the wrist but to the thumb side, by

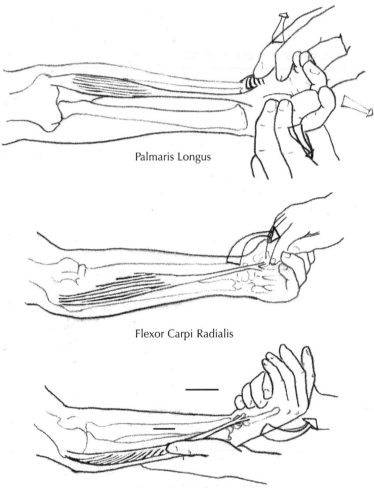

Palmaris Longus

Flexor Carpi Radialis

Flexor Carpi Ulnaris

Figure 7.3 Palmaris longus, flexor carpi radialis, and flexor carpi ulnaris.

attaching to the index and middle finger bases and thus pulling on the wrist on one side only (fig. 7.4). Flexor carpi ulnaris pulls on the other side only, because it is attached to the two wristbones under and including the base of the little finger. All these movements are used in almost all instrument playing at some time or other, as part of the wrist flexibility. Weakness leads to weak wrist grasp, wrist forearm and elbow pain, carpal tunnel and tunnel of Guyon problems, and can be mistaken for golfer's elbow. There is a possible meridian link with diabetes.

Test position: Palmaris longus—Testee sits with bent elbow and wrist and cupped palm. The back of the hand is supported with the Tester's thumbs, as the Tester opens and flattens the Testee's palm. Flexor carpi radialis—The elbow is bent, the fist is clenched, and the wrist bent maximally and half turned palm in, the forearm is supported while pressure is put on the thumb side of the palm as though to straighten the wrist toward the little finger side. Flexor carpi ulnaris—The elbow is bent, the fist clenched, and the wrist is bent maximally and half turned out. The forearm is supported while pressure is put on the little finger side of the palm to straighten the wrist toward the thumb side. Other muscles to test if weak: supinator, opponens pollicis.

Antagonist muscles: Extensors of the wrist.

Meridians: Flexor carpi radialis—Spleen. Flexor carpi ulnaris—Heart.

Holding points: Flexor carpi radialis acupoints are Sp-2 and H-8. Sp-2 is on the nail end of the big joint at the base of the big toe, on the side of the foot. Hold it with H-8, which is on the palm of the hand in the crease under the ring finger.

Flexor carpi ulnaris acupoints are H-9 and Lv-1. H-9 is on the nailbed of the little finger. Hold it with Lv-1, which is on the inside nailbed of the big toe.

Nutrition: Vitamin B complex and slippery elm.

Emotion: Unwilling/willing, empty/fulfilled, unaccepted/accepted, nervous/restful.

Bach flower: Mimulus and Hornbeam.

Extensor Carpi Ulnaris, and Extensor carpi radialis longus and brevis

These muscles work as a group to bend the wrist straight back, or singly to bend it back one side only. The longus and brevis of extensor carpi

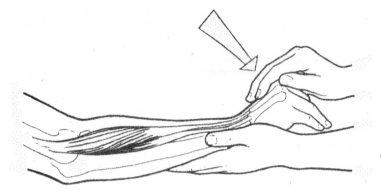

Extensor Carpi Radialis

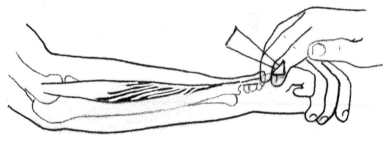

Extensor Carpi Ulnaris

Figure 7.4   Extensor carpi radialis and extensor carpi ulnaris.

radialis (ECR) lie side by side and can really be considered as one. They run from the outside of the elbow (the extensor tendon that inflames to become tennis elbow), across the forearm to the knuckles of the index and middle fingers.

Extensor carpi ulnaris (ECU) starts in the same place but, as the name implies, stays on the same ulnar (little finger) side and goes to the knuckle of the little finger. These muscles between them are responsible for the arch of the hand and the ability to move the hand sideways when the forearm is still. They are used in all sorts of bowing techniques in string playing and reaching and extension fingering techniques in almost all playing. As a consequence, too much extended and sideways stretching during playing can cause forearm and wrist pains, and tennis elbow, though you never touch a racquet! Weakness may cause poor grip or poor hand alignment, excessive tension from overpracticing fast passagework or computer use may cause elbow pain. Because of meridian associations, there may also be itchy skin under the hair and dizziness if you stand suddenly.

Test position: The Testee sits with arm extended almost straight on a table and wrist extended off the table. The wrist is supported underneath, while pressure is applied to the back of all the knuckles to push the hand on to the table. This tests all extensors together. To test ECR alone, the index and middle fingers should be raised highest with the deviation of the hand toward the thumb. Pressure is applied to their knuckles only. To test the ECU alone, the little finger side of the hand is raised highest and the hand is deviated to the little finger side. Pressure is applied to the back of the little finger knuckle only. These are important muscles to test if there is a nerve entrapment syndrome. Other muscles to test if weak: supinator, pronator teres, latissimus dorsi, triceps, and anconeus.

Antagonist muscles: Flexors of the hand.

Massage points: Along the back of the forearm from the outside of the elbow to the knuckles.

Meridians: Pericardium (Cx.) and small intestines. Spleen and stomach.

Holding Points: Cx-9 and Lv-1. Cx-9 is at the end of the middle finger pad on the side nearest the index finger. Hold it with Lv-1, which is on the corner of the nailbed of the big toe that's nearest the other toes.

Nutrition: Vitamins A, B5, B6, B complex, and E, potassium/iodine, lecithin, cayenne, mustard seed and greens, alfalfa, apricot, banana, nettles and slippery elm, brown rice.

Emotion: Unwilling or obligated/willing, frustrated/satisfied, confused/confident, tongue-tied/expressive, nervous/peaceful, unappreciated/appreciated, deceived/truthful, difficult/easy, upset or restless/calm, concerned/trusting.

Bach flower: Holly, Star of Bethlehem, Mimulus, and Willow.

LONG HAND MUSCLES

1. Flexor digitorum (superficialis and profundis)
2. Extensor indices, extensor digitorum, and extensor digiti minimi
3. Flexor pollicis longus (and brevis)
4. Extensor pollicis longus (and brevis)
5. Abductor pollicis longus (and brevis)

It may seem surprising that the strongest muscles of the hand are not located on the hand itself. This is for practical reasons. Large muscle bulk would fill up the palm space available, and long muscles exert better leverage and so are stronger. The forearm is an obvious place to park them. There are, of course, lots of muscles on the hand, but they are mainly used for light and fine movement and speed, not movements requiring strength of grasp.

Flexor Digitorum Superficialis and Flexor Digitorum Profundis

These muscles both flex the fingers (fig. 7.5). Flexor digitorum superficialis (FDS) flexes the middle bone of each finger and flexor digitorum profundis (FDP) flexes the last bone on the middle bone of that finger. Just occasionally, the tendons or nerve supply of one becomes inflamed or squashed by muscle bulk and then the joint it supplies won't work. Weakness of FDS decreases grip strength and interferes with finger function, so that the middle bone is flexed, but the last one is straight or even bent backward. Weakness of FDP means difficulty in flexing

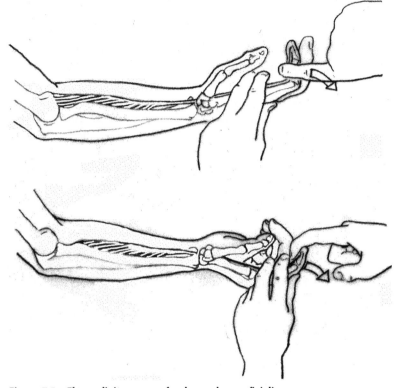

Figure 7.5   Flexor digitorum profundus and superficialis.

the last joint on the finger, affecting any precision movement, especially intonation in string playing and balancing tone on a piano.

If finger weakness is not affected by gentle pressure on the base of the palm, half an inch beyond the wrist crease, then there is no carpal tunnel problem. The tendons of both can become subject to nodules on the palm of the hand in both trigger finger and Dupuytren's contracture, which shorten the tendons. Smoothness of finger action is affected, and the palm gradually closes over time; correction is possible with very delicate surgery. The ring and little fingers of men aged forty and over are most commonly affected. Because of its meridian associations, there may be digestive disorder, nausea, and headaches; alcohol or sugar handling difficulty; feeling irritable, or cold and hating drafts; varicose veins, sore gums, and easy bruising.

Test Position: FDS—The Testee is seated, the elbow slightly bent. All fingers are flexed except the one being tested. The knuckle is firmly held while the next joint away on the finger is flexed. Pressure is applied to the middle bone of each finger in turn to straighten it. You can't always isolate the action of the middle finger. A sign of weakness may be a very weak handshake or there is carpal tunnel syndrome.

FDP—Test position is the same but now the middle bone of the finger is held firmly, the last joint flexed, and pressure is put on the finger pad to straighten the finger. Difficulty in picking up small objects, playing in high positions, needing weaker springs for key pads or having difficulty with heavy action keyboards are sign of weakness. Other muscles to test if weak: interossei, palmaris longus.

Antagonist muscles: Finger extensors.

Massage points: (a) Massage the muscles from inside the elbow to the wrist. (b) Between the seventh and eighth ribs on the left side of the ribcage in the soft cartilage. (c) Either side of the spine, level with the bottom of the shoulder blade.

Meridian: Heart.

Holding points: Acupoints H-9 and Lv-1. H-9 is found on the nailbed of the little finger. Hold it with Lv-1, which is on the inside of the nailbed of the big toe.

Nutrition: Vitamin B6, B12, and E, lecithin, potassium/iodine, calcium, alfalfa, banana, nettle, slippery elm, cayenne, strawberry leaf tea, apple cider vinegar, licorice.

Sensitivity: Turmeric.

Emotion: Nervous/peaceful, restless/calm, defeated/successful, unwilling/willing, not needed/needed, confused/confident, sour/agreeable, hungry/full, incapable/understandable, unloved/loved, speechless/communicative, grief for others/fellow feeling, unconcerned/caring, revolting/attractive, undesirable/pleasant.

Bach flower: Hornbeam.

Extensor Indices, Extensor Digitorum, and Extensor Digiti Minimi

These muscles all straighten bent fingers (fig. 7.6). The last two are so close together they almost work as one, except that we can extend each

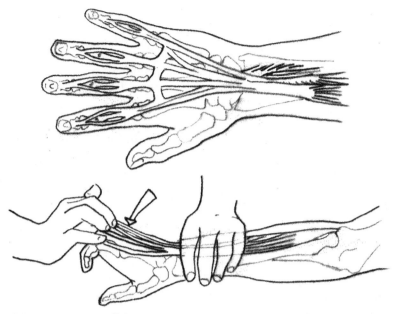

Figure 7.6   Extensor digitorum.

finger separately. They run from the common extensor tendon on the outside of the elbow to the tips of the fingers. There is an extra muscle for greater strength going to the index finger (extensor indices [EI]), which joins from the forearm near the wrist. These muscles are involved every time we pick up the fingers in any kind of fingering work on any musical instrument. Signs of weakness are constantly clenched fingers. Singly, there may be focal distonia, where there is imbalance/uncoordination between flexors and extensors of the fingers (see chapter on reactive muscles).

Test Position: The testee's wrist is stabilized and the knuckles are arched back. Pressure is put on the back of each knuckle in turn to flex it.

Massage points: Same as for ECR and ECU.

Meridian: Same as for ECR and ECU.

Holding points: Same as for ECR and ECU.

Nutrition: Same as for ECR and ECU.

Emotion: Same as for ECR and ECU.

The Long Thumb Muscles

Once again, these main longus muscles are not on the hand but on the forearm, to gain extra strength through longer leverage. They are backed up by smaller, local brevis muscles, which are found on the hand. In each case the longus muscle goes the furthest distance (i.e., crosses the furthest joint, and brevis crosses the nearest). Harpists and guitarists tend to use the last joint to play, so that the longus muscles are vital. Some schools of brass playing bend the fingers more from the knuckles, so for them, brevis muscles are more important. Keyboard players use both.

Flexor Pollicis Longus (FPL)

FPL runs mainly from the forearm, but there is a small, strong connection that crosses the elbow joint (fig. 7.7). It then goes under the wrist fibers through the carpal tunnel to the base of the last bone of the thumb. Flexor pollicis brevis (FPB) runs underneath it and connects the base of the thumb to the strong fibers that cross the inside of the wrist. Surprisingly, FPL is not affected by carpal tunnel syndrome, because although its tendon runs through the carpal tunnel, its nerve supply doesn't. FPB is affected, because although the muscle is beyond the tunnel, its nerve supply goes through it—differentiation here is a definitive test. Both FPL and FPB bend the thumb toward the elbow, and away from the back of the hand. Cramps can occur if you hold your instrument tightly for too long, or do too many exercises that pass the thumb under the other fingers on a keyboard instrument. Weakness will make holding a full cup difficult, and there will be poor fine control of grip, and a sore or bent back thumb. Because of the meridian association, there may be a tendency to irritability and low-grade systemic infections.

Test position: FPL—Hold the base and first joint of the thumb while the Testee bends the last joint. Pressure is put on the pad of the last bone to straighten the thumb.

FPB—Hold the base of the thumb only. The Testee bends the thumb enough for it to lie straight, alongside the base of the index finger. The ball of the thumb is stabilized and pressure is put on the second bone to move it away from the index finger. Other muscles to test if weak: adductor pollicis and opponens pollicis.

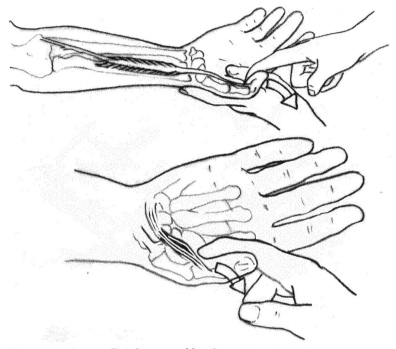

Figure 7.7 Flexor pollicis longus and brevis.

Antagonist muscles: Extensor pollicis group.

Massage points: (a) Behind the areola on the chest wall (go gently!) (b) Immediately under the point of the bottom of the shoulder blade.

Meridian: Stomach.

Holding points: (a) Frontal eminencies—Over the center of each eye, halfway between the eyebrows and hairline. (b) Acupoints S-41 and SI-5. S-41 is on the top middle front of the foot in a small dip in the center of the ankle crease. Hold it with SI-5, which is on the little finger side of the wrist, on the end of the forearm bone.

Nutrition: Vitamins B6 and B complex, beetroot, brown rice, aloe vera juice, calcium, apple cider vinegar, cayenne, garlic, parsley.

Emotion: Unwilling/willing, stubborn/yielding, defensive/listening, nervous/restful, disorganized/organized, proud/humble.

Bach flower: Willow.

162 Chapter 7

Extensor Pollicis Longus and Brevis

These two muscles work together to straighten the thumb (fig. 7.8).
They start on the forearm: extensor pollicis longus (EPL) on the thumb
side, and extensor pollicis brevis (EPB) on the little finger side. As
usual, longus goes to the end of the thumb whereas brevis doesn't. Both
muscles are also attached to the membranes that connect the two forearm bones and so will be badly affected if either is misaligned, as can
happen with an overpronated forearm (as in some schools of string and
keyboard playing, or poor hand position in flute and guitar playing).
Abnormal protrusion of either forearm bone will cause irritation to tendons that pass over them. Typical problems might cause tenosynovitis,
tenderness, inflammation, and swelling, all of which could be prevented
by better positioning during playing.

Test position: The thumb is extended in line with the wrist and forearm. For EPL, the base of the thumb is held on either side and pressure

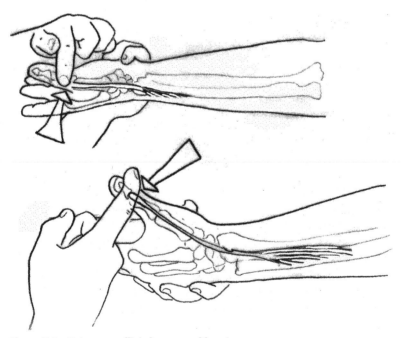

Figure 7.8   Extensor pollicis longus and brevis.

is put on the nail to bend the last joint. For EPB, the little finger side of the hand is held while pressure is put on the back of the thumb to bend the joint at the base of the thumb. Other muscles to test if weak: abductor pollicis longus and supinator.

Antagonist muscles: Thumb flexors and opposers.

Massage points: Massage down the inner forearm toward the thumb.

Meridian: Pericardium (Cx).

Holding points: Cx-9 and Lv-1. Cx-9 is at the end of the middle finger pad, on the index finger side. Hold it with Lv-1, which is on the nailbed of the big toe, on the corner nearest the other toes.

Nutrition: Vitamin E.

Emotion: Confused/confident, deceiving/truth.

Bach flower: Holly.

Abductor Pollicis Longus and Brevis

If the hand is palm up, the abductor pollicis longus (APL) muscle moves the thumb away from the palm and the floor (whereas the extensors move it out to the side, away from crossing the palm, while keeping it the same distance from the floor) (fig. 7.9). Its main use to musicians is as an antagonist to both the flexor and opponens group of muscles. Since it crosses the wrist joints on the thumb side, it also assists extensor carpi radialis in bending the wrist laterally. Abductor pollicis brevis (APB) assists APL and is rarely weak except where there are multiple allergies or wrist fracture, both of which are beyond the scope of this book. Because of meridian associations, there may also be accompanying rectal irritation.

Test position: The little finger side of the wrist is stabilized, the thumb moved about 70° away from the flattened palm and plane of the other fingers. Pressure is placed on the side of the lower of the two thumb bones nearest to the base of the thumb, to push it back toward the index finger. Other muscles to test if weak: extensor carpi radialis longus and brevis.

Antagonist muscles: Abductor and opponens muscles of the thumb.

Massage point: Massage from halfway down the thumb side of the forearm to the middle joint of the thumb.

Meridian: Triple warmer.

Holding points: TW-3 and GB-41. TW-3 is on the back of the hand

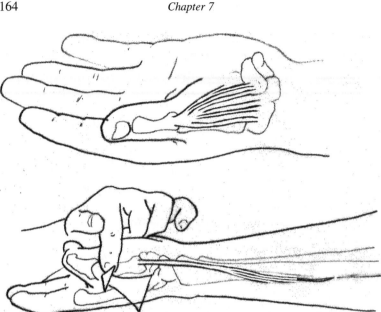

Figure 7.9   Abductor pollicis longus and brevis.

halfway between the base of the ring finger and the wrist, on the little finger side of the bone. Hold it with GB-41, which is on the top of the foot, halfway between the base of the fourth toe and the ankle.

Nutrition: Zinc, lecithin.

Emotion: Concerned/trust, self-centered/kind, disrespect/respect.

Bach flower: Mustard.

Intrinsic Hand Muscles

1. Adductor pollicis and opponens pollicis
2. Abductor digiti minimi, flexor digiti minimi, and opponens digiti minimi
3. Interossei (dorsal and palmar)
4. Lumbricals

These are the little muscles on the palm and the back of the hand. Great care should be taken when testing them, not only because they are small and therefore easily overpowered, but also because your livelihood depends on them. In testing them, the tendency is to use a group of the strongest muscles of both hands to test one poor little muscle. This is where it is vital to remember that you are testing for quality of *reaction, not gross strength*. This applies particularly when testing single fingers, especially the little finger. Don't cause problems for yourself as Schumann did!

I know of no musician who hasn't complained about his or her little finger at some time or other. So often it has to reach further, or is at a disadvantage because of leverage distance, quite apart from the fact that it is the smallest finger. Those who have a large discrepancy between finger lengths definitely do have a greater coordination problem that those with "square" hands. The fifth finger is blessed with its own set of muscles and this helps, but the tendency is to damage it by overtraining or overcompensation. This upsets the balance of the hand, and even upsets wrist or elbows at the extremes. If you look for it in other books, the little finger may be listed as digiti quinti.

Adductor Pollicis and Opponens Pollicis

These muscles bring the thumb toward the palm and bring the thumb inward at the level of the webbing; adductor pollicis (AP) going to the middle of the palm bones, and opponens pollicis (OP) going to the flexor retinaculum—the band of tough cartilage that covers the carpal tunnel (fig. 7.10). They work closely with flexor pollicis brevis (see earlier entry). Weakness may cause difficulty gripping things and illegible writing. All these thumb muscles are vital to smooth scale playing on keyboard instruments. With weakness, the only other way to pass the thumb under the fingers is to lift and pronate the wrist to bring the fingers into a more vertical position, which makes for a bumpy legato and general lack of control due to differing finger lengths. Tension in these muscles causes pain in the ball of the thumb.

AP and OP are also vital to changing position in the left hand of string and guitar players, for holding most wind instruments, all drum sticks and so on in percussion, and even for holding a pencil to mark your music! Little is known specifically about symptoms associated with weakness of these muscles other than toxic headaches. However, being able to test specifically which one is weak is useful in diagnosis

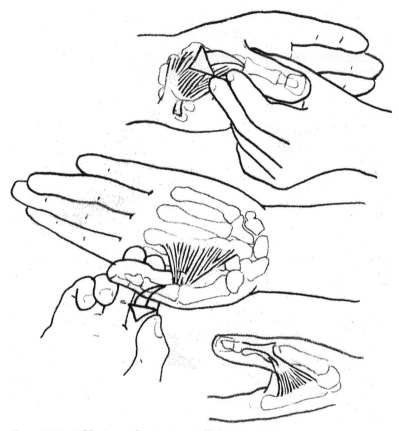

Figure 7.10 Adductor and opponens pollicis.

of carpal tunnel syndrome, which unfortunately, frequently afflicts musicians. Chronic tension in these muscles may often lead eventually to arthritis.

Test Position: For AP, the straight thumb lies on top of the index finger and palm (whereas with FPB it lies next to the index), and with OP the ball of the thumb lies across the palm. In all cases, the little finger side of the palm is stabilized. To test AP, tuck two fingers between thumb and the base of the index finger, and pull the thumb away from the palm toward the inner elbow. To test OP, the ball of the thumb is pulled out sideways to flatten the palm. As adductor pollicis has nearly the same function as opponens pollicis but a different nerve supply, it is important to asses both where there is a possibility of carpel or Guyon tunnel syndrome. Other muscles to test if weak: all the other thumb muscles, longus, and brevis.

Antagonist muscles: All the thumb extensors

Massage points: (a) Under the front of the pelvic bones (above the very tops of the legs and more centrally than the groin). (b) On the back of the top of the pelvis in between the two dimple marks either side of the base of the spine.

Meridian: Stomach.

Holding points: (a) The frontal eminences—over the center of each eye, halfway between the eyebrows and hairline. (b) Acupoints S-41 and SI-5. S-41 is on the top of the ankle crease in a small dip. Hold it with SI-5, which is just below the little finger side of the wrist, on the end of the forearm bone.

Emotion: Unwilling/willing, restless/calm, revolting/attractive.

Bach flower: Willow.

Abductor Digiti Minimi, Flexor Digiti Minimi, and Opponens Digiti Minimi

The first of these muscles, the abductor digiti minimi (ADM), moves the little finger from lying next to the ring finger out to the side (fig. 7.11). It runs from the forearm bone on the same side to the outside of the bone nearest the palm. Next to it is the flexor digiti minimi (FDM). This muscle is further around on the palm and runs from the wrist to the same bone at the base of the little finger. Further around still, and even shorter, is the very important opponens digiti minimi (ODM), which runs from the wristbones to the base of the little finger, still on the palm. This may also be weakened by Guyon tunnel syndrome, where the nerve is squashed between two wristbones (pisiform and hammate).

Test position: ADM—The straight little finger is moved away from the ring finger in the same plane. Support the rest of the hand and put pressure on the outside of the finger to push it toward the ring finger.

FDM—The straight little finger is flexed from the knuckle nearest the palm. The rest of the hand is supported, and pressure is put on the palmar surface of the base of the little finger to flatten the hand.

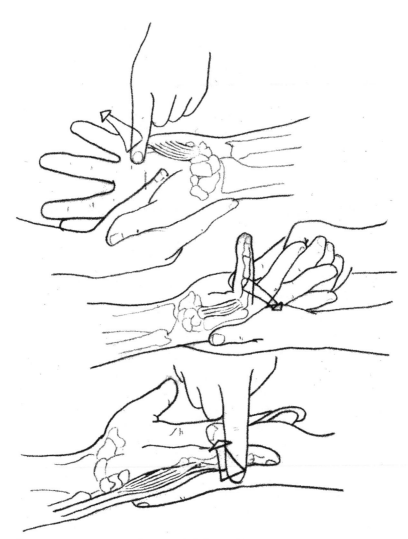

Figure 7.11   Opponens, flexor, and abductor digiti minimi.

ODM—The straight little finger is flexed toward the base of the thumb. The rest of the thumb is supported, and pressure is put on the palm under the little finger to flatten the hand. Other muscles to test, if weak: other digiti minimi muscles, finger flexors and extensors, supinators and pronators for which it may be compensating.

Antagonist muscles: Extensor digiti minimi, palmar interossei.

Massage points: Same as short thumb muscles.

Holding points: Same as short thumb muscles.

Nutrition: Vitamins B6, B12, and B complex, magnesium, lecithin.

Emotion: Nervous/peaceful, not needed/needed, unwilling/willing.

Bach flower: Willow.

Interossei

There are two sets of interossei: the palmar (on the palm), which brings the fingers together, and the dorsal (on the back of the hand), which spreads the fingers (fig. 7.12). You can see them on the palm if you flatten your hand and hold the fingers close together, or on the back of your hand if you spread your fingers (fig. 7.13). They are the little bumps between the bones near the base of the fingers. In musicians, they are likely to be well developed, but overstretching for big chords or playing an instrument that is too large may cause weakness, hand pain, and poor coordination. Because of meridian associations, there may also be sciatica and poor dental health.

Test position: Palmar interossei—Hold the thumb and finger straight and close together. To test, pull each finger away from the next.

Dorsal interossei—Spread the fingers, keeping them straight and in line with the palm. Test them by pushing each pair together.

Antagonist muscles: The other interossei.

Meridian: Triple warmer and spleen.

Holding points: TW-3 and GB-41 . TW-3 is on the back of the hand, halfway between the base of the ring finger and the wrist crease on the little finger side of the bone. Hold it with GB-41, which is on the top of the foot, halfway between the base of the fourth toe and the ankle.

Nutrition: Vitamin B6, iron, lecithin, garlic and parsley, thyme and marjoram, apricot, apple cider vinegar, asparagus, cabbage, grapes, citrus fruits, figs, soy, and yogurt.

Sensitivity: Potatoes and foods containing zinc.

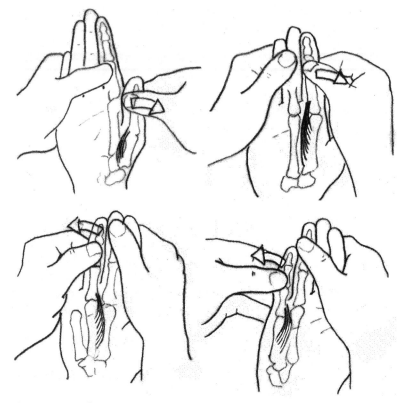

Figure 7.12   Palmar interossei.

Emotion: Unwilling/willing, defensive/listening, concerned/trust.
Bach flower: Mustard and Mimulus.

Lumbricales

These muscles are used to bend straight fingers at the knuckle by flexing the joint at the knuckle while extending the last joint of the fingers,
as when holding a piece of paper or a fan of cards between the flat pads
of the fingers and thumb (fig. 7.14). They run from the tendons of flexor
digitorum to the base of each finger just beyond the webbing. With
marked weakness, it's very difficult to hold a book or paper in one hand.

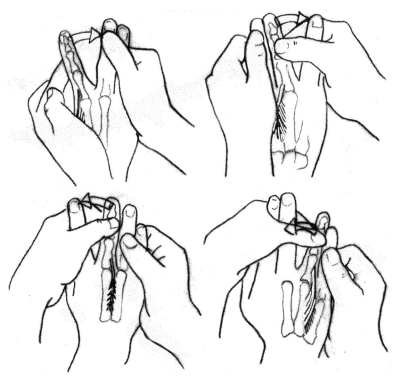

Figure 7.13   Dorsal interossei.

This results in claw hand deformity, such that the finger with the weak muscle will not flex in all joints completely if the palm is flat, giving pain at the base of the fingers. These muscles are specifically used in heavy brass playing by the three middle fingers.

Test position: This requires two tests because of the double action. With straight fingers bent only at the knuckle, pressure is simultaneously put on the palmar surface on the fingers next to the palm to straighten the knuckle and also the nailbed of the same finger to bend the last joint.

Antagonist muscles: Finger extensors and flexor digitorum profundus.

Massage points: Massage between the bones of the hand from the wrist to the fingers.

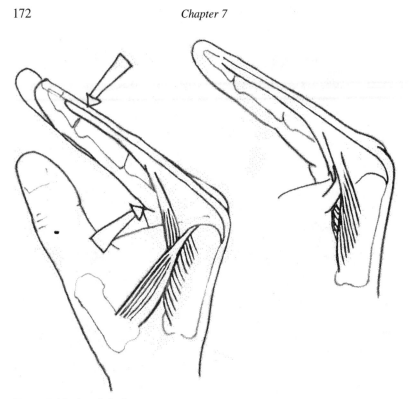

Figure 7.14 Lumbricales.

Meridian: Spleen.

Holding points: Sp-2 and H-8. Sp-2 is on the nail end of the big joint, at the base of the big toe, on the side of the foot. Hold it with H-8, which is on the palm of the hand on the first crease below the base of the ring finger.

Nutrition: Vitamin B3, cayenne.

Emotion: Unwilling/willing, unaccepted/accepted.

Bach flower: Mimulus.

8

Muscles of the Torso, Abdomen, and Back and Other Postural Muscles

1. Torso muscles
2. Serratus anterior
3. Abdominals
4. Diaphragm

Serratus Anterior

This muscle is serrated as it fits between the ribs on the side of the chest wall (hence its name) (fig. 8.1). It holds the shoulder blade on to the rib cage, and weakness creates difficulty in raising the arm both to the side and to the front. At the same time, the shoulder blade "wings" out at the back. It is used for bowing in all stringed instruments, wind, brass, percussion, harp, and conducting. It is also used when turning pages while seated at a keyboard instrument and playing the upper registers of the harp where raising the shoulders would upset the position of the harp resting in the shoulder. Weakness can cause bursitis, unequal chest expansion, upper backache, pain in the bottom corner of the shoulder blade and armpit, or pain on deep breathing or reaching across to the opposite side. Because of its association with the lung meridian, it is often weak in wind and brass players when under stress. It is involved in almost all shoulder problems.

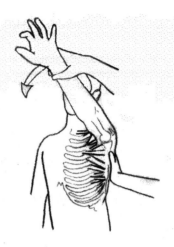

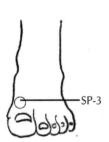SP-3

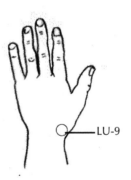LU-9

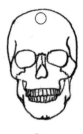

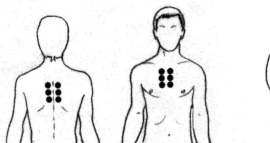

Figure 8.1   Serratus anterior.

Test Position: The Testee is sitting, the straight arm is raised 45° above horizontal and 45° to the side, thumb up and palm in. The lower tip of the shoulder blade is lightly stabilized while pressure is put on the forearm to push it to the floor for the middle division. Push the arm forward to test the lower division, and backward to test the upper division as the muscle follows the curve of the rib cage. However, the test can be done lying down. This is the most stable position. The Testee lies down and raises a straight arm at 90° above horizontal and 45° to the side, with the thumb up and palm in. The aim of the test is not to test arm strength but to see whether the shoulder blade remains stable. Other muscles to test if weak: diaphragm and levator scapulae.

Antagonist muscles: Anterior deltoid, coracobrachialis, rhomboids.

Massage point: (a) Between the third, fourth, and fifth ribs, either side of the breastbone. (b) Between the third, fourth, and fifth ribs next to the spine, level with the top down to the middle of the shoulder blade.

Meridian: Lung.

Holding point: (a) Anterior fontanel—one thumb's width back from the vertex of the head. (b) Acupoints L-9 and Sp-3. L-9 is at the end of the wrist crease, at the base of the thumb. Hold it with Sp-3, which is on the ankle side of the big joint at the base of the big toe.

Nutrition: Get lots of fresh air and avoid smoky, dirty, or mouldy atmospheres. Avoid all dairy products as these can be mucus forming. Increase intake of foods high in vitamins A, B complex, and C, kelp, alfalfa, ginger, apple cider vinegar, garlic, parsley, maple syrup, chamomile.

Emotion: Nervous/restful, discontented/contented, depressed/expressive, confused/confident, futile/assured, unwilling/willing, grief/fellow feeling, scared/courageous, useless/useful, haughty/meek, smug/compassionate.

Bach flower: Water violet.

Abdominals

There are many parts to this group muscle (fig. 8.2). Rectus abdominis (the six-pack) runs straight up the front in a series of bands from the pelvis to the ribs and is involved with breathing control. On either side there are the transverse abdominis and oblique abdominis, which are involved in holding a slightly twisted posture when playing a one-sided

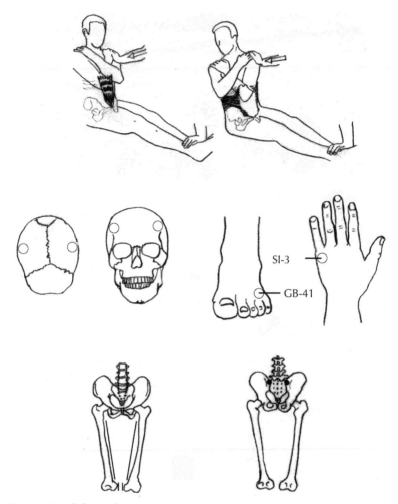

Figure 8.2 Abdominals.

instrument; anchoring them all at the bottom is the pyramidalis, which
is not discussed except to say that it is involved in counterbalancing the
pull of the back muscles against gravity. The abdominal muscles protect the soft abdominal contents, which are vulnerable between the ribs
and pelvis in the front, but protected behind by the ribs, which reach

down lower, and the spine. A flabby belly or distended "stomach" area is a sure sign of muscle flaccidity. Abdominal muscle weakness is the most usual cause of back pain, because the back muscles have to take up the chronic slackness and so go into spasm. The lower abdominals are also particularly subject to herniation in men, through a natural developmental anatomical weakness, and this can be exacerbated by lifting heavy instruments or poor technique in brass playing. Pain may occur in the groin or the pubic area, on top of the hips and lower ribs at the side, or on twisting the upper torso, or there may be difficulty in breathing deeply when side bending. It is quite common to find reactive muscle patterns in wind and brass players. (See chapter 10.) Bladder infections may occur concurrently.

Test position: All abdominals. The Testee sits leaning back slightly, with legs straight out in front, head up and arms crossed to the shoulders. The legs are stabilized, while pressure is put on: (a) the midchest of crossed arms to push the Testee straight backward; (b) the same position but with pressure on the right shoulder directly backward; (c) the same position again but with the pressure on the left shoulder directly backward. For (d) the Testee now twists so that one shoulder is pointing forward and pressure is put on the forward shoulder to push it directly backward. (e) is the same as (d) but the other shoulder forward. The degree of backward lean in the starting position determines at what level on the abdominal wall the muscles are being tested, although of course they are all working to some degree all the time. To test the lowest level, test with the least backward lean. Other muscles to test if weak: psoas, iliacus, sacrospinalis, latissmus dorsi. (Also reread the section "Breathing Misconceptions" in chapter 2.)

Antagonist muscles: Sacrospinalis, quadratus lumborum, latissimus dorsi.

Massage points: (a) The inside of the thighs on a broad band stretching from the groin to the knee. The lower part of this broad band helps the rectus abdominis and pyramidalis most, and the upper part the transverse and oblique abdominals. (b) The most prominent knobs at the top back of the pelvis on either side of the spine (L-5, PSIS).

Meridian: Small intestine.

Holding point: (a) Three inches (4 cm) above the ear at the widest point of the head. (b) Spread your fingers out either side of a line running from the centerback of the skull, and as the Testee breathes in and pushes the head upward, gently pull the spread fingers outward along the center line as though to widen the head between the ears. Do this five times. It assists the normal motion of the skull during breathing. (c) Acupoints SI-3 and GB-41. SI-3 is on the side of the hand midway between the base of the little finger and the end of the wrist crease.

Nutrition: Arnica. Foods rich in vitamin E, kelp, lecithin, calcium and zinc; avocado, cucumber, raisins, radish will help. Avoid spicy food, caffeine, alcohol, sugar, white rice, and white flour.

Sensitivity: White flour, celery, cinnamon, sugar intolerance.

Emotion: Nervous/restful, vain/useful, unsuccessful/successful, confused/confident, resentful/appreciative, unwilling/willing, hopeless and helpless/trusting and powerful, hard/adaptive, rebellious/accepting, discontent/content, frustrated/able.

Bach flower: Star of Bethlehem.

Diaphram

The diaphragm is one of the rare, almost horizontal muscles. It divides the torso into two parts, the upper part containing the heart and lungs and the lower containing the liver, spleen, stomach, and other digestive organs. It is attached to the inside of the lower ribs on the front and back and has large centrally placed holes in front of the spine, through which passes the main blood vessels, and the gullet, and some smaller holes for nerves and other vessels. Being a muscle, its natural elasticity is occasionally lost. Overelasticity can cause digestive problems such as heartburn and hernia, due to laxity or constriction of the passage to the stomach. Because it interdigitates with psoas as it attaches on the inside of the spine, chronic diaphragm tension can set up reactive muscle patterns by preventing proper contraction of psoas and giving rise to low back pain; the opposite is also true but less likely in musicians that a psoas in spasm will affect diaphragm function. Diaphragm weakness is indicated when the Testee is unable to hold his or her breath for forty seconds or is unable to blow out a match from a 15-cm distance with the mouth open. It is the main muscle of breathing, its contraction altering the pressure around and within the lungs to draw air in, and it also helps to hold the breath in and control its release in a long musical phrase. Most breathing out is done by gravity, but can be assisted by the diaphragm pushing up and decreasing the available lung space.

Obviously good control and function is essential to all wind and brass players and singers. The most frequent misuse occurs in other instrumentalists, however, particularly players of upper strings and keyboards who have a bad habit of holding many muscles in tension including the diaphragm (and therefore the breath) in anxiety states. To temporarily weaken the diaphragm when it is hypertonic and causing reactive patterns (see chapter 11) of weakness in psoas or SCM (sterno cliedo mastoid, or neck flexors), feather the massage points, rub the holding points hard (i.e., reversing normal treatment). To reset the muscle after this, take a deep breath in and out.

Test position: Inaccessibility makes this muscle difficult to test without a spirometer, which is usually only available in hospitals. However, in the interests of simplicity, a fairly good indication of normal function is the ability to hold a good breath in for forty seconds without releasing it. Any wind or brass player or singer should beat this easily. It might be helpful to note your own "normal ability" in seconds, and compare it with your ability when stressed. There is a further possibility of gently pressing three fingers up under the bottom of the breastbone while testing an indicator muscle. This will only indicate that the diaphragm is weak in a general way. Some control of today's all-too-prevalent asthmatic spasm can be achieved by learning to breath through a straw, but oboe players who do this habitually as they play are occasionally subject to sharply painful air leaks into the space outside the lungs and this needs immediate medical attention. Other signs of weakness include hiccup, pain in the lower rib cage, and pain upon deep breathing. Because of its meridian association there may also be accompanying sciatica. Other muscles to test if weak: abdominals, upper trapezius, pectoral muscles, teres minor, and psoas.

Antagonist muscles: Abdominal muscles.

Massage points: (a) The whole length of the breastbone. (This can be very painful.) (b) On the right-hand side of the spine, level with 2 inches below the lowest part of the shoulder blade.

Meridian: Lung.

Holding points: (a) Bregma back to 2 cm above lambda—one thumb's width back from the vertex of the head for three finger's width backward. (b) Acupoints L-9 and Sp-3. L-9 is on the end of the wrist crease at the base of the thumb. Hold it with Sp-3, which is on the inside of the foot, on the heel side of the large joint at the base of the big toe.

Holding these acupoints can increase the length of time you are able to hold your breath by half as long again!

Nutrition: It goes without saying that smoking reduces lung capacity. It constricts the blood supply, as well as clogs the airways and causes spasm of the delicate and very fine lung tissue. Ninety percent of the smoking habit is psychological dependency rather than drug dependency, so it's much easier to give up if you reduce the panic, stress, and psychological need. Increase intake of foods high in vitamins B3, C, and E.

Emotion: Unwilling/willing, not needed/needed, tongue-tied/expressive, confused/confident, barrier/clear, undesirable/pleasant.

Bach flower: Water violet.

BACK MUSCLES

1. Latissimus dorsi
2. Erector spinae (also called sacrospinalis)

Latissimus Dorsi

This is one of the more easily visible large back muscles and often works together with lower trapezius (fig. 8.3). It is joined to the pelvis and middle and lower spine by a strong sheet of cartilaginous tissue. This wide muscle narrows down to a single very strong tendon, which catches the bottom tip of the shoulder blade as it passes and twists round on itself as it goes under the armpit to attach to the front of the upper arm. Its action is to twist the arm inward, toward the buttocks and the lower torso and down to the floor. It is used by upper string players in the upper half of the bow on all down strokes, especially at the tip of the bow. Weakness causes shoulder and low back pain and elbow pains (which can be mistaken for tendonitis or tennis elbow), due to forced overuse of synergistic muscles. There may be low back pain or a deep ache at the lower corner of the shoulder blade or on the front of the shoulder. Because of its meridian association, there is often an accompanying sugar intolerance. There may be a raised shoulder on the weak side and flatulence shortly after eating, dizziness, or tiredness.

Test position: The straight arm is held to the side and turned palm

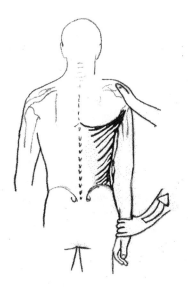

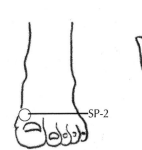

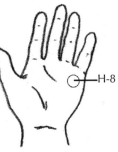

SP-2

H-8

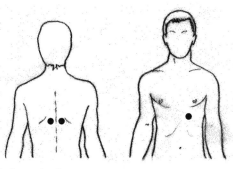

Figure 8.3   Latissimus dorsi.

out with the thumb facing backward. Stabilize the shoulder, and be sure the elbow is locked straight as you pull the forearm away from the body to the side and 45° to the front. Pull from the forearm, not the wrist. Some women can overstraighten the arm, some men can't completely straighten it. This is of no consequence as long as it is held as straight as possible, with the feeling of holding the elbow in, not the wrist. The most common fault in testing is to let the Testee bend the elbow or shoulder. Where there is elbow pain, pull from above the elbow. Weakness on both sides may cause constant raised shoulders and spasm in the upper trapezius muscles. Other muscles to test if weak: upper trapezius, PMC, triceps.

Antagonist muscles: Posterior deltoid and trapezius.

Massage points: (a) Between the seventh and eighth ribs on the right side of the ribcage 2 inches (5 cm) below the nipple and an inch toward the breastbone. (b) Between the seventh and eighth ribs on the left side of the spine and level with the bottom of the shoulder blade.

Meridian: Spleen.

Holding points: (a) Either side of the head at about 1 inch (2.5 cm) above the back of the ear. (b) Acupoints Sp-2 and H-8. Sp-2 is found on the side of the foot at the nail end of the large joint at the base of the big toe. Hold it with H-8, which is on the palm crease, under the ring finger.

Nutrition: A consistently weak latissimus dorsi may indicate sugar handling difficulty whether hyperinsulinism, diabetes, or low bloodsugar. Avoid all quick-release "empty calorie" sugars such as sucrose and glucose like the plague! Be aware that these occur in all sorts of disguises in processed, packaged, and canned foods, in most soups, smoked meats, hams, sausages, bacon, and salamis as well as bottled concentrates or reconstituted juices, pies, sweets, cakes, and biscuits. Learn to read labels or only eat fresh foods! Keep your blood-sugar supply constant by eating slow-release carbohydrates such as whole grains and meusli bars and avoid all stimulants such as tea, coffee, cola, and alcohol as they raise blood-sugar levels too fast. Increase intake of foods containing vitamin A and essential fatty acids, B complex, zinc and chromium, lecithin.

Emotion: Unwilling/willing, bitter/forgiveness, unaccepted/accepted.

Bach flower: Mimulus.

Erector Spinae (Sacrospinalis)

This muscle has at least two names because it is a composite of muscles, combining most of the complicated structural support of the back against gravity (fig. 8.4). It joins ribs to spine, ribs to other ribs, and ultimately the pelvis to the spine, neck, and back of the head. Despite common ideas, it is rarely weak, but very frequently in spasm, which is the cause of the pain felt. Sitting still on long journeys or watching TV may cause spasm but 90 percent of back pain is due to weak, stretched, and flaccid abdominal muscles that the erector spinae has to counterbalance. Its main function is to bend the spine backward when both sides contract, or to assist side bending when only one side contracts. True weakness of erector spinae causes many areas of pain and dysfunction, arthritis, referred pain, shoulder and elbow problems due to compensation, spinal curvature ("C" curves and "S" curves), sciatica, and pain and tingling in the legs and feet. It is also noticeable that emotional feelings of lack of support (whether in the family or professionally) certainly add to back pain and may compound problems due to poor seating, prolonged standing, practicing for hours, or playing a one-sided instrument—notably the double bass, a heavy viola, or bass trombone. Upper back problems may result in breathlessness for wind and brass players and singers. Other typical back problems are caused by poor lifting techniques where, because the person tends to bend from the waist instead of the hips, the tiny muscles between the bones of the back take the strain, instead of the thigh muscles, which are built for the job. If there is a "back" problem, reread chapter 2 to learn how to adapt chairs and concert platforms to fit you, and how to counteract wearing high heels. Bladder infections and prostate problems due to meridian associations are less common causes of erector spinae malfunction. To help this, always wear cotton underwear and follow the dietary advice below.

Test position: The Testee lies face down and clasps hands over the back of the pelvis. Both shoulders are then lifted off the table. The Testee then looks over and raises one shoulder. The hands are stabilized on the pelvis and pressure is put on the raised shoulder to push it back to the table. Swap head turn and shoulder to test the other side. Other muscles to test if weak: Latissimus dorsi, quadratus lumborum, psoas, gluteus maximus, tibials, and peroni.

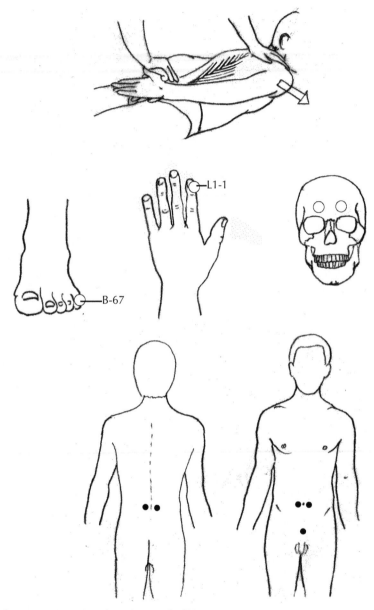

Figure 8.4   Erector spinae (sacrospinalis).

Antagonistic muscles: All abdominal muscles.

Massage points: (a) One inch (2.5 cm) either side of the tummy button and over the middle of the pubic bone—rub the bone, don't squash the bladder! (b) Either side of the spine, 2 inches (5 cm) below the lowest ribs.

Meridian: Bladder.

Holding points: (a) The frontal eminences—over the center of each eye and halfway between the eyebrows and hairline. (b) Acupoints B-67 and L-11. B-67 is on the nailbed of the little toe. Hold it at the same time as L-11, which is on the thumb side of the nailbed of the index finger.

Nutrition: Increase intake of foods containing vitamins A, C, and E and calcium. With bladder problems, drink chamomile tea and barley water (water in which barley has been boiled, not squash or fruit juice!), and eat melon, pumpkin seeds, and garlic. If you have to take antibiotics for some reason, watch out for rashes, nausea, depression, diarrhea, and headaches and when the course of antibiotics is finished, eat lots of live yogurt.

Sensitivity: Caffeine, chocolate, rhubarb and purple fruits, spicy foods.

Emotion: Frustration/peace, unsupported/supported, not needed/ needed, unhelpful/helpful.

Bach flower: Impatiens.

LUMBAR MUSCLES

Most of the muscles which follow, in this and the remaining two sections, are not directly connected with playing a specific musical instrument. They are included because they are vital for posture, are jeopardized by a musician's lifestyle and can be the foundation cause for compensatory tensions in muscles used in playing.

1. Psoas and iliacus
2. Quadratus lumborum

Psoas and Iliacus

Psoas connects the inside of the lower spine to the top of the thighbone, running across the edge of the pelvis as it does so (fig. 8.5). It is a hip

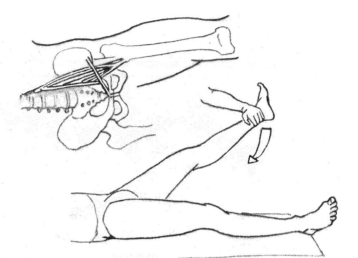

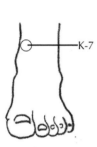K-7

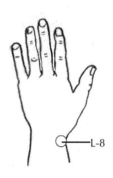L-8

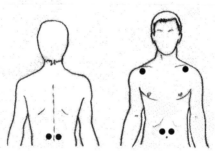

Figure 8.5   Psoas.

flexor, and on it depends the low back curvature. When weak it causes "sway back." Feet that splay like Alice's fish footman and won't walk "Indian file" are often compensating for sway back by dropping the arches that cause "flat feet."

Iliacus connects the inside of the pelvic rim, on either side of the spine to the top of the thighbone (fig. 8.6). Its tendon melds with psoas. Both psoas and iliacus can be the cause of low back pain, burning leg pains, spasms and sciatica, skin irritations, and digestive upsets. If you frequently suffer from constipation or diarrhea, see a kinesiologist for iliacaecal valve syndrome (IBS) correction. Weakness and spasm also appear to have an effect on general coordination.

Test position: Psoas—The Testee lies flat on his or her back. One straight leg is raised 45° up and 45° out, with the foot maximally turned out. The opposite hip is stabilized to prevent rocking, while pressure is applied to the lower leg to push it down and out. Do not put pressure over the knee joint or ankle joints. Great care should be taken if there is severe low back pain. The Testee should at least be able to hold the testing position. If there has been an injury to the back of the head or the muscles, or both sides are weak but strengthen when the Testee puts a hand behind his or her head, go to see a cranial specialist.

Iliacus works very closely with psoas and shares its tendon; it is tested the same way, but the leg is lifted up 60 to 70°. Other muscles to test if weak: TFL, gluteals, erector spinae (sacrospinalis).

Antagonist muscles: Gracilis, pyramidalis, and sartorius.

Massage point: (a) One inch (2.5 cm) out and up from the tummy button. (b) On the midback at the level of the last ribs, either side of the spine. (c) Inside the front, side edge of the pelvic bones. (d) In the dip on the front of the shoulder joint.

Meridian: Kidney.

Holding point: (a) Find the little bump on the skull over the valley at the top of the neck. Go diagonally up and out 1 inch (2.5 cm). (b) Acu-points K-7 and L-8. K-7 is three fingers' width up and one back from the inner anklebone. Hold it with L-8, which is on the side of the forearm, three fingers' widths below the wrist crease, thumb side.

Nutrition: The muscles are very badly affected by caffeine and dehydration, so don't go and drink coffee or alcohol, which are both diuretics when working in a dry centrally heated studio! Drink water! The same applies to long-haul flights where there is a similar atmosphere.

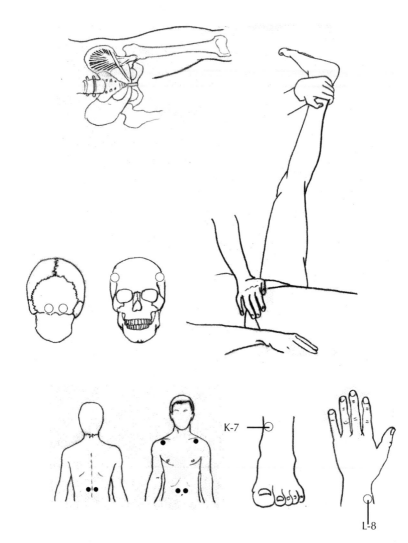

K-7

L-8

Figure 8.6   Iliacus.

Increase intake of foods high in vitamins A, B complex, and E, zinc, iron, kelp, Brazil nuts, cabbage, lecithin, molasses, cayenne.

Emotion: Unwilling/willing, unhelpful/helpful, confused/confident, suppressed/encouraged, irritated/tranquil, failure/success, nervous/restful, argumentative/agreeable, hard/adaptable, embarrassed/modest, frustrated/satisfied.

Bach flower: Scleranthus.

Quadratus Lumborum

This muscle is found either side of the lower back and joins the back of the pelvis to the lumbar spine and lowest ribs (fig. 8.7). It stabilizes the lower back with the lowest fibers of erector spinae (sacrospinalis). It helps the diaphragm with breathing by stabilizing the lowest ribs and can either pull the pelvis up to the ribs or pull the ribs down to the pelvis during side bending. This muscle can be badly affected by hours of sitting on a poor fitting chair or car seat, when under stress. There may be pelvic pain and shoulder blade pain, and it is also blamed for back pain, spasm (lumbago), and sciatica, when the problem is really caused by taking up the slack from lax abdominal muscles. Because of its meridian association, there may be bowel upset and flatulence, ear drainage problems, dry, irritated eyes, and anemia.

Test position: The Testee lies face up and holds the treatment table for upper body stability. The legs are held together and swung out to the near side. The opposite hip is stabilized, as the legs are pushed back to the midline of the table. Watch that there is no swivelling of the pelvis to bring other synergistic muscles into alignment. Other muscles to test if weak: oblique abdominals, erector spinae, psoas, iliacus.

Antagonist muscles: Abdominals and other quadratus lumborum.

Massage points: The end of the last rib, and between the last two ribs on either side of the spine.

Meridian: Large intestines.

Holding points: (a) Three inches above the ear at the widest part of the head. (b) Acupoints LI-11 and S-36. LI-11 is found at the end of the elbow crease on the thumb side. Hold it with S-36, which is 2 inches (5 cm) outside the bump below the knee cap, on the front of the shin.

Nutrition: Increase intake of foods rich in vitamins A, C, and E, lecithin, calcium, zinc, garlic, arnica, yarrow, apple cider vinegar, alfalfa.

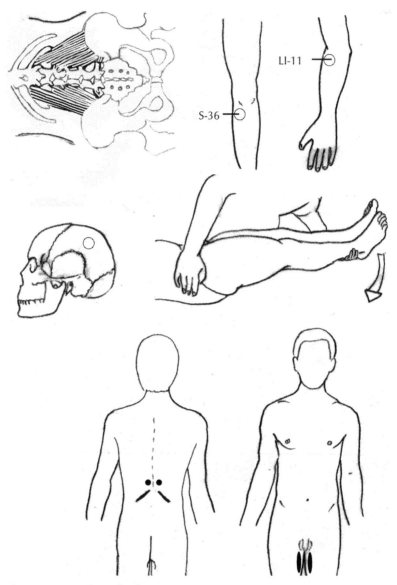

Figure 8.7 Quadratus lumborum.

S-36

LI-11

Sensitivity: Yeast, eggs, figs, olive oil, hypersensitivity to chlorinated water.

Emotion: Unwilling/willing, irresponsible/responsible, nervous/restful, grief for self/fellow feeling, confused/confident, insignificant/important, disappointed/satisfied, bored/enthusiastic, discontent/tranquil, incapable/success, sour/agreeable, proud/humble.

Bach flower: Pine.

9

Muscles of the Pelvis, Thigh, Calf, and Foot

PELVIC AND THIGH MUSCLES

1. Piriformis
2. Gluteals
3. Quadriceps
4. Sartorius
5. Hamstrings
6. Tensor fascia
7. Adductors and pectineus
8. Popliteus

Piriformis

This is one of the inner buttock muscles (fig. 9.1). It is a postural muscle in that it helps support the transference of upper body weight through to the thighs. The musician's interest in it is due to its variability. Under stress everyone "holds on" with some part of the anatomy. Some clench and grind their teeth, others' shoulders go up around their ears, others clench their buttocks and with them, piriformis. Since musicians have to keep their arms free (and some are even aware of shoulder tension), piriformis tends to be the main tension victim. The variability of piriformis is that the sciatic nerve may go under, through all or part

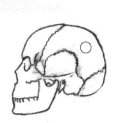

CX-9

LV-1

Figure 9.1   Piriformis.

of it. Any chronic tension in this muscle will therefore compress the sciatic nerve nine times out of ten and ultimately causes excruciating sciatica. The muscle is employed when you sit and spread your knees sideways, and so is particularly used by organists. However, most orchestral musicians sit knees apart, with their instrument or bow between their knees. This doesn't mean that you should not sit like this—far from it—ask any Alexander teacher! What it does mean is that you need to be aware of excess tension, buttock clenching, and holding on in this area. Given ideal posture and chair, it should not be necessary, but one-sided instruments like the violin tend to foster tension on one side to get the knees out of the way of the bow. This also twists the pelvis and lumbar region chronically. Weakness of the piriformis may be the cause of deep pelvic pain (especially during intercourse), a turned-in foot, and/or ankle pain.

Test position: (a) The Testee lies face down and the knee is flexed at 90°. The outside of the knee is stabilized and pressure is put on the inner ankle to pull the lower leg out to the side. (b) The Testee sits, hips bent at right angles only (not more), knees also bent at a right angle. Watch that the Testee does not lean forward during the test. The lower leg and ankle is taken across over the ankle of the other leg (not knee over knee), the knee is stabilized, and pressure is placed on the inner shin to push it out sideways. Other muscles to test if weak: Gluteus maximus, tensor fascia lata, hamstrings, and adductors

Antagonist muscle: Iliacus.

Massage points: (a) Top of the pubic bone. (b) The most prominent bumps on the top back of the pelvis (PSIS).

Meridian: Pericardium (Cx).

Holding points: (a) Parietal eminence—3 inches (7.5 cm) above the top of the ear at the widest point of the head. (b) Acupoints Cx-9 and Lv-1. Cx-9 is the end of the middle finger on the side nearest the index finger. Hold it together with Lv-1, which is on the big toe nailbed on the side nearest the other toes.

Nutrition: Foods rich in vitamins A, B complex, and E, zinc, and magnesium will help.

Emotion: Unwilling/willing, forsaken/accepted, weary/refreshed, nervous/restful, unmotivated/motivated, confused/confident, incapable/understandable, arrogant/listening, belligerent/agreeable.

Bach flower: Holly.

Gluteals: Gluteus Maximus, Gluteus Medius, Gluteus Minimus

These are the buttock muscles. Gluteus maximus is at the back and provides the mass of the bottom, shielding the pelvic bones from the shock and compression when you sit (fig. 9.2). It also stabilizes the knee with tensor fascia lata (TFL), so weakness could cause knee pain.

Gluteus medius and gluteus minimus are around at the sides and provide the "panniers" (fig. 9.3). They are large, strong muscles that connect the pelvis to the legs and prevent forward flop or excess sideways sway of the torso when you walk. They are part of the chain of muscles—erector spinae, gluteals, hamstrings, and calf muscles—which pull top to toe down the back of the body to counteract the lack of bony support on the front of the body and keep it upright. If you play a heavy instrument (e.g., bass trombone or tuba) that has to be carried, these muscles have to counteract that as well. Gluteus maximus is mainly used to stabilize the back and hips when going upstairs or running. Gluteus medius and minimus are used to take the leg out to the side (as in organ playing) and stabilize the side of the pelvis and hips. These muscles can spasm if you tend to put most of your weight on one leg when standing (particularly in upper strings and flute to counterbalance the instrument weight), when telephoning, waiting for a recording playback, or at bus stops, or doing household chores such as sweeping or washing up. Unless you switch sides frequently, unequal use of this sort twists the entire pelvis and sets you up for uneven hip and shoulder heights, back, and buttock pain! If there is a constant weakness, meridian association may mean a glandular imbalance and depressed appetite.

Test position: Gluteus maximus—(a) The Testee lies face down with the knee bent at 90°, foot in the air. Raise the whole leg off the table. Pressure is put on the back of the thigh to press it back to the table, whilst stabilising the opposite side of the pelvis. Watch there is no "hip rolling" or change in knee flexion to recruit quadratus lumborum or hamstrings. (b) The Testee lies face up and resists a pull to lift the straight leg off the table. This test is faster but less good as it is impossible to prevent the hamstrings helping.

Gluteus medius and minimus—(a) The Testee is side-lying. Lift the straight leg 45° for gluteus minimus but back slightly, with the toe out for gluteus medius. The hip is stabilized and pressure is put on the lower

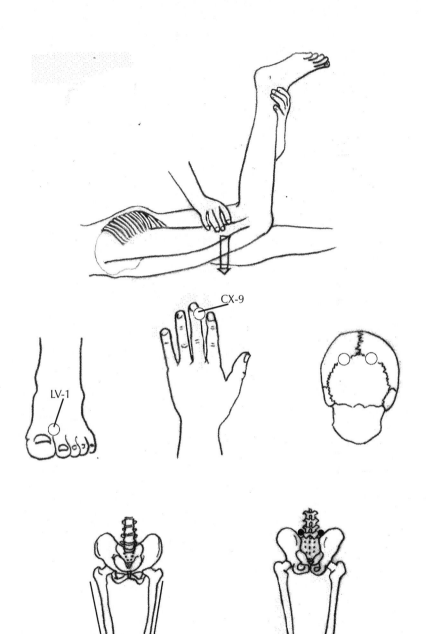

Figure 9.2   Gluteus maximus.

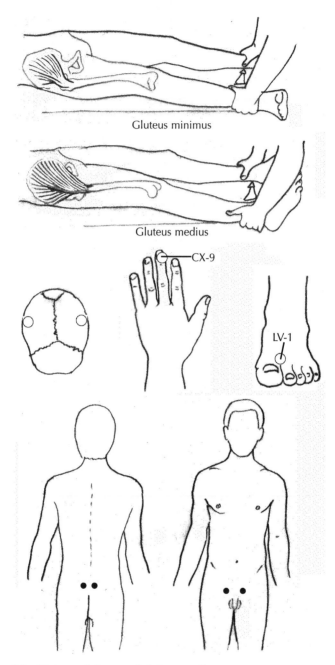

Gluteus minimus

Gluteus medius

CX-9

LV-1

Figure 9.3   Gluteus minimus and gluteus medius.

leg to push it back to the other leg. (b) The Testee lies face up at the edge of the table to allow the leg to drop below the table level. The straight leg is taken out to the side with toe out 45° for gluteus medius and toe straight up for gluteus minimus. Pressure is put on the lower leg to bring it back next to the other leg, while the other leg is stabilized (watch for hip twisting to recruit tensor fascia lata). Weakness will frequently be present if there is piriformis malfunction.

Massage Points: Gluteus maximus—(a) The whole of the outside front of the thigh. (b) The most prominent bumps on the back of the pelvis (PSIS).

Gluteus medius and minimus—(a) Upper edge of the front of the pubic bone 1 inch (2.5 cm) either side of the midpoint. (b) The most prominent bumps on the top back of the pelvis (PSIS)

Holding points: Gluteus maximus—(a) Directly above the ear. (b) Two inches (5 cm) behind the ear on an imaginary line extending from the corner of the eye through the top of the ear.

Gluteus medius and minimus—Three inches (7.5 cm) above the top of the ear at the widest part of the head.

Meridian: Same as for piriformis.

Holding points: Same as for piriformis.

Nutrition: Foods rich in vitamins B complex and E, kelp, zinc, lecithin, honey, calcium.

Sensitivity: Garlic.

Emotion: Unwilling/willing, undesirable/pleasant, confused/confident, guilty/innocent, insecure/secure, not listening/attentive, abhorrent/adoring, impatient/patient, concerned/trust, irritated/tranquil, obdurate/submissive, unhelpful/helpful, hungry/fulfilled, forsaken/accepted.

Bach flower: Holly.

In the muscles that follow, quadriceps bring the knee forward; hamstrings take it back. Tensor fascia lata (as well as the gluteals discussed earlier) take the leg out to the side, adductors bring the legs together.

Quadriceps

This is a group of four muscles that make up the front of the thigh (fig. 9.4). Their main function is to straighten the knee, but one part also helps psaos to flex the hips. The lower tendon contains the kneecap, which acts as a fulcrum to give extra strength. Quadriceps, together

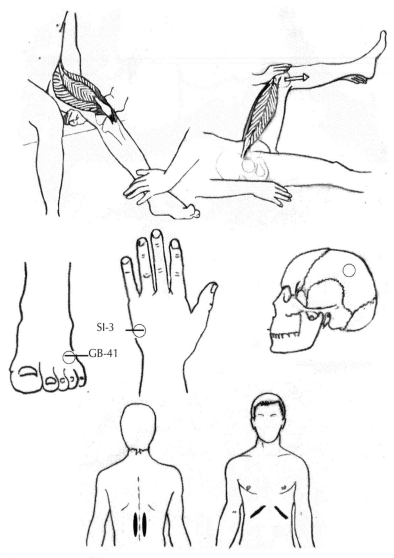

Figure 9.4   Quadriceps.

with the shin and calf muscles, are mainly used in walking, but also in any form of pedaling (all keyboards, timps, and harp), and in driving most vehicles. These are the muscles that should be used for lifting heavy cases, not the little inter-spinal muscles. Make the quadricepts work by bending your knees, and then, keeping your back straight, take hold of the heavy weight. Lift by straightening your knees. (See also chapter 3.) Similarly, move a piano on its castors by bending your knees first, then lean your weight against the piano and push, with the strength coming from your thigh muscles, not your back or arms.

Remember, the thigh muscles are well trained, each one singly lifts your entire weight every step you take! Weakness causes knee and thigh pain and fatigue climbing stairs; there may also be leg cramps.

Test position: (a) The Testee lies face up with one leg bent 80° and the shin just above horizontal. Support the lower leg under the ankle. Horizontal pressure is put on the thigh just above the knee, pushing straight toward the feet, straightening both knee and hip joint. (b) The Testee sits on a table with legs dangling over the side, one leg is horizontal and straight. The Tester puts one hand under the knee of that leg to protect the hamstrings from the table edge and pressure is put on the shin to bend the knee. It is also possible to use this test standing while leaning back against a wall to assist stability. Weakness on both sides may indicate allergies or a Candida overgrowth problem. Other muscles to test if weak: sartorius, TFL, psoas, abdominals.

Antagonist muscles: Hamstrings.

Massage points: (a) All along the underneath border of the front of the ribcage. (b) Either side of the spine, level with the bottom of the shoulderblade and three rib-spaces below.

Meridian: Small intestine.

Holding points: (a) Parietal eminence—three inches (7.5 cm) above the top of the ear, at the widest part of the head. (b) Acupoints SI-3 and GB-41. SI-3 is on the back of the hand, halfway between the ring and little fingers, knuckles, and wrist. Hold this with GB-41, which is similarly placed on top of the foot, halfway between the base of the fourth and little toes and the ankle crease.

Nutrition: This muscles group reacts badly to stress, particularly mental overload, so it needs support with the B complex vitamin group, vitamins D and E, zinc, magnesium, safflower oil, apple cider vinegar, poppy seed, and tarragon.

Sensitivity: Avoid all spicy foods, refined sugars, caffeine, and alcohol. You may also find milk products difficult to digest, and there may be a temporary hypersensitivity to many foods.

Emotion: Nervous/restful, injustice/justice, sour/agreeable, defeated/success, unwilling/willing, irritated/tranquil, upset/calm, depressed/cheerful, confused/confident, barrier/clear.

While this test for quadriceps is a good general test, pedal users may wish to test the inner and outer portions more specifically. These are vastus lateralis and medius, and they help stabilize the knee on either side. Use the lying down test. Bend both knees to 90°. The Tester holds one knee above the kneecap with his or her hand nearest the head. The Testee's other leg rests on the Tester's forearm. With his or her other hand, the Tester then puts pressure in the shin to bend the knee more. To test vastus lateralis, the shin should start slightly outward and be pulled down and in; to test vastus medialis, the shin should start slightly inward and be pushed down and out. The correction massage and holding points and nutrition apply as above.

Sartorius

Because it runs diagonally across the front of the thigh, the sartorius helps to stabilize both the outside of the hip joint and the inside of the knee (fig. 9.5). Because it crosses both hip and knee joints, it helps the quadriceps both as a hip flexor and knee extensor, too. You use the sartorius most when you sit cross-legged "tailor fashion" as in playing some Indian instruments. Cellists and viol players use it to support the lower bouts of their instrument, and organists, harpists, and harpsichord players use it to control the lower leg when doing complex peddling. When weak, this muscle can cause knee pain and a twist in the pelvis so you don't face the front squarely or you have one leg apparently shorter than the other.

Test position: The Testee lies face up with the leg turned out and knee bent, so that the ankle lies on the other knee, or just below it. The Tester holds the bent knee with one hand to stabilize it and pushes inward slightly. The Tester's other hand then pulls against the ankle to straighten the leg. Take care there is no hooking of the toes over the shin or around the knee!

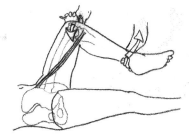

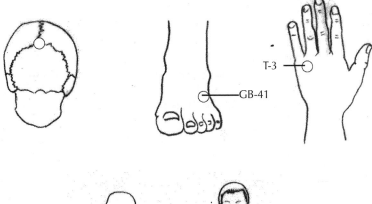

T-3

GB-41

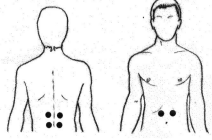

Figure 9.5   Sartorius.

Other muscles to test if sartorius is weak: adductors, quadriceps, hamstrings, neck flexors, soleus, latissimus dorsae, pectoralis major clavicular, psoas, peroneus, sacrospinalis, and anterior tibials.

Massage points: (a) On the belly 2.5 cm to the side of the belly button and 2.5 cm toward the head. (b) Just above the lowest rib on the back, right against the spine.

Meridian: Pericardium (Cx) or triple warmer.

Holding points: (a) The lambda—the spot on the back of the head where the occipital and the two parietal bones meet. (b) Acupoints T-3 and GB-41. T-3 is between the knuckles of the ring and little fingers and the wrist, one-third of the way down from the base of the ring finger. Hold this together with GB-41, which is in a similar place on the top of the foot, between the base of the fourth and little toes and ankle.

Nutrition: Typical signs of nutritional causes of weakness are (a) feelings of tiredness in the mornings, but improving energy levels as the day goes on, (b) the blood pressure doesn't vary when standing up after lying down, (c) swelling ankles and wrists due to water imbalance, and d) recurrent minor infections. This may all be due to adrenal stress or a low blood sugar problem and doesn't mean eating lots of sugar in tea, coffee, and sticky cakes! Doing that causes a "sugar dump" into the blood stream, and the body overreacts by pumping in insulin, with the result that about an hour later you end up with even lower blood sugar. Eat whole grains such as whole wheat bread and meusli bars with high B complex that release sugars slowly into the system in a form the body can handle. Foods with a high vitamin C content are also good (citrus fruits and green peppers). Avoid all caffeine-containing foods such as coffee, chocolate, and cola, and get plenty of sleep to replenish the adrenal system drained by too much stress.

Sensitivity: Sugar.

Emotion: Boyant/depressed, generous/stubborn.

Bach flower: Holly and Mustard.

Hamstrings

There are three muscles in this group (fig. 9.6). All three start on the bottom back of the pelvis (on the bones you sit on) and hold it down toward the back of the knee. They cramp easily because (a) the muscles on the front of the leg (quadriceps) tend to be more developed, and (b) because they cross two joints, they tend to contract in waves rather than

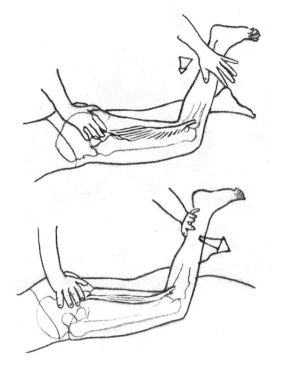

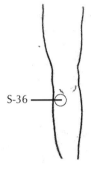

S-36

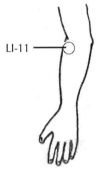

LI-11

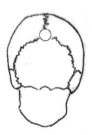

Figure 9.6   Hamstrings.

ends to middle (like most other muscles). Cellists have difficulty sitting on chairs with seats that slope back, as the front edge then tends to cut into this muscle group most uncomfortably. They are also particularly active in pedaling. These muscles together with the calf muscles also become permanently shortened in women who habitually wear high heels for performance and do not stretch afterward. This eventually causes chronic knee, back, and neck pain. Because of the meridian association there are frequently accompanying symptoms of fatigue, restlessness, toxic headache, and constipation, colitis, or hemorrhoids, the last thing you need on tour!

Test position: (a) The Testee lies face down and bends on knee 60–70°. The buttocks are stabilized while the lower leg is pushed straight down on the table. If there is a tendency to cramp, then stabilize the midthigh instead. (b) The Testee lies face up, knees bent. The knee is stabilized while the lower leg is pulled away from the buttock to straighten the limb. Lateral hamstrings can be tested lying face down by turning the foot out while the Tester pushes down and in; the medial hamstring by turning the foot in and pushing down and out. Frequently weak hamstrings strengthen while the Testee holds his or her breath. If this is so, there may be a breath-assisted cranial fault that will need a cranial osteopath's assistance. Other muscles to test if weak: gluteals, abdominals, TFL, and adductors.

Antagonist muscles: Quadriceps.

Massage points: (a) On the inside of the thigh as high as you can near the groin, yet still be on the thigh. (b) The bones of the pelvis at the back that you sit on. (c) The most prominent bumps at the top back of the pelvis (PSIS)—put your hands on your hips and slide them around to the back of the pelvis until you find them.

Meridian: Large intestine.

Holding points: (a) Draw an imaginary line from the corner of each eye, which passes through the top of each ear and goes round to the center back of the head (1 inch or 2.5 cm above the posterior fontanel). This point is often in the hair whirl. (b) Acupoints LI-11 and S-36. LI-11 is at the outer end of the elbow crease. Hold it with S-36, which is 1 inch (2.5 cm) below the knee cap and 1.5 inches (3 cm) out to the side in a little dip.

Nutrition: Avoid laxatives if possible by eating a high-fiber diet and avoiding refined sugars and starches. Food rich in vitamins B complex and E, zinc, alfalfa, garlic, parsley, kelp, lecithin, paprika, ginger, and dill seed are good. Drink lots of plain pure spring water.

Sensitivity: Carrots.

Emotion: Unwilling/willing, restless/calm, nervous/restful and peaceful, concerned/trust, self-centered/ kind, irritated/tranquil.

Bach flower: Pine.

Tensor fascia lata (TFL)

This muscle runs down the outside of your thigh (exactly under the seam of your jeans) and stabilizes both the hip and the side of the knee joint (fig. 9.7). As a musician, your only interest in it is as a postural muscle. However, weakness is often accompanied with low back ache and knee problems, constipation and colitis, diarrhea, menstrual problems and breast soreness because of its meridian association.

Test position: The Testee lies face up with straight leg raised 30–45° and taken out to the side about 30°. The foot is turned in. The other hip or leg is stabilized, as pressure is put on the outer shin to push the leg back down next to the leg on the bench. Sort out your test position in your mind before testing as the leg feels very heavy in this position and will tire easily before you have even tested it if you are inefficient— especially if it is weak! It is possible to do this test standing but involves good balance. If both sides are chronically weak, there may be a problem with anemia, which needs professional nutritional help. Other muscles to test if weak: quadriceps, gluteus medius and g. minimus, psoas.

Antagonist muscles: Adductors.

Massage points: (a) Along the entire length of the outer thigh from 1 inch (2.5 cm) below the knee, to above the hip joint. (b) A triangular area either side of the bottom of the spine, just above the pelvis.

Meridian: Large intestine.

Holding points: Same as for hamstrings.

Nutrition: This is another muscle that reacts badly to dehydration, so no diuretics (no caffeine, coffee, or alcohol), and increase intake of vitamins B complex and D, magnesium.

Sensitivity: Garlic, rice, pecans.

Emotion: Confused/confident, unsociable/sociable, cut off/united.

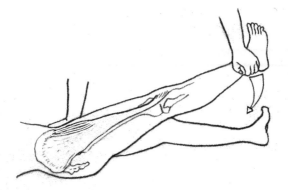

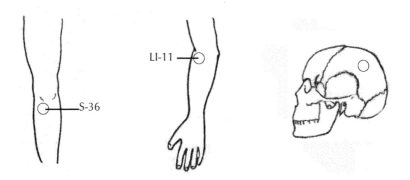

LI-11

S-36

Figure 9.7   Tensor fascia lata.

Adductors and Pectineus

Yet another group of muscles! They are all attached to the bottom of the pubic bone, and at the succeeding places along the inner part of the thigh bone, which means that they all pull the legs inward (fig. 9.8). They are used by cellists to hold the lower bouts of the viol, tuba and euphonium players and by women wearing short black skirts, and others

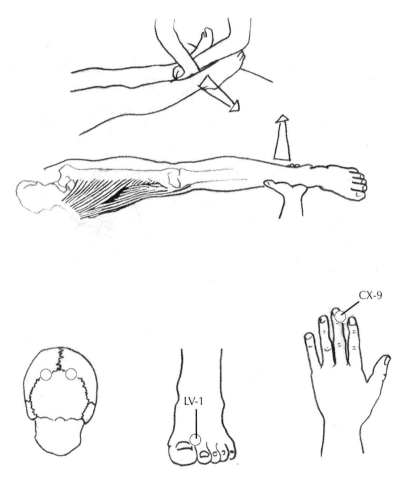

Figure 9.8   Adductors.

to hold the knees together to make a platform for the instrument (fig. 9.9). The saphenous nerve and vein pass through the lower part of the adductor muscles and can therefore become crushed by gripping the cello (or viol) too hard; this causes burning inner thigh, knee, or calf pain often occurring at night, and there may be a loss of feeling during the day. Pain in the area may also be due to a low back problem or lymphatic congestion from flaccid abdominals and sitting cross-legged for hours, compressing the area. If it doesn't clear with a reduction in grip pressure, go and see a chiropractor or osteopath. Weakness can cause leg length difference, low backache, walking difficulty especially in moving legs forward, groin pain, pubic bone pain, and pain during intercourse.

Test position: (a) The Testee lies on the side to be tested. The uppermost leg is bent and placed on the bench in front of the leg to be tested to stabilize it. The underneath leg is held straight and lifted off the bench as far as possible. The Tester stabilizes the shoulder while contacting the underneath shin and pushing the leg back to the table. (b) The Testee lies face up, legs together. One ankle is stabilized while pressure is put on the inside of the other to pull that leg away. Watch for hip rock as the Testee tries to use other muscles. Other muscles to test if weak: gracilis, quadriceps, and hamstrings.

Antagonist muscles: Gluteals and TFL.

Massage points: (a) Directly below the nipple. This may be very tender. (b) On the back below the lowest part of the shoulder blade.

Holding points: (a) Lambdoidal suture. Draw an imaginary line from the corner of the eye to the top of the ear, extend it 2 inches (5 cm) behind the ear, and hold this point. (b) Acu-points Cx-9 and Lv-1. Cx-9 is on the nailbed of the middle finger. Hold it with Lv-1, which is on the nailbed of the big toe, on the side nearest the other toes.

Nutrition: Foods rich in vitamins A, B complex, and E, iron, calcium, magnesium, banana, slippery elm, mint, kelp.

Sensitivity: Melon, cabbage family.

Emotion: Self-centered/kind, grief for self/fellow feeling, sorrow/joy, irresponsible/responsible, unfulfilled/fulfilled, confused/confident, deceiving/truth, sad/glad, nervous/peaceful, tongue-tied/expressive.

Bach flower: Holly.

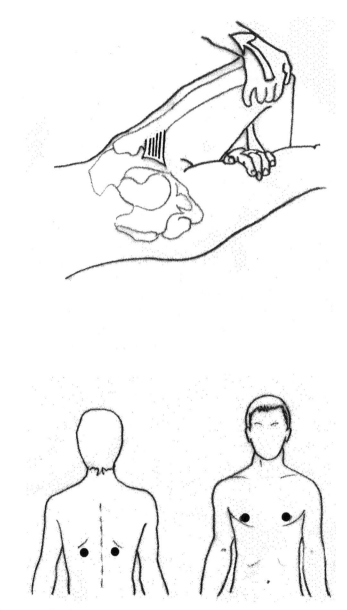

Figure 9.9   Pectineus.

Popliteus

This muscle stabilizes the back of the knee joint with a screw-home action so it won't bend backward (fig. 9.10). It is attached to the lowest part of the thigh bone (femur) on the outside and to the cartilage in the knee joint, and then extends across the back of the knee to the shin bone (tibia). It is used by singers and all instrumentalists who stand to play. Many knee aches can be attributed to this muscle, and its strength can be affected when there are low neck problems and sore gums, gallbladder problems, and feeling sleepy after eating fats.

Test position: (a) The musician lies face down, face up, or sits and bends the knee at right angles. The foot (and shin) is turned in so that the big toe points across to the other leg. The heel is stabilized and pressure is put on the inside of the foot on the big toe side (but not actually on the big toe joints) to twist the shin back straight inline with the thigh bone. Other muscles to test if popliteus is weak: sartorius, quadriceps, anterior deltoid, pectoralis major clavicular, and sternal.

Massage points: (a) Between the fifth and sixth ribs just under the nipple on the right-hand side of the breastbone. (b) On the right side only, 1 inch to the side of the spine, just below half way down the length of the shoulder blade at the level of the fifth and sixth ribs

Meridian: Gall bladder.

Holding points: (a) Inside the knee halfway along a line between the top of the kneecap and the knee crease (on the medial meniscus). (b) Acupoints B-66 and GB-43. B-66 is on the outer edge of the foot at the base of the little toe. Hold it together with GB-43, which is similarly placed at the base of the fourth toe.

Nutrition: Eat nonfatty foods containing vitamin A such as dark green fruits and vegetables, melon tomatoes, and liver.

Sensitivity: Fatty foods.

Emotion: Unwilling/willing, imposed upon/accepted, rage/forgiveness.

Bach flower: Cherry plum.

CALF AND FOOT MUSCLES

1. Gastrocnemius and soleus
2. Tibials and peronei

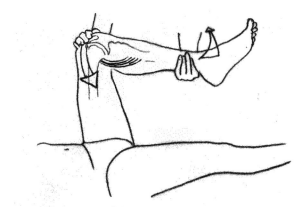

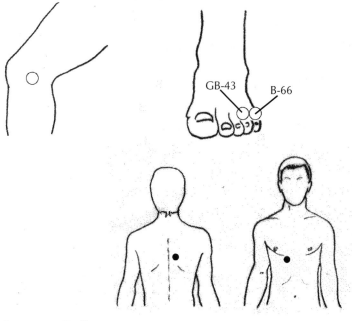

GB-43   B-66

Figure 9.10   Popliteus.

Gastrocnemius and soleus both pull on the Achilles tendon and point the foot (fig. 9.11). To point the toes up and in, you use anterior tibial, to point down and in you use the posterior tibial. To point the toes up and out, you use peronius tertius, and down and out you use the other peronius muscles.

Soleus and gastrocnemius are the two main back calf muscles and lie one under the other sharing the Achillies tendon (fig. 9.12). Together they are known as triceps surae. Gastrocnemius crosses the knee joint, soleus doesn't. They are part of a chain of muscles that pulls from the head downward to counteract the forward flop of the body that would occur otherwise due to gravity. They both react badly to the habit of wearing high heels, by cramping, and leg twitch, unless stretched when you take those shoes off. They are both very strong, and singly they have to lift your entire weight when you walk. Weakness will cause a forward-leaning posture; spasm will cause a chain of events that may start off as calf pain and progress to low back pain and neck pain as each part of the body tries to compensate for the basic postural fault. Because of the median association, there may also be poor digestion. Soleus and gastrocnemius are used by any musician who has pedals on the instrument (i.e., harp, organ, timps, vibraphone, harmonium as well as the more common keyboards).

Test Position: (a) Mainly gastrocnemius: The Testee stands on the ball of one foot. Pressure is put on the shoulders to pull the heel back to the floor. (b) Mainly soleus: The Testee lies face down and the knee is bent 90° toes pointed. The heel is pulled upward at the same time as downward pressure is put on the ball of the foot to bend the ankle. Other muscles to test if weak: thigh muscles.

Antagonist muscles: Tibials and peronei.

Massage points: (a) One inch (2.5 cm) out and 2 inches (5 cm) up from the tummy button. (b) Between the lowest three ribs on the back, either side of the spine.

Meridian: Triple warmer.

Holding points: (a) Lambda. Draw an imaginary line each side, from the corner of each eye passing through the top of the ear. Hold the point where the continuation of these two meet at the back of the head. (b) Acupoints TW-3 and GB-41. TW-3 is found on the back of the hand between the ring and little finger, and halfway between the base of the fingers and the wrist crease. Hold it with GB-41, which is in a similar

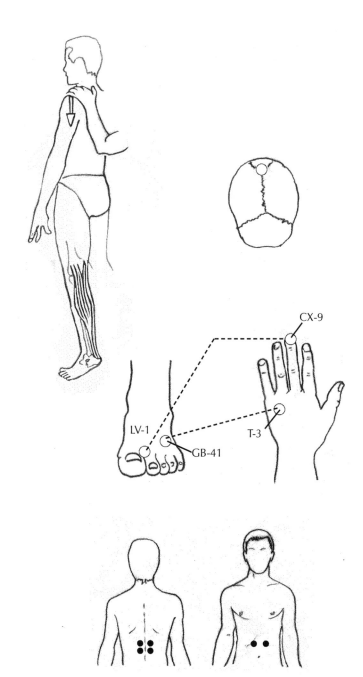

Figure 9.11 Gastrocnemius.

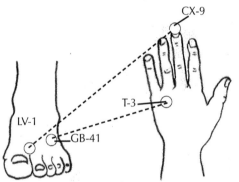

Figure 9.12   Soleus.

place on the top of the foot—between the base of the last two toes and the ankle crease.

Nutrition: Vitamins B and C, manganese, alfalfa, apricot, banana, garlic.

Sensitivity: Tobacco, excess vitamin A, plastics, PVC, polystyrene and polythene, cellophane, and rubber.

Emotion: Unwilling/willing, restless/calm, confused/confident, cut off/united, not needed/needed, ungiving/cooperative, forsaken/accepted, incapable/understandable, disappointed/satisfied, forced/helpful.

Bach flower: Mustard.

Anterior and Posterior Tibial, Peronius Longus, Brevis and Tertius Tertius

These two muscles work against gastrocnemius and soleus in pedalling (see earlier); posterior tibial and peronius longus (and brevis) work with them (fig. 9.13). All of them are important to organists, harpists, and harpsichordists to manipulate and move from one pedal to the next. All but one of the muscles cross the ankle joint, running from the shin bones to the foot (fig. 9.14). They are very strong and proportionately short; therefore they tend to cramp. Weak shin muscles may cause flat feet, and because of their meridian association are frequent indicators of bladder problems and "foot drop," which trips you up. Weak peronei may also predispose to twisting or turning the ankle over. There may also be foot and knee pain and poor balance (fig. 9.15).

Test position: All are tested with the Testee lying face up. (a) Anterior tibial. The ankle is maximally flexed, with the toes up and in, the heel is supported underneath, while pressure is put on the top of the foot to point the big toe. Suspect weakness if there is a tendency to stumble, and there may be loud foot contact with the ground or chronic calf pain. (b) Peronius tertius. The ankle is maximally flexed with the toes up and out. The heel is supported underneath and pressure is put on the top outside of the foot to point the toes down and in. Weakness in this muscle also causes a stomping gait. (c) Posterior tibial. The toes are held pointed down and in. The heel is supported underneath and pressure is put on the ball of the foot to push it up and out. Adrenal dysfunction may accompany chronic weakness. (d) Peronius longus and brevis. The

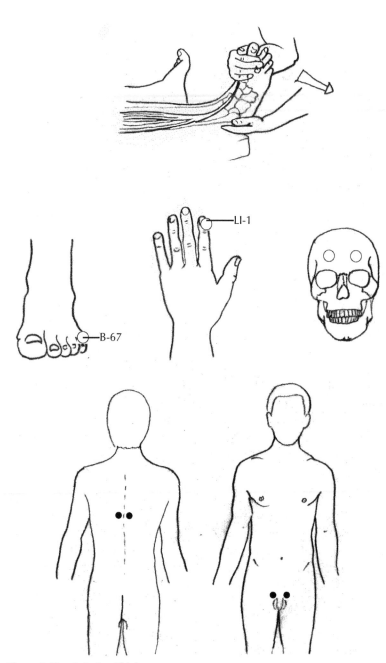

Figure 9.13 Anterior tibial.

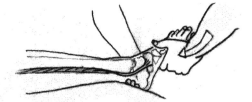

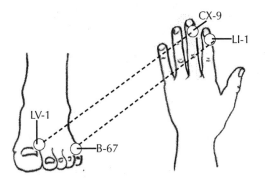

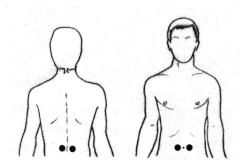

Figure 9.14   Tibialis posterior.

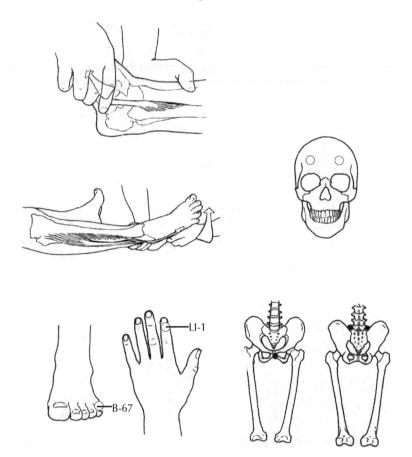

Figure 9.15 Peronius longus and brevis.

toes are pointed down and out. The heel is supported underneath and
pressure is put on the ball of the foot under the toes to push the foot up
and in. Other muscles to test if weak: piriformis, psoas, gastrocnemius,
and soleus.

Antagonist muscles: Muscles tested in (a) and (b) earlier work as
antagonists to those in (c) and (d).

Massage points: (a) One inch (2.5 cm) above the center of the pubic
bone. Under the pubic bone. (b) Either side of the spine below the

lowest rib. L-5 to PSIS the most prominent bumps at the top back of the pelvis.

Meridian: Bladder and Pericardium (Cx).

Holding points: (a) The frontal eminence's—over the center of each eye and halfway between eyebrows and hairline. (b) The glabella—between the eyebrows. (c) Acupoints B-67 and LI-1. B-67 is on the nailbed of the little toe. Hold it with LI-1, which is on the outer edge of the nailbed of the index finger.

Nutrition: Vitamins A, B complex, and E, calcium, potassium, magnesium, buckwheat, sunflower seeds, cayenne, lentils, rice, tarragon, lemongrass, and ginseng.

Sensitivity: Wood smoke, apples and cider, grapes and raisins.

Emotion: Nervous/restful, forgotten/remembered, unwilling/willing, wasted/invigorated, confused /confident, arrogant or defensive/listening, too much responsibility/responsible, hopeless/trusting, unsupported/supported, defeated/success, undesirable/pleasant, paranoid/secure, disorganised/organised, impatient/patient.

Bach flower: Impatiens.

Please realize that although the muscles discussed here may seem many and various, they are only the most important few that are most relevant to musicians.

10

Emotions and Muscles

STAGE FRIGHT

Stage fright is perhaps the most common reason for muscles feeling weak and incapable or tight as a drum and immovable when playing to an audience. The feeling can creep up on a player, or hit one suddenly with a shock when it accompanies some other trauma. It is no respecter of age or ability. The thoughts crowd in and absorb almost all your concentration. You terrorize yourself. You think and feel so "attacked" you can't give out, only defend and go through the motions of playing, longing for it all to end, and the blessed release when it's all over. It amounts to mental malpractice, self-torture, or something worse!

The causes are often multiple and difficult to pin down. Our undoubted ability is cut down again and again because we are concerned that we haven't done enough practice, we won't please our parents/teachers, it's too hot/cold, past injuries will show up again, unusual conditions will occur, other players have to be considered, the instrument will break down, and so on. Rarely is it about lack of courage. Unremedied, the list of causes tends to form a vortex of anxiety, a vicious circle that drags you down to incapacity, possibly even to a phobia that then rules your life, unless you have a means of stopping it in its tracks.

So many artists identify their art with the "self." They talk about what they are (e.g., I am a violinist) not who they are (e.g., I am Jane/ John and I play the violin). It's not so much that "the show must go on" but that *they are the show.* They die a little every time they can't perform to perfection and only feel really alive when they do. This is unrealistic and obsessional, yet in a crowded profession, many think one has to be that way to get anywhere. On stage, you feel as if you are in a glass cage.

The skin is an excellent demarcation line between inside and outside, between "me" and "not me," or between "them" and "us." Performance is about communication bridging that gap. Most of the concern is with the outer environment and how to adapt ourselves to it, but in so doing, the inner is affected, too. Stage fright seems to be about "them" (whoever "they" are). Actually, it is about you and the mental baggage you have heaped on *your own back*, and with which you have shackled, poisoned, and terrified yourself. It is a terrifying, very real black hole. Some people compensate by throwing themselves about, giving the audience a poor theatrical show instead of spellbinding, sublime music. Others "do the expression marks" 150 percent so the stupid audience "gets it." Some even project the well-practiced, hypercritical relationship they had with a strict teacher onto the audience and blame them for being "mistake hounds" before they have even sat down—yet the poor audience only paid good money to enjoy themselves! They want the artist to succeed, or they wouldn't have come.

It isn't that people are unfeeling and can't project. Far from it. Either the personality and feeling get squashed because the player is shrunk to nothing with nerves, or the artist puts on such armor plating that the sound can't get out and blossom; or there is communication, and the medium is the message, but what communicates is fear in terms of "the perlies," split notes, wrong notes, or quavery tone. And the audience is extremely uncomfortable.

Stage fright is usually worst immediately before going on stage, but there can be a long "preburn" of panic and equally long "after-burn" of self-castigation, especially if you are the perfectionist most musicians are trained to be. *Capacity is a state of mind.* The belief that you can't do something can simply be a rationalization for not being willing to take risks. The sad thing is that while arguing for one's limitations, one tends to keep them!

This is where some musicians resort to beta-blockers, which block the effects of adrenaline on the body. However, be aware that what often comes out is often a conveyor belt of tasks completed, not a true communication musically that has emotion deep enough to go past the edge of the stage. Be aware too that these drugs can precipitate asthma attacks and heart failure, nausea and diarrhea, lightheadedness, and insomnia in susceptible people. Taking Prozac for the depression such fear chops the top and bottom off all feeling but can have similar side effects and can also cause blurred vision. Either is better than alcohol, which makes you clumsy, but none solve the problems of stage fright, they just shelve them.

When a musician stops taking such drugs, there are all the problems again staring them in the face, plus the added complication of side effects to cope with as well. "Psychoactive medications must be used judiciously with artists, keeping in mind that certain side effects—drowsiness, dry mouth, insomnia, tremor—may interfere with high level performance," suggest Oswald and colleagues (1994). Look up medications' side effects in the British National Formulary in your library before taking them so you can discuss the whole situation with your general practitioner from an informed point of view. If you are driven to taking these drugs, it is strongly recommended you have psychological counseling at the same time. To have counseling doesn't mean you are "off your rocker," it means you are being responsible and helping yourself with a temporary dysfunction.

If you wish to help yourself without the use of drugs, you need to be clear about which are useful states of mind and which not. At the European Quaker Peace Consultation in Geneva, Nelson Mandela was quoted as saying, "Our deepest fear is not that we are inadequate. Our deepest fear is that we are powerful beyond measure. It is our light, not our darkness, that frightens us. We ask ourselves 'Who am I to be brilliant, gorgeous, talented, fabulous?' Actually, who are you not to be? You are a child of God. Your playing small doesn't serve the world. There is nothing enlightened about shrinking so that other people won't feel insecure around you. We are all meant to shine as children do. We are born to manifest the glory of God that is within us. It's not just in some of us, it's in everyone. And as we let our own light shine, we unconsciously give other people permission to do the same. As we are liberated from our own fear, our presence automatically liberates others."

The opposite of love is not hate but fear and indifference, and *90 percent of fear is not justified by the facts, or by what is actually happening.* There is a natural excitement about performance. There should be, but that's not real "nerves." A performance is a celebration of your ability and love of music, but it's often quite difficult to tell the difference between suppressed excitement, fear, hunger, and sickness. These feelings all happen in the stomach region, so we "comfort eat" or starve ourselves when what we actually feel is a heightened arousal state. If the state of arousal is in proportion to the task to be performed, we do well, but too much or too little and our performance suffers. The confusion arises because all these signals are carried by the sympathetic nervous system, and one nerve in particular, the vagus nerve. Confusion in understanding the signals is always worst with a new task.

There should be a balance between the sympathetic (fight or flight) and its opposite number, the parasympathetic (repair and conserve) nervous system, the level being set according to what you are doing. One of the two is always dominant. Highly strung perfectionists, living on the edge, have a nervous system already set with high sympathetic levels, and it only takes a little extra stress to send them over the top into stage fright patterns. Laid-back, dozy people who can't seem to get going are set too low, and "need a bomb under them" or at least performance conditions before they perform their best. They don't get stage fright; they need that extra stress.

Typically your tummy gurgles when you sit relaxed after a meal because digestion is a parasympathetic function. However, when sympathetic function is dominant, digestion is one of the first things to be shut down, because there is increased blood flow to the muscles involved in instant action or reaction—fight or flight. You get "butterflies in your stomach," which is actually the slight ache produced by too much stomach acid made for the digestion that's no longer happening.

Just like Pavlov's dog, you learn. Just as Pavlov's dog who so associated the sound of a bell with the arrival of food that he eventually salivated at the sound of a bell even when there was no food, you learn a habit of reaction, too. Eventually just thinking of playing "that bit" to "those people" causes the panic reaction. It is a normal survival technique that has become out of synchronization with actual fact and actual need. When you are just thinking about it, you are not in actual danger at all. No one is actually going to kill you for not performing perfectly, let alone just thinking about it!

Reason has nothing to do with emotional reaction. Factual accuracy and emotional truth are not the same thing, but both are equally valid to a trained nervous system. The original incident (the first time you did it "wrong," perhaps due to a freak accident and highly unlikely to occur again) becomes an assumption that you will always do it wrong. Survival techniques are based on the assumption that you only have one life and need to protect yourself against any possible repeat of that awful mistake. Such protective memory strategies proliferate—you only touch a boiling kettle once and remember not to for the rest of your life.

You are also particularly vulnerable to such small mistakes when you are tired, have poor endurance, are not on top form physically, have high stress levels for other reasons (e.g., at home), or for chemical reasons (mild overdose or sensitivity to some food), are suddenly faced with unexpected extras or lacks or poorly timed/destructive criticism (whether justified or not).

Suddenly you doubt your ability; you become afraid of losing control; you remember that passage you haven't studied enough, worry you will forget it or lose your place; you think the audience members are bored; the accompanist is late or makes a mistake; your shoulder rest falls off or the music stand collapses; someone blocks your view. Your mouth goes dry, your breathing is short and shallow or you even hold your breath; your heart races, your hands are cold and sweaty; you shake, you have loss of feeling, seeing, hearing, but muscular tension or sickness and a heightened awareness of other outside stimuli (like someone shuffling their feet, or a mobile phone). Your concentration goes to the winds. You do lose your place because your mind is wavering between the experience itself and the opinions you are forming about it all. The chatter in your head is like a radio going full blast in your ears, doom laden and telling you the worst will happen. You, poor victim, you believe it! You can't analyze anything objectively any more, and so go straight into paralysis like a deer caught in car headlights, and then the worst does happen. Again. And your self-esteem goes another ten notches lower. Things can even get to the physical state where the physical symptoms are worn like a badge that shows that the person no longer has to be responsible, and they can then legitimately give up performing.

What can you do about it? The first thing to realize is that *your reaction is absolutely normal*, just a bit over the top, and so are all the symptoms that you feel, whether they seem useful or not. The second is to evaluate which aspects are the frightening trigger factors in your case, and what removable stresses there are in your life.

Research has shown that musicians whose parents were professional musicians generally have a much harder time than those whose parents were interested nonprofessionals. Second-generation musicians have to cope with expectation, covert persuasion, overt coercion, and even persecution to get them to practice, with consequent anger and guilt resulting in either rebellion or failure, depending on the character of the child. The film *Shine* admirably demonstrates this. There may be social deprivation if children have to spend hours indoors practicing alone and not playing/socializing with their contemporaries (who will be their future audience/promoters/employers). Children of amateurs have high motivation, concentration, and devotion, springing out of self-confidence of doing something of their own well. They are supported for the love and fun of it but not pushed mercilessly. Which were you? What spooks you?

The third is to diffuse old bogies, replace them with good successful experiences and keep away from new infectious bad ones. This is done by cleaning up practice methods (see the chapter on best practice) and retuning the blaring destructive radio in you head to another station with the help of self-talk and visualization or Neuro-linguistic programming (NLP), facing the problem in a graded way with the help of a sympathetic colleague. Of course, you can duck the issue and resort to beta-blockers but they only deal with the symptom not the cause. They tend to make your playing rather flat (apart from other side effects) and the problem is still there if you stop taking them.

Self-reliance comes from two things: a positive orientation toward your goal and a reduction of inhibiting dependency patterns that crucify your mental and muscular control. Face it and move on. You can recapture the excitement and wonder of music! Collect information. Make a private list of all the times you had problems with "nerves." Look for recurring patterns and trigger factors. Evaluate them on a scale of 1–10 for scariness. If a specific thing happened, go back to the first time and write it down in all its gory detail using as colorful language as you like. Typically "I can't/if only I could" is tacit, negative acceptance of this, crippling your best intentions and sabotaging your talent and ambition into mediocrity. The list is an outward form of the negative "self-talk" program you have in your head. No one else is going to see the list and you can have the satisfaction of burning it later! Identify or work out which words have the most negative power over you and use the techniques from behavioral barometer section to defuse them. Remember that Shakespeare said, "There is nothing either good or bad but thinking makes it so." In other words, what you think about something is how it is for you, unless you change your mind. Stress isn't the problem, but how you react to it. With a scary situation that is coming up in the future, write down the best/worst and objectively, the most likely outcome. Find solutions for each scenario. Now!

Listen to what you tell yourself: the names you call yourself when something small goes wrong. Do you mutter "stupid idiot," four letter words? Worse? *Much worse*? Make a note of who first said that to you, and who goes on saying it now. It's a known fact that if you are told something often enough without investigating it, you will eventually believe it, if not consciously, then subconsciously, especially if you set it up and get agreement from others. Look at Hitler; he persuaded a whole nation! You are being a little Hitler to yourself and you believe it. Then you act out what you tell yourself because the subconscious is programmed to do what you tell it; it doesn't know the difference between truth and lies. So if you tell your mind to act like a stupid idiot, that's what it does.

Affirmations are a bit like the lines people used to have to write for misdemeanors at school. To a lively mind, they are exceedingly boring. You decide on some undesirable aspect/behavior/habit you wish to change (e.g., I'm always late) and rewrite it in a positive form (e.g., I always leave the house with plenty of time and enjoy arriving with time to spare to look at the music). The idea is then to write this out in first second- and third-person singular at least twenty times a day.

You can imagine how many people would stick to that, let alone believe it will change them! It's embarrassing. You might find it more helpful to put a cluster of positive affirmations on tape on improving self-esteem or coping with stage fright and play them to yourself on waking and before going to sleep and when washing up or doing any other mindless activity. Attaching the affirmation to a ditty can make all the difference. Hum the ditty in your head and the words come without effort. I chose Clementine for "I am always in the right place at the right time, and successfully engaged in the right activity." I was never late through my own fault again and it calmed me down when I was stuck in traffic. From someone who used to get detention after detention at school for lateness, I suddenly realized how rude and selfish it was. Through the affirmation I developed a reputation for reliability. It meant that on the very rare occasion that I was late, no one turned a hair. I just apologized later, and never got "het up" and all tense about punctuality again. I didn't arrive in a state of high anxiety and muscular tension but kept all my energy for the performance.

After examining how you talk to yourself, take another look at how you react to others' helpful suggestions. Are you a *"Yes, but"* person? That "but" ever so politely dismisses everything before it, and means you haven't really listened to what was said to you. Get off your "but" and replace it with "and" and notice how it changes the communication by including both old and new ideas. Now you have a choice and are open to learning, which is hard if you are all buttoned up!

Other judgmental words you might look at are "right" and "wrong." How right, how wrong? It is more productive to break the problem down into small steps and then think in terms of goals that you update. Go for excellence and satisfaction for a good job done, not perfection, because that's never obtainable. If you do attain perfection, there's nothing more to improve and that's boring and rather inhuman. Give yourself clear positive guidelines, not "put downs"—"right" is simply the next goal.

"Should" and "ought" are also words to beware of. They can contain resentment and definitely no responsibility because they always imply someone else's directives rather than your own. If you do something for any reason other than that you want to do it, then you are doing it to manipulate someone else. Who? Incidentally, that person does not have to be still alive, but they are alive in your head, and are probably the source of the loud voice that's blaring at you in your head. Don't get hardening of the "oughteries"—it shortens life.

Control (of yourself), usefully interpreted as "loving mindfulness," sometimes becomes equated with "holding on," whether mentally or muscularly. It is then accompanied by jamming the diaphragm and consequent lack of breathing, or jamming the anal muscles, causing constipation. Both come from fear that "they," who are not to be trusted, will take over and take all from you, or that if you let go of what you have, there isn't any more left for you. This causes total confusion and disruption subconsciously and scrambles the messages from your brain to your muscles, giving a predisposition to mistakes. Control when understood in the sense of "hold" is therefore the opposite of spontaneity, intuition, and joy at being here.

"Try harder" is the most useless request I know. It is actually physically impossible to carry out. Think about it for a minute. Then try to think about it, then try to do it. "Try" is the last of the commonly used words that triggers stage fright, How does one succeed at trying to do something? It's either possible to do it or not possible, that's all. Fritz Perls' statement that "trying fails, awareness cures" sums this up beautifully.

Living for approval of others, playing to please them, is another way of lying to yourself, yet this is what all artists do to a greater or lesser extent, unless they realize that you must play for yourself and then give that playing away by sharing your joy and love of what you do. Then it's your authentic voice that speaks, and there's nothing so catching as enthusiasm!

> Responsibility starts with the willingness to experience yourself as cause in the matter. It is not burden, fault, praise, credit, shame, or guilt; all these include judgments and evaluations, they are not responsibility. Being responsible means being willing to deal with a situation from the point of view that you are the source of what you are, what you do and what you have. This point of view even extends to what is done to you (and ultimately what another does to another). It is a context of Self as the source for the content and interpretation of what is, in your awareness. (Erhardt).

When you think about it, no one will ever breathe one breath for you, or ever stand in your body, feel your fears, dream your dreams, or cry your tears. We are born, live this life, and leave it entirely on our own. That self and the divine spirit within are what we have to work with. So decide now: Are you going to be at the mercy of your fears and let them run your life, "fire fighting" as you go or will you take charge, maybe be afraid but do the thing you fear anyway? It shows you who is in command, and that what you feared was the fear itself. Responsibility is the basis of individual determination to accept life as an opportunity and to fulfill ourselves within it. For each possible course of action, consider: (a) What does it cost? (b) What does it buy me? (c) What are the possibilities I am missing by taking or not taking this action? Then act or don't. This is all there is.

People think there is "something" that will make them happy, if only they could get hold of it. If they have that something, they could then do something, then they would be something. Have, do, be. It's the other way around. In your own mind, you must "be" first, then you can "do," then "have" comes later by itself. They have the patience to learn how to operate their instrument but not how to operate themselves. They diminish themselves by saying "I couldn't help myself" when what they really mean is "I didn't help myself." "I can't" mostly means "I won't." Halfway is "I won't/can't yet." Now is all there is. The saying "the best place to look for a helping hand is the end of your arm" is annoyingly true. So if "they" make you nervous, you are acting like a victim and giving away your power. "They" are not doing it, you are the one creating the pain. You only react in the way you do because you don't see that you have a choice in the matter, and that their opinion is no more valid than yours. It takes two to make an argument, and if one side doesn't respond but goes its own way, then there's no argument. You don't see that how you react is a learned response from childhood when it was a matter of survival to obey your "elders and betters." You don't see that how you react is a learned response that you can unlearn, an interpretation of signs and symptoms that you can change, that you can replace the reaction you don't want with one that you do want.

It's the worrying about you and the fear of them rather than communication that causes the problems. Curiously, when you try to succeed, you fail, and when it's OK to fail, you succeed. The only difference between humming a tune to yourself at home and singing at the Albert or Carnegie Hall is the opinion you have about the audience and the volume. In other words, you need to talk to your overprotective ego so that it doesn't interpret the situation as dangerous. That done, you simply go and do the job, trusting the practice you have done. You will then have X amount of success. The result will be excellent or need more help—that's all there is to it, and without the ego terrorizing you, the former is more likely. The secret is to separate the person from the deed.

By the way, if you look at all I have said and find you don't want to let go of old habits, that's fine, too, but remember that then you have no moral right to complain about it all any more, because you have made a choice. It's hard to move on if you dig your heels in! Choice in itself has no goodness or badness, it's just choice, as trivial as choosing between chocolate or vanilla. The power and the growing comes in what you do with the choice you make.

BURNOUT AND TATT

Your arms feel like lead weights, you are exhausted all the time yet you sleep badly, you are listless, depressed, and irritable, your blood pressure is up, and you feel at the same time drained and driven. You have no interest in doing the things you normally love doing and shut down any will to give out to other people, other than as duty. Often it is accompanied by poor feeding habits/junk food; overreliance on stimulants, calmatives, or other over-the-counter drugs; poor general health with irritating coughs and colds that just won't go away. This is a recognizable overstressed state and may need medical help.

Burnout is indicative of a one-sided lifestyle. Too much work, stress, travel, and performing, and not enough playing, recreation, and feeding the soul/spirit with other interests. It definitely needs rest. There is life outside music but because you work unsocial hours, you rarely meet anyone who isn't in the music business.

The only way to deal with it is to take a long-term view. Decide how many weeks of holiday you deserve a year and then how many years since you have had a really restorative holiday. Add them together and jolly well take that holiday. Go where you are very well looked after, stop the over-the-counter drugs, coffee, and booze, eat well, banish guilt, and above all, rest. It will be hard at first because it's so unusual for you.

"But what about my dates/concerts/fixers?" I hear you cry. If you broke your arm and couldn't play, or suddenly had to go to the Australian outback, what would you do? Tell them when you will be back. So do the same now. This is a similar crisis. Recognize it as such—your body already has! It tried to attract your attention by posting signals in the form of all those symptoms you feel. If you don't listen now, eventually it will shut down completely and make you listen.

If you are in any doubt, ask your GP. It's no good earning all that money if you have no energy left to enjoy it, if you are too ill to enjoy your life. Burnout ignored makes everyone around you miserable too as you become more and more difficult to live with, even though you think you are doing your best for your family. It often leads to strokes and heart attacks or unforced but lethal accidents because you are just not "with it," are too tired to recognize it, and make bad mistakes.

There are 101 other reasons for being tired all the time (TATT). Internal chemistry may be a cause. Check out hepatitis, liver cirrhosis from long-term alcohol overload, gall bladder and fat absorption problems, irritable bowel syndrome with its attendant chronic diarrhea and constipation and metabolite and malabsorption problems, peptic ulcers, and even parasites from strange food on tour. Tiredness can also be a sign of kidney malfunction, hormone imbalance and anemia, or emphysema from years of smoking. Externally, you feel tired mostly from side effects from drugs, such as antibiotics and especially chemotherapy, but also airborne phenols like formaldehyde in paints and furnishing materials, heavy metals (such as lead in water in old pipework or your own old tooth fillings that are leaking mercury into your blood stream).

Systemic infections mean the whole of you is under par. Best known of these are postviral syndromes, but Candida and hormonal imbalances can drag you down. Common psychological reasons for feeling constantly tired, apart from those already mentioned, include depression, marital problems, and grief. These only scrape the surface of the more common reasons. It's really worth talking to your GP and asking for help before you become more seriously ill.

If your GP gives you a clean bill of health, learn to say "No." Energy and self-esteem are not inexhaustible. They are more like a bank balance. You have to put something in before you can draw out. Don't overdraw too often or your body/bank manager will foreclose the account. If possible, aim for no more than three main stressors a week, rather than all on one day! How do you say "No"?

Fixers want a good band with minimum hassle. If you have to turn a job in after accepting it, it works best to be straightforward. Fixers are just as good as you at smelling rats! Ask who they would like you to get, and offer to do the "phoning round" yourself. In the long run, it's cheaper.

Have a good spread of freelance work that includes more than only one sort. Regular orchestras have free time written into their contract, but freelance players don't. You have to be firm if you want time off. If you don't, you will pay in poor health. Mad as the idea is, maybe you could save 10 percent of all you earn so that in seven years you have enough to take a sabbatical year off. Think about it—a year's paid holiday!

PSYCHSOMATIC ACHES AND PAINS

The popular understanding of psychosomatic pain is that the pain is imagined and that the sufferer must be a bit neurotic. Not so. The pain is very real and the person is probably perfectly normal. What the word actually means is "psycho" (mind) plus "soma" (body). In other words, what your mind won't/hasn't resolved, your body will try to save you from as part of your survival mechanism. Even physical tension stemming from mental stress is "psychosomatic." Your muscles are tense because you are in constant mentally unresolved fight/flight situation.

Pain in any form is a call for help—your body's way of getting your attention. So thank it and give it attention.

1. Sit quietly, breathe deeply, close your eyes and focus on the pain, allowing it to be there. Rest your hands lightly on your forehead.
2. Describe out loud as accurately as possible, the pain's precise location and size; its shape (round/oblong); its density (soft/hard, like steel/wood/stone, rubber/woolly/misty); its edges (rind/hairy/misty/melting); its color (green/red/brown).
3. Watch as it changes. Sometimes it's helpful to have a friend ask for descriptions ("How is it now?") as you look with your mind's eye.
4. Keep breathing and observing and "being with" the pain and describing the changes as if seeing them for the first time, continuing until it either contracts to nothing or spreads out and evaporates.
5. If it returns later, notice what the trigger factor was and deal with it.

While on the subject of psychosomatic aches and pains, there are people who never admit to any pain no matter how bad, but it is also important to recognize that there are definite attitudes that predispose one to noticing pain. This is known as "illness mentality." The person concerned takes little or no responsibility for how they are, and ills and hurts are rehearsed and exaggerated. (See chapter 1.)

BEHAVIORAL BAROMETER

This is a wonderful technique taught me by Gordon Stokes. It consists of a list of ordinary negative words and associated words that people find disturbing somatically (i.e., their muscles go "weak" when they think of them). To use this technique you need to know how to test muscles (see chapter 4) and the location of emotional stress relief points. These are found on the forehead over the center of each eye and halfway between the eyebrows and where the hairline is (or should be, if the musician is balding). You may need a friend to help.

1. On the list below, test the words in capitals (especially the second list) by saying them out loud at the same time as a strong indicator muscle is tested by your friend. When the strong indicator muscle goes weak, that is the section of the list to concentrate on.
2. Test the negative words in that section to find the specific words that cause weakness and need help.
3. Your friend now holds the points on your forehead lightly (just stretching the skin) while saying these words (it seems to help if they are said in as many different ways as possible—crossly, pleadingly, smugly, sorrowfully, etc.). Intersperse these with as many rhetorical prompts as possible like:

> When did you last feel XXX?
> How does it feel to be XXX?
> Who around you is XXX?
> Who else is XXX?
> What's it like to receive XXX?
> Who else makes you XXX?
> Where in your body do you feel XXX?

Think of a time long ago when you felt XXX.

When was the first time you remember feeling XXX?

Who was there and what would you like to have said/not said or done/undone then that you didn't?

What would have made it alright then? How about now?

None of these questions need to be answered out loud; it's an entirely private matter for the person being helped and no one else. The idea behind the prompts is to keep you thinking about the word and stop your mind wandering—it will not want to stay concentrated because the words are uncomfortable and have had such power for such a long time. You may get a bit emotional—even want to cry, as you let go of such a long-held grief, but it's worth it as you feel so much better afterward, and the words have lost some if not all of their power over you.

4. When you run out of questions, check for reactions by muscle testing with the positive counterparts, and, if need be, repeat stages 1–3 above.

5. You have finished when none of the words weaken your muscles any more.

6. You can also use this technique to destress a future event, because what you fear will be a reflection of a past event.

- ONENESS FOCUS ON UNFOLDMENT AT PEACE calm peaceful composed safe comfortable quiet equilibrium contented tranquil serene sustained satisfied in balance ENLIGHTENED enriched fulfilled visionary transformed transcended majestic UNITY at-one-ment complete undivided

- ATTUNEMENT APPRECIATIVE fortunate thankful grateful benevolent perceptive responsive GRACIOUS outgoing unselfish kind gentle tender merciful soft-hearted HARMONIOUS in-tune with flowing graceful congruent coordinated JOYFUL creative happy rejoicing glowing elated jubilant cheerful

- EQUALITY/COOPERATION ACKNOWLEDGED recognized respected validated esteemed EMPATHETIC aware involved tolerant concerned courteous compassionate EQUAL balanced poised patient impartial placid just on a par with PURPOSEFUL productive gifted motivated lucky energetic imaginative SINCERE honest reliable trustworthy dependable attentive

- ASSURANCE ASSURED valued looked up to certain confident COURAGEOUS bold spirited self-reliant brave daring audacious INSPIRED uplifted transported impressed motivated LOVED cared for loving affectionate supported trusted desired protected considered SUCCESSFUL triumphant proud positive exhilarated exultant
- ENTHUSIASM ALIVE vibrant bubbly animated effervescent buoyant vivacious invigorated enchanted bewitched ATTRACTIVE lovely beautiful handsome glamorous thought well of appealing admirable DELIGHTED amused captivated jubilant exultant EXCITED enthusiastic eager elated ecstatic thrilled stimulated TRUSTING loving supporting encouraging
- INTEREST CARING concerned sympathetic being there interested genuine CORDIAL friendly warmed welcomed hospitable FASCINATED stimulated turned on tuned in NEEDED appreciated wanted essential necessary meaningful vital UNDERSTANDING considerate conscientious solicitous thoughtful
- WILLINGNESS ENCOURAGING perceptive aware responsible receptive REFRESHED renewed revitalized invigorated ANSWERABLE capable competent adequate prepared communicating
- ACCEPTANCE ACCEPTIVE acceptable choosing to want to, approving nonjudgmental ADAPTABLE open affable amiable supportive approachable COMFORTABLE at ease clear focus agreeable unconcerned OPTIMISTIC outgoing hopeful cheerful positive worthy deserving valuable useful befitting honorable proud
- CHOICE, ACCEPT WHAT IS, AS IS, CREATE ANEW FROM THERE, RESIST WHAT IS AND CONTROL
- ANTAGONISM ATTACKED questioned interrogated put on the spot BOTHERED pestered annoyed troubled irritable disagreeable BURDENED put up with endured tolerated in the way inadequate INDIGNANT right/wrong have to ought to should must controlling I win/you lose UPSET agitated shaken bothered frantic unbalanced distressed worried

- ANGER FUMING seething overwrought fiery incensed irritated belligerent gruff OUT OF CONTROL furious violent raging savage explosive outraged reckless hysterical
- RESENTMENT EMBARRASSED mortified ashamed shamed HURT wounded injured stung harmed offended maltreated broken sad unappreciated REJECTED demeaned belittled censored stifled put down RESENTFUL repelled indignant foolish dumb lost face disgusted SUPPRESSED used maneuvered imposed on disrespected abused exploited rigid manipulative
- HOSTILITY FRUSTRATED trapped cornered caged put on overworked picked on pressured HOSTILE aggressive unfriendly depraved pugnacious quarrelsome vindictive HYPOCRITICAL two-faced deceitful pretender hateful contrary SARCASTIC uncaring sniping critical fault-finding tactless WITHHOLDING stubborn held back resisting perverse veiled hostility
- FEAR/LOSS ALONE left out unwelcome lonely apart neglected severed endangered friendless DISAPPOINTED let down overlooked passed over misunderstood discontent BITTER jealous envious insecure anxious covetous FRIGHTENED afraid scared terrified fearful horrified cautious suspicious HYPERSENSITIVE self-conscious unsure uncertain overly reactive
- GRIEF/GUILT BETRAYED victimized destroyed devastated ruined deceived DEFEATED discouraged failing weak resigned submissive overpowered conquered despondent GUILTY blame-worthy unacceptable anguished reprehensible self-punishing self-pity INFERIOR inadequate unworthy poor bad impoverished second-best naughty childish THREATENED weak helpless tormented powerless susceptible vulnerable
- INDIFFERENCE DISINTERESTED indifferent apart lukewarm callous unconcerned denial bored FRIGID pessimistic cynical deadly destructive stagnant SHOCKED numb shaken stunned immobilized depressed listless resigned UNFEELING cold undemonstrative insensitive emotionless disconnected
- SEPARATION FOCUS ON FAILURE, ABANDONED

excluded left out unwanted unworthy desolate forsaken HOPELESS helpless unable to think dull detached separate dejected dismal INCAPACITATED immobilized incapable catatonic depressed aphasic DESERTED uncared for unacceptable unloved loveless unimportant melancholy

PSYCHOREGULATION

This is a Russian technique explained to me by Professor Vladimir Ilyn, sometime deputy Minister for Health in USSR. It is basically positive medical sports psychology translated into musical terms. It entails observing the uniquely personal signs that occur when you perform at your optimum. This is when your breathing rate, blood pressure, and psychological arousal state best fit the performance required. In international competitions (whether music or sports), millions may be watching/hearing you represent your country, and you will need the right level of confidence, courage and aggression, endurance, and sensory awareness to win, not to mention play like an angel. It's also useful for playing in public to a normal-sized audience.

You need to know your emotional quotient. In your daily life, are you someone with a low level, who is laid back/phlegmatic, placid, bored/depressed/lazy, leave it all to the last minute? People like this need the stimulus of performance and never do their very best unless up against it. Or are you always living near the top with a high level, a perfectionist in a state of tension, anxiety and worry, making unreasonable demands of everyone but especially of yourself? The slightest extra load sends such people into a state of overload where they cannot cope. They have a preburn of worry about what might happen, panic when it does, and an after-burn of self-castigation. People like this are hypersensitive and need time, reassurance, and good preparation. These people need Best Practice (see chapter 3) and psychoregulation desperately to be able to take control.

Stress is not in things out there, it's in us. Chronic stress is characterized by a host of symptoms (in no particular order): increased sensitivity to light, increased urination, dizziness on prolonged standing or on getting up from lying down, recurring infections, allergies and sensitivities, stomach symptoms, diarrhea, chronic fatigue and depression, low motivation, trembling and twitching, memory loss, confusion and poor concentration, insomnia but daytime sleepiness, jaw clenching, teeth grinding, neck pain and headache, low back pain, significantly increased or decreased appetite, chronic aches and pains, a need for stimulants/coffee/alcohol, yo-yoing moods and energy levels.

What a horror list! We all have a few of these but where they are part of your lifestyle, look again at what you can do to help yourself. You know when perhaps once a year your playing hits a purple patch! It's when you are totally inspired and in a Zen-like state, and your instrument seems to play you rather than vice versa. You communicate directly and effortlessly. That is what you need to harness and learn about—not what you do wrong/isn't good enough and so on, but how you do it right!!

1. Immediately after you finish, get a stop watch and ask someone to count your breaths per minute while you count your pulse (by putting three fingers on the thumb side of the inner side of your wrist, just below the wrist crease). To recreate that state at a later date you might have to either run round the block or meditate.
2. Observe your state of mind. What is your mood? Are you calm, excited, exultant, aggressive, angry? Find one word that encapsulates the feeling. Whatever it is that you felt, that is the state of mind that, specific to you, needs to be recreated to play as well next time.
3. Make a note when you felt so inspired of what you were thinking about, and where in your body you felt it. Remember and recreate that too.
4. Make a note of what food you have ingested and how long after eating you played.
5. Make a note of how long you slept and how long since you woke up. Do you function best early or late?
6. Make a positive habit out of your findings as a preparation for your next performance. Then harness your natural optimum state by consciously emphasizing what works for you.

FEEL-GOOD FACTORS

Other feel-good factors you can add into your daily life to help muscles work well are often best when slotted into the odd few minutes when you can't do anything else. Doing them gives you the feeling that you are filling your life with good things. Here are a few ideas for home and hotels:

1. At any time you can stretch and wriggle. Use the time at traffic/ stop lights, during TV commercials, when talking on the phone. Dance when you hear music (when off the platform!).
2. Head squeeze, neck squeeze, and facial massage for relaxation, then wring out a face cloth or hand towel and put it over your face for five minutes, then brush your hair 100 times with a bristle brush to wake up.
3. Massage all the muscles in your feet and calves and then pop them into warm water.
4. Do eye exercises and breathing exercises.
5. Rub some massage points (chapter 4).
6. Do a memory rehearsal (chapter 3) or clarify some technique quietly in your mind so your mind is clear on what to tell your muscles.
7. Plan your next leisure time. Let go and be exotic!
8. Take a five-minute holiday (see the section later in this chapter).
9. Keep an inspiration scrapbook for browsing. Collect articles and sayings that have inspired you over the years to reread and interpret in the light of your present situation and inspire/excite you to be positive about yourself and your future. Keep something handy that makes you chuckle!
10. Keep an interest book. Every night make a list of the things you hope for tomorrow, and the good things both expected and unexpected that happened today. It will relax you so that you go to sleep happy with a daily sense of accomplishment. You can live off that interest. It's worth investing in you and what's good about you. When you finally settle down to sleep, give yourself that extra tender loving care by asking each bit of you if it is entirely comfortable exactly where it is. Would it prefer to be slightly more this way or that, bent or straight, more curled up or tucked in. Start with your toes, then ankles, and work up through each joint to your head, by which time you will probably be asleep!

Work out what are the main energy drainers and energy givers in your life. Where you can, plan to only have two drainers a week. Aim to resolve the worst by Monday night if possible, then the rest of the week is easier. Axe everything that doesn't give you a feeling of accomplishment or satisfaction and replace it with what is ennobling, empowering or energizing.

For some people, finding things that help them feel good about themselves is a real challenge: It's as if they wore blinders that shut out all the bright and joyous things! Perhaps there are hidden payoffs for them in continuing to suffer. Any compliment fades quickly or is given short shrift and helped on its way with denial. It's because there is no sense of achievement from within. Doing what makes you feel good about yourself is not self-indulgence, but the opposite. It doesn't mean gratifying an isolated part of you, it means satisfying your whole self, which includes feelings for, ties to, and responsibilities to others. Self-indulgence means satisfying only the smallest part of you and that only temporarily. No one wants the fruit of someone else's self-denial It's the worst kind of self-indulgence. Doing something because you want to has integrity. Doing it without that and only to please someone else is manipulation and resentment is very close under the surface. Take a look at yourself. Is some of your muscle tension coming from this area? It's imperative to know what makes you feel good, really good, on top of the world, light and free, full of bounding joy and energy, not what advertisements tell you you should feel. When you have identified something real that does feel good, and for which you have a name, write it down. Now remember what you were doing the last time you felt like this, even if it was so long ago you were a child, and write it down. What makes you feel utterly relaxed, soft, and dreamy or any other special feeling? Write it down. If you don't know clearly what you like best right now, how can you ask for it or give it to yourself?

Really get in touch with your sense of pleasure so that you know what makes you glow authentically from inside, what recharges you, restores your self-esteem, and wipes away all the hurt and buffeting you have received. Write them all down somewhere—it's so easy to forget them in the hurly-burly of life and you can change them the minute you want to. If you rely on others to supply your treats, those treats will definitely be too few.

VISUALIZATION

There are various areas in which this is particularly useful. You can either just close your eyes, or you can go into a meditative state. To do this:

1. Sit or lie down and breathe deeply with your eyes closed. (Note Bene: You are not going to sleep, so you may prefer to sit.)

2a. Imagine yourself sitting outside in the shadow of a large cloud. Watch the cloud dissolve slowly as it passes over and relax bit by bit as you feel the sun's warmth sinking into each part of your body, starting with your toes and going gradually, gradually upward until you are basking in its gentle, golden light.

    Or

2b. Imagine you are sitting under a huge tin of golden syrup. The gooey sticky syrup is slowly trickling down and down your face, nose, lick a bit as it passes your mouth! It goes on over your shoulders and down your arms, it goes down your back and chest, past your waist and down your legs and trickles off your toes. You are one glorious golden blob of happiness.

    Or

2c. Imagine you are in a garden and there is a path in front of you in the warm sunshine. Follow the path and slowly float up to the top of a mountain where you will find a person with a beautiful face who is your guru. Feel the beauty of the place, the view, the safety, the serenity.

    There are many lovely options.

3. From there take yourself to your favorite, secret, totally safe place and enjoy the luminous silence for a five-minute holiday. Hear the quiet sounds from the birds or the stream or the sea, smell the perfume from the flowers, see the colors in the butterflies wings.

    You can now go on and do your chosen visualization.

4. When you have finished, remind yourself where you are before you open your eyes and smile.

Useful Visualizations

1. Go through in your mind and be absolutely clear about every single detail of a specific piece of music you intend to play. Any foggy bits will show up in your performance, so clear them out now. A good memory aid, this can be hard work the first few times round. Persevere; it's worth it. Some people find it helpful to picture their most admired performer and play (without instrument) as though they were that person, with all the skills, sound, and brilliance of that person. Be clear in your mind about the character the composer wished to portray rather than the written dynamics. Get under the skin of the specific animal that has the characteristics you wish to emphasize in the piece you intend to play. Be a growling tiger—fur, claws and all—or a flower, a tree, a bird, a snake. It will add immediacy to your playing.

Use visualization to prepare you for playing in new, unusual, or difficult circumstances. See the room/hall, see who will be there, give them happy interested faces. Play about and imagine the worst that can happen. Embellish it until you make it so grotesquely awful that it becomes funny. Laugh gleefully if you like! Next make it the absolute best that can happen until it's unbelievably wonderful in a way that is special to you. Then visualize it being so easy and enjoyable that you look forward to it.

You can also use visualization to plan your "Golden Future." Stress-free and fulfilling. Imagine, if you could wave a magic wand with money, time, and energy no object, where would you be and what would you be doing? When you have that clear, put it say five years into the future and plan backward so you know exactly where you need to be in three years, and from there in one year, three months, one month, by this evening, and so on. Then even what you do today is in line with your ideals and gives you a sense of lightness and purpose that transcends problems in a single leap. Visualization increases in value the more you do it. Above all, it gets you away from victim status into being in charge, of being the cause of how you are and how you will be.

REFERENCES

Andrews, E. *Muscle Management*. New York: Thorsons/HarperCollins, London 1991.

Bandler, R., and J. Grinder. *Frogs into Princes*. Moab, Utah: Real People Press, 1979.

Bartley, W. *Werner Erhard: Transformation of a Man*. New York: Clarkson N. Potter Inc., 1978.

Cooke, D. *The Language of Music*. Oxford: Oxford University Press, 1964.

Evans, A. *The Secrets of Musical Confidence*. New York: Thorsons/HarperCollins, 1994.

Gardiner, D., and G. Beatty. *Never Be Tired Again*. New York: Harper and Row, 1988.

Green, B., and T. Gallwey. *The Inner Game of Music*. London: Pan Original, 1986.

Hay, L. *Love Yourself, Heal Your Life Workbook*, ed. Eden Grove. London: Airlift Books Co., 1982.

Helmsetter, S. *What to Say When You Talk to Yourself*. New York: Pocket Books, 1982.

Jamplosky, L. *Healing the Addictive Mind*. Berkeley, Calif.: Celestial Arts, 1997.

Ostwald, P., B. Baron, N. Byl, and F. Wilson. Performing Arts Medicine. *Western Journal of Medicine* 160 (1994): 48–52.

Salzer, F. *Structural Hearing in Music,* Vols.1 & 2. New York: Dover Publications, Inc., 1962.

Storr, A. *Music and the Mind*. New York: Flamingo, HarperCollins, 1992.

11

More Useful Techniques

Emergencies shouldn't happen. But they do. They usually occur as the "straw that broke the camel's back"—as an accident waiting to happen. Because the warning signs have been ignored and because of a chronic "just one more" attitude. Obviously they are less likely, and less dire with good preparation. We are not talking here about fainting or falling off the stage. Such matters are for the St. John's Ambulance or Red Cross personnel present, and the concert hall management, and after such an accident, you should not consider playing unless they have cleared you as fit. Having said that, there's nothing to stop you learning First Aid. And all orchestral managers accompanying orchestras should be proficient in at least the basic course. But suppose someone bumps into you as you bend to lift your instrument case, causing you to stumble awkwardly and strain a muscle? Suppose your preconcert meal threatens to resist the digestive process? What if the dull ache around your left thumb suddenly becomes a shooting pain?

Much of what follows would not apply if you were a rank-and-file string player in a large symphony orchestra, because there are other players on the same part so you can opt out without wrecking the show. However, here we are mainly talking about small ensemble work, or the wind or brass section of an orchestra, where each player is a soloist.

"It" has happened and you have a very short time before going on stage. What to do? The first thing is to decide is *if* you can continue, not do you want to continue. Typically problems are mental (panic), physical (pain or muscle strain), chemical (nausea, dizziness), environmental (too hot/cold, no air, no room), or instrumental (I leave that one to your lurid imagination).

1. Remember that people will want to help you and will want you to continue. But the *final decision is yours*, not theirs.
2. Ask for what you want or need. If it has to do with the venue, get hold of the top person available who can actually do something about it (usually the stage manager). As time is short, don't waste time complaining to anyone else. When you are performing, you are king—the whole outfit (both back stage and front of house audience) is there because of you, so don't be shy. Act like a king but be polite. You always have the choice of not going back on stage.
3. Be specific. People cannot be expected to read your mind.

You've had a shock. For that take Arnica 6 (two tablets every hour for six doses and then three times a day until you feel normal again), or Rescue Remedy (see instructions later). Later, when you have finished playing, reassess the situation. Realize that so far you have been "symptom treating." The cause of the breakdown must be found and treated ASAP after the concert if you don't want it to recur and become a chronic problem.

Mental problems—you panic. (a) Sip water with four drops of Rescue Remedy per glass. (b) Sit down, hands in lap, and breathe deeply and quietly in and out. (c) Visualize a time of success. (d) When you get out on stage, concentrate on what you want the music to say as you play each bit—it's too late to worry about technique. Trust all the hours of work that you have done. Remember that living for approval is just another way of dying; do it for you; go out and give the audience yourself, the person they came to hear, not a load of "oughts and shoulds."

Physical problems. These are the most common you will encounter. For a cramp, "Feather" the muscle. Brush it lightly and fast backward and forward with your hand as though you were brushing crumbs off it, until the cramp goes. This disperses the excess energy stuck in the muscle. Now gently stretch the muscle.

Muscle strain (pain that gradually gets worse as you play). (a) Ask for ice. (b) While you wait for it to arrive, rub the massage points for that muscle hard for thirty seconds (not more!). (c) Pinch the muscle belly together and gently pull its ends apart (see origin/insertion technique later in this chapter). (d) Wrap the ice in a hanky and hold it over the muscle. You may also massage it gently with the ice cube. Do not continue with the ice beyond ten minutes, and less if it starts to hurt from the cold. (e) Take Rhus tox 6x.

Muscle weakness (weakness and/or lack of feeling, which comes on slowly during performance). (a) Rub the massage points for that muscle. (b) Push the ends of the muscle together. (c) Massage it from body (center) to extremity, to help blood flow. (d) Keep it warm. (e) Make sure all joints of the limb that are nearest the heart are working well, and that your head and neck posture is the best it can be. (f) Take Arnica 6x.

Muscle tear (pain usually happens suddenly, with immediate decrease in function). (a) If you must continue, realize that you do so at the risk of being unable to play for a while afterward (maybe one week or two weeks depending on severity). (b) Ask for a paramedic if available, ice, and a crepe bandage (or other type of flexible strapping) or borrow a limb support. Meanwhile, hold the muscle under a running cold tap. (c) Use the ice wrapped in a hanky over the painful area for ten minutes to stop swelling. (d) Bind it gently so you can move, but it feels supported, taking care not to cut off the blood supply (i.e., make sure it doesn't turn blue). This is much easier for a paramedic to do than you, unless you are trained already in bandaging and strapping. (e) Take Rhus tox 6. (f) Rearrange the program to lessen physical stress. (g) After the concert, see a trained therapist ASAP.

Blinding headache. (a) Make sure that you are not staring into spotlights on stage. Get them properly angled by the lighting manager (before he goes home, usually about 4:30 PM). (b) Do some palming (see chapter 4). (c) Use acupoint GB-31. Press in hard for ten seconds on the point on the outside of the thighs where the end of your straight arm and middle finger would touch the seam of your jeans (if you were wearing them). This point can be excruciatingly tender. Press for ten seconds, rest for ten seconds. Repeat this three times. (d) Search in the webbing between thumb and index finger for a sore point and squeeze it for thirty seconds. (e) Massage hard all round that base of your skull at the top of the neck from ear to ear, giving extra attention to all the sore spots. This will help your neck muscles to relax. (f) Hold your frontal eminences (see chapter 8), and give the pain your complete attention. Stop when it has gone. This is a good technique for any pain anywhere in the body that originates in tension.

Chemical problems—Nausea. Decide if it's caused by food or fear. If from food (a) allow yourself to be sick if possible, to get rid of the poisons and excesses. (b) Take Arsen Alb. 6 if it's mild food poisoning and diarrhea, Nux Vom. 6 if it's indigestion. If the nausea stems from fear, sip some cold (not iced) water, into which you've put Rescue Remedy or Arnica.

Allergy. Asthma is the only one that needs instant help, and you will probably know already what to do. However, (a) ask that the cause (scent or smoke) be removed and ask for a straw. (2) Sit quietly, calm yourself as best you can, and breathe through the straw. If it hasn't settled down in two minutes, do not go back on stage. Ask the paramedic for help. You will know if you are going to collapse. Demand a doctor, and don't even think about continuing to perform. Lumps and bumps that come up can be covered with Rescue Remedy cream and covered against friction until after the performance. All allergic reactions are increased by mental stress, so breathe as deeply and as slowly as you can, visualizing peaceful situations in all breaks, and don't be tempted to have any caffeine.

Dizziness. (a) Breathe deeply and get your feet above your head by lying on the floor with your feet on a chair. (b) If you haven't eaten for more than three hours, ask for a lump of sugar. (c) If neither of these work, don't go back on stage. You may trip and hurt yourself seriously, and probably smash your instrument as well.

Environmental problems. Find out who has real control in the building (usually the stage manager) and be specific, be polite, and be firm about your needs and why it's essential to get something done now, rather than next week. If necessary, get back-up from your concert manager.

Instrument emergencies. Decide to (a) borrow what you need. (b) Invent—maybe the house technician can help. (c) Change the program order or swap parts with someone capable. (d) Change the program and play what is possible, given the limitations you now have, and tell the audience so they can sympathize. (e) Never travel without your spare kit again.

Postmortem. While you are nursing yourself back to health, be responsible for your future, and make a written assessment. The breakdown occurred. Why?

1. The losses and gains and long-term effects accruing from the emergency—what I did too much/too little of that predisposed me to breakdown?
2. What I can do/change technically to forestall another such emergency, such as less technical crowding, or more stamina building?
3. Given the risks, what must I now know/learn/do/delegate? Do some things need to be delayed or reprogrammed?
4. Who can be trusted in such circumstances to help/take over?
5. To what expense am I prepared to go to keep my health/job/instrument going now and in the future?
6. What should I now add to my emergency pack?
7. Who are the local experts for this problem? Who would be available on tour?
8. Who will come to me if I'm incapacitated (doctor, dentist, physiotherapist, chiropractor, osteopath, instrument repairer)? Who does emergency repair work, who does the best work, and who has an instrument like mine that I can borrow?
9. What exactly does my insurance cover (read the small print)?

MASSAGE

There as many types of massage: Swedish, remedial or sports, aromatherapy, reflexology, and shiatsu, as well as erotic "with extras," and books are available on all of them. I shall not discuss the last; I leave that to you. Straight, Swedish or remedial massage can be either invigorating or calming, and to some extent depends on the practitioner and on your personal likes and dislikes as to pressure and which area. Some people do not feel they have had their money's worth unless they feel tired afterward and equate heavy pressure and pummelling with getting in touch with and straightening out parts of their body they normally ignore because they live in their heads. For them, massage is a lazy form of passive exercise. Others would be shattered by this, and want the lightest of esoteric strokes to lead them into a relaxed, meditative state. Sports people often only want the parts of the body they have exercised worked on as part of a warm-down regime because they know it will lessen stiffness later. Some only want their back worked on or hate having the head of feet touched. Whatever you choose, when you go for a massage, realize that it is your time and you do not have to have any "extras" you don't want.

To find a reputable practitioner, apply to one of the massage schools offering a certified course, and ask for their best student. All others will have full diaries if they are any good. Alternatively, you and your spouse or best beloved could learn together, and then you are set up for life. The ideal for a soloist on a concert tour might be an invigorating massage before, and a calming one after the performance as part of the warm-up/down procedures from a tame traveling masseur, but that is as expensive as taking your own grand piano with you and can't be done on the bandroom floor! Some have been known to research and carry a list of all the Turkish baths on tour, or Japanese massage parlors. Top hotels may have a resident masseur if they have a fitness center. It's worth an inquiry at the reception desk.

Shiatsu incorporates the important acupoints relevant to your condition, and brings about both relaxation and healing. Very often acupoints coincide with areas of muscular tension that a chiropractor, osteopath, or physiotherapist will work on using trigger point therapy. Many muscle facilitation techniques are available (see later section). Tougher than trigger point massage is *Rolfing*, which can be exquisitely painful, and works on releasing and stretching tight fascia (the sort of sausage skin that encases every muscle), thereby having dramatic effects on posture and allowing muscles, which for years have been held in contraction, to relax. Generally, this is done as an integrated course of ten treatments, concentrating on specific areas each session.

Self massage. You know your own areas of cramp, spasm, and tension. Find the places and use deep firm, but gentle and slow circular motions on these (making sure the rest of you doesn't become tense while you do it!). A useful exercise is to massage the entire scalp with your outstretched fingers, really moving the skin against the bone, and also going gently round the eye-sockets. Next, working with your thumbs, pay particular attention to the jaw joint in front of your ears, and the top of the back of the neck under the skull. Follow this by clasping hands behind the neck and squeezing between finger and palm down one side; then change hands and squeeze down the other. For awkward places on your back, you can use a golf ball, positioning it so it rests under the center of a tight muscle when you lie down on it. Relax in this position until the muscle tension goes.

Aromatherapy is at the gentle end of the massage scale. Essential flower essences are added to a plant oil, which acts as a carrier, and the volatile oils are absorbed through the skin. They work through their subtle chemistry and through emotional associations, likes, and dislikes. Lavender is one of the most popular because of its many healing and relaxing properties, but you will find a full list in Raymond Lautie's book (see references). Sometimes it is very pleasant to have just your face done by someone else, to melt away the world's tensions, and finish with a hot towel over you to help soak in the oils.

Reflexology is a form of foot massage and can be extremely relaxing as well as usefully diagnostic in a general way. This is also true for a head, hand, and jaw massage. It all depends where you hold tension or screw up in knots with playing, or which you ignore in normal daily living.

Tired muscle or "overuse" injury? How do you know the difference? Fry (1986) has defined five categories that should act as alarm bells and stop you playing. (a) Pain at one site only. (b) Pain at multiple sites. (c) Pain that persists beyond the time of playing, with some loss of coordination. (d) All of the above, plus pain in normal activities of daily life. (e) All the above, where all activities using the affected body part cause pain.

You should never let things get to this state, and you will not if you throw out the notion of "No pain, no gain." Instead of charging on, hoping the pain will go away, use your brains for silent practice and thoughtful consideration of your technique.

ANTICRAMP

Cramp is usually due to trying to force a cold muscle to work before it is properly warmed up, or lack of warm down after a lot of exertion. Night cramp is said to be due to calcium imbalance. When a muscle cramps, it is because mechanically the microscopic ratchet system of fibers is jammed in contraction. Chemically the waste products are clogging the electrical control or the muscle ratchet, and meridian energywise cramp is interpreted as too much energy in one place.

The traditional method of release is to stretch the muscle forcibly or massage it deeply and, as a last resort, inject it with botulinum toxin (which is a very drastic remedy). However, where there is ordinary cramp (and not a serious incurable problem like motor neuron disease), the most effective method is "feathering," which is painless, better than heavy massage and often far faster, and can relieve all cramp symptoms. Simply disperse the excess energy by brushing the muscle with your fingers very fast and very lightly, backward and forward and end to end, as though you were brushing off the dust. It usually only takes ten seconds, but may need to be repeated after using the muscle again until it settles.

Reread chapter 4 before proceeding further, to familiarize yourself with basic muscle testing. If, when you have worked on all the massage points and holding points, there is still a problem (such as pain, spasm, twinges or stiffness, the posture looks distorted but the muscles test strong, there is a restricted range of movement or there are overenlarged flabby muscles, or there is a persistent recruiting of muscles that shouldn't normally be used to carry out a specific function), the problem may lie in the balance between the relative tension settings of those muscles. For instance, muscles may be chronically contracted because you habitually use them that way. Typical of this is the raised left shoulder of so many violinists. It causes a switch-off of all the muscles that work against it, because they then have to work at half strength, and can cause joint malfunction. The first technique to work on is: Hypertonic muscles/muscle energy techniques/neuro-muscular relaxation—these are all different names for basically the same thing.

This is a simple muscle technique, often used by physiotherapists, osteopaths, and chiropractors, but with the addition of breathing and indicator muscle testing, as discovered by Frank Mahoney, DC, which vastly increases its effectiveness. Use it when you find a muscle that feels tight and sore and doesn't want to relax when you finish playing.

1. Find a strong indicator muscle (see chapter 4).
2. Put the sore muscle in extension by stretching it gently as far as it

will go, or to the point where discomfort starts, but before there is real pain. Then bring it just a little back from that.

3. Hold it there, while you retest the indicator muscle, which will now be weak if this technique is needed.

4. Keeping the problem muscle in extension by holding it, ask the Testee to take a deep breath and, while exhaling, gently and slowly contract the muscle against the resistance the Testee is providing over a count of eight to ten seconds.

5. The Testee then relaxes the muscle gently and the Testee can now take up the slack, to reach a new starting position.

6. Stages 3 to 5 are repeated twice more.

7. Retest stages 2 and 3 but now the indicator muscle will stay strong.

It is particularly important that the muscle is only worked on with resistance when the Testee breathes out. Many people stop breathing, or push when inhaling, and this will only worsen the problem and may jam the muscle completely. This technique is particularly successful where problems recur as a result of repetitive movements, requiring specific muscle contraction. The muscles will have a greater potential than is being used in this repetitive action. It is as if the brain thinks that the small range of movement used repetitively is the maximum range of movement, and erroneously resets other muscles accordingly.

ORIGIN/INSERTION AND SPINDLE
CELL TECHNIQUES

These techniques always work, but the effects can be short-lived as you are working on the sensory nerve cells of the muscle itself. There are two ways to strengthen the muscle mechanically. The first is to push the two ends of the muscle (the origin and insertion) together. This has the general effect of shortening the muscle artificially and thus strengthening it. (The reverse is also true—if you pull the two ends of a strong muscle apart, it will then test as weak.)

The second technique (seemingly opposite to the first) is to pull apart the fibers (spindle cells) within the belly of the muscle so they are not overcrowded and can work more efficiently. This will strengthen the muscle (naturally, the reverse is true—if you push the belly of the muscle together it will weaken strong muscle). These effects will not last if you haven't sorted out the underlying problem of how the muscle got in that state. However, the technique is particularly useful to switch a muscle off temporarily when working with reactive muscles (see later) and in emergency, midconcert.

SWITCHING

Optimal development of the nervous system does not always occur in a growing child by the age of seven. The left hemisphere of the brain is normally dominant so the child is right-handed, right-footed, and so on. Right-brain dominance leads to left-handedness. Failure to achieve complete dominance leads to neurological disorganization and is almost invariably present in dyslexics. When testing muscles, this becomes important when the problem is obviously on one side of the body, but seems to show on the other in an unpredictable way.

Procedure:
1. Find a strong indicator muscle in the lower half of the body (e.g., quadriceps).
2a. Testee holds K-27, both sides, one with a finger from each hand (K-27 is found under the collarbones on either side of the breastbone).
2b. The Testee changes hands, making sure the hands do not touch each other. This tests right/left switching.
3a. The Testee holds GV-27 and CV-24 (top and bottom lip).
3b. The hand positions are reversed. This tests superior/inferior switching
4a. The Testee holds the tummy button and the very tip of the spine between the buttocks.
4b. The hand positions are reversed. This tests front/back switching.

None of the above hand positions should cause the indicator muscle to become weak. Temporary corrections: rub the points concerned. If the Testee has a lot of stress before rubbing the points, find the relevant

Bach flower remedy that also returns the indicator muscle to strength. Chronic switching needs the help of an applied kinesiologist.

GAIT

Another syndrome causing intermittent muscle weakness and poor coordination is the gait mechanism. Normally when walking, to keep balance and appropriate facilitation of muscle groups, while a main muscle group is contracted, the antagonistic group is inhibited. When walking, the opposite arm and leg will swing forward when taking a step forward; neck muscles will contract on the side of the forward arm so that the head is always looking forward. Signs of weakness include a rolling gait and arms held by the sides instead of swinging when walking or running. Any such uncoordination will mitigate against good playing and make learning harder as the body has to compensate for poor balance against gravity. The six groups are as follows: The Testee lies on the bench face up. All muscle groups should be strong when tested separately. The Testee:

1. raises the shoulder and opposite leg forward,
2. holds opposite shoulder and hip down against the bench,
3. holds opposite arm and leg 45° out to the side,
4. holds opposite arm in to the side of the body and leg against the other leg,
5. contralateral psoas and pectoralis major sternal,
6. contralateral gluteus medius and abdominals.

The Tester tests both groups simultaneously. If one group now tests weak, correction can be obtained by deep massage between the furthest joints of the toes on the outside of the big toe and little toes and in the center of the ball of the foot. Massage each active point for thirty seconds daily. Retest the weak muscle groups. Active points may well be very tender and get more tender before getting better. Chronic problems require cranial and/or pelvic treatment from a kinesiologist.

VISUAL INHIBITION

If you have a feeling of insecurity when going up or down stairs, on and off the concert platform; if you feel tired when you look at a piece of music or the conductor; if you trip over curb stones yet there's nothing wrong with your feet, you may be suffering from visual inhibition. It could be that you have learned so much stress while you were using your eyes in a specific way, while looking in a specific direction that your natural "switch off" protective mechanism has come into play. It will continue to do so even when you are looking in that direction but not in that stressful situation. Dyslexic stress (see later) is another cause of visual inhibition

Test positions: The Tester finds an indicator muscle (see chapter 4). Check that it is strong while looking forward normally. Retest as the Testee looks up, down, right, left, far to near, and near to far (conductor to music and back) or at the specific focal length distance of the music stand. Do all this without moving the head. It's also worth testing while swivelling the eyes clockwise/counterclockwise, right/left/right/left to simulate the movements made in score reading. Whichever direction weakens the indicator muscle, that is the one that needs treatment. When the Tester watches the eyeball, it appears to jump rather than move smoothly through that area, and that is the direction the Testee should look while the corrections are being done.

Massage points: Immediately under the collarbones on either side where they join the breastbone, at the same time as the tummy button. The Testee may try to look in another direction while being treated. Pay attention.

Holding point: Both sides of the head 2 inches (5 cm) behind the top of the ear.

Nutrition: Adrenal glands may need support so avoid anything containing caffeine and eat foods high in vitamins A and B complex.

Dyslexia and Music

Dyslexic children need special help or they become discouraged and find themselves on the scrap heap of life. They can use the left brain for logic and calculation or the right brain for color, spacial awareness, and sentient things, but cannot integrate them. They get locked into one or other mode. Unfortunately the world of music needs and uses both together.

At pre-reading age suspect a problem if: (a) the child missed the crawling stage and went straight from bottom shuffling and creeping to walking, missing out the crawling stage, (b) when walking there is no arm swing, (c) the child is very clumsy, late learning to dress, tie shoe laces, or has difficulty knowing right from left, (d) has poor memory and concentration although apparently very intelligent.

All aspects of learning hold traps for dyslexics and will make strong muscles feel weak.

1. Reading music. Learning that G is followed by A not H; words and music together; different clefs and score reading; enharmonic equivalents; groups of notes that are beamed together for instrumentalists but broken up for singers; ledger lines; crotchet and quaver rests that are mirror images of each other; whole bar, minim and semibreve rests.
2. Left/right confusion. "Up and down" a keyboard (vertical—as on the music) is actually right/left (horizontal); hand pattern reversal—playing 1-2-3-4-5 with the right hand moves "up" but the same pattern in the left hand moves "down."
3. Rhythm. Poor coordination in clapping, even though the rhythm is clearly felt.
4. Language. Confusion between American and English terminology (quarter note equals a crotchet, not a quaver). Use of Italian, French, and German terms.
5. Accuracy. Missing out complicated bits and words like hemi-demi-semiquaver; poor sight-reading; inaccurate counting of bars rest.
6. Conductors. Looking at the conductor and then back at the music, being unable to find the place on the page.

Solving these problems requires great tact and patience, consistency and repetition, multisensory learning, and no surprises (as this causes panic). Holding the emotional stress points while thinking about the particular stress mentioned earlier will help. These points are found on the forehead, midway between the center of each eye and the hairline.

It can be seen from this earlier list that the correct choice of instrument is vital. It must use one stave and one clef only, or learning must be done by rote and separated from score reading. Specialist teachers can be contacted through the British Dyslexic Society and specific help found with techniques set forth in J. Goodrich's *Natural Vision Improvement* and "EK for Kids" (Dennison).

REACTIVE MUSCLES

If the desired result is achieved with the use of the two techniques described earlier, but the effect lasts only for a few seconds, you may have a reactive muscle syndrome. This problem usually occurs in muscles that are very frequently used (as in playing), or in a combination of a muscle and its antagonist. It can also apply where a muscle affects its twin on the opposite side of the body (e.g., right latissimus dorsi affecting left latissimus dorsi). The syndrome occurs because one of the two muscles is set too high (i.e., is too contracted) and thereby inhibits or weakens the other, causing poor coordination. The way to find this syndrome is to test the two suspect muscles in very quick succession. If they are both strong if tested singly, but when tested quickly one after the other, one now becomes weak, then the balance between them needs resetting.

1. Work on the muscle that remains strong.
2. Switch it off by reversing origin/insertion technique (see earlier), or by "misusing" the relevant massage points by feathering them instead of massaging firmly (Note Bene: The massage points are not usually on the problem muscle itself.), or by gently hitting the holding points (not the acupoints!).
3. The muscle that was weak will now have strengthened since it is no longer inhibited. Contract it gently several times to reset it.
4. Tap on the Testee's forehead in a small clockwise circle. This will reset the muscle you purposely weakened.
5. Test the two muscles again in quick succession. Both should now remain strong.
6. Any pair of muscles can get "hooked up" like this, and for musicians a frequent occurrence involves the eye muscles and feet, causing tripping up over curbs (see section under eyes). Another frequently found pair is psoas and diaphragm or neck flexors (SCM) and diaphragm. Wind and brass players often have jaw muscle involvement with low back muscles. String players and pianists often have forearm pronators or supinators and the muscles of the hand. There also appears to be a correlation between opposite muscle groups on a joint basis (e.g., biceps with quadriceps on the opposite side, hamstrings to opposite side triceps).

FOCAL DISTONIA

Also known as "disobedient fingers," this syndrome may well be a chronic result of the reactive muscle syndrome. This syndrome only happens when playing and usually takes the form of middle fingers bending at the same time as the outer fingers, creating havoc. The most common sufferers are pianists (either hand) and guitarists (right hand). There is an imbalance between the flexors and extensors of the fingers due to learned neural pathways in the brain. Classically, retraining takes time, and may involve injections in the muscles concerned. However, the sufferer can help himself or herself by learning where the bellies of the affected muscles are in the forearm and inhibiting the hypertonic muscles and strengthening the weak muscles, while holding the emotional stress relief (ESR) points on the forehead found over the center of each eye halfway between the eyebrow and hairline. This is a reactive muscle technique (see earlier). John Thie, DC, suggests testing for this syndrome by holding one hand an inch above the top of the head and testing a strong indicator muscle. If this muscle now becomes weak, suspect reactive muscles. Correction is done by massaging K-27 (a point found at the base of the front of the neck between the first and second ribs, just under where the collarbones meet the breastbone) at the same time as massaging with five fingers around the naval. Repeat switching hands. Check out correction by wriggling and twisting every bit of you but especially the parts concerned and retesting with the hand over the head. Repeat the correction until there is no weakening of the indicator muscle.

PAIN CHASING

This technique is useful when there are shooting pains that come and go and seem to wander or progress from muscle to muscle.

1. Start with the muscle that is giving pain now.
2. Find a strong indicator muscle.
3. Bit by bit, feel the territory of muscle that hurts, retesting the indicator muscle as you do so.

4. The point you touch that causes the strong indicator muscle suddenly to test weak is the next point to work on.
5. Firmly pinch together either side of that spot several times for a few seconds.
6. If you have been successful, touching the spot will now no longer cause the indicator muscle to weaken.
7. Go through the entire muscle and remove any other points.
8. Tap clockwise in small circle on the Testee's forehead to reset the mind-muscle connection and ask where the Testee's pain has now gone; if there is no further pain, stop. This technique often unravels old injury patterns and compensatory tension chains built by the body in order to try to solve the problem itself.

AEROBIC/ANAEROBIC

Playing often involves repetitive use of a muscle that becomes fatigued or weaker sooner than expected, after sustained or repeated action.

1. Test the suspect muscle. It will be strong.
2. Now test it lightly but quickly ten times in succession and it becomes weak.
3. If it now becomes and remains strong when the Testee holds the massage points or holding points for that muscle (see chapter 4), these points need working on for at least three or four minutes as there has been inadequate lymphatic clearing of the muscle. Waste products are clogging it, causing shortage of oxygen and consequent weakness.

INJURY REVERSAL TECHNIQUE

Just as you retain a mental memory of the accidents that happen to you so there is also a tissue memory. At its most basic level, the self-preservation mechanism of the body remembers at a subconscious level that when you got into that position, something nasty happened, and there was injury. It therefore resists that position, and goes into "switch-off" protection mode, even when the danger is long past, every time that position is repeated. It is that subconscious memory that will cause hesitancy and lack of confidence, incomplete healing, or delayed return to normal use when there is no other apparent reason for it. Typical injuries are an old forgotten whiplash, falling on your hands, breaking or dislocating a limb (especially the shoulder), tooth extraction, and so on.

1. Find a strong indicator muscle.
2. The Testee must describe the accident in as lurid a detail as possible, physically getting into the positions they were in, with instrument, too, if that is relevant. What matters is not so much mental recall as body recall.
3. Test the indicator muscle, which will now be weak if this technique is relevant and the event still active in the subconscious.
4. You may need to support the Testee in this position with cushions and furniture. It doesn't matter what the support is made of; it's the position and contact points with other structures that's important.
5. Hold the Testee's frontal eminences—over each eye and midway between the eyebrows and hairline, while the story of the accident is told three times.
6. Retest the indicator muscle that should now be strong. If not, there may be further positions with stored memories.

This technique may uncover defensive "switch-off" reactions—patterns that have been affecting the body for years that it built up as a safety measure. These remain unhelpfully active, when all they are actually doing is holding up progress and confidence. If the accident is recent, obviously the Testee must be checked by a competent physician. More often than not, however, the body may be reflecting the last stages of healing from surgery, and you will have been told that you will now just have to live with the lesser function.

SPONTANEOUS POSITIONAL RELEASE

Although this technique is useful on many large muscles, the greatest use to a musician is probably to undo tensions in the small intrinsic muscles of the spine that are otherwise difficult to negotiate or feel.

Symptomatic might be a sharp pain or tenderness at one spot, a "crick in the neck," or sudden inability to turn the head.

1. The Testee lies face up. The Tester then holds the head, taking its weight and placing a firm finger over the painful spot (usually somewhere in the neck).
2. While receiving continuous feedback from the Testee, Tester and Testee together find the most comfortable and pain-free position of the erstwhile painful spot by moving the head. This can be any and often extraordinary position of the head and neck! Search until you find it.
3. Holding the position, pressure is then placed over the crown of the head to push the head "into" the base of the neck and held for thirty seconds. The principle behind the method is to contract the muscle more, so that its natural release mechanism comes into play, not unlike undoing a hook and eye—the more you pull it the more it holds, but push it together and it releases easily.
4. The same technique may be used on any of the small muscles of the spine, by moving the torso until the pain disappears, and then applying pressure.

SCARS

Scars can have an extraordinary effect, even keyhole surgery and stitch scars, particularly if they happen to cut across a meridian. This is because scar tissue is different from normal skin and hasn't the same stretch or conductive properties. Scars also often contract, pucker, and itch, pulling on muscles in an abnormal way. When they occur internally they can also cause adhesions, with an occasionally very disruptive effect. There is nothing that can be done here about internal scars (so talk to your GP); external ones can be easily helped, however. Postoperative carpal tunnel scars (see later) are typical of these.

1. Immediately after the operation dressings are permanently removed, smooth vitamin E cream all over the site. It will help skin healing and reduces puckering.

2. Do not work on a scar that has not healed properly yet. When the scar is really strong and well healed, say six months later, find a strong indicator muscle.
3. Work along the scar bit by bit, testing the indicator muscle as you go. Any weakness indicates that that place is out of sync with the rest of the surrounding tissue, and needs treatment.
4. Use PR (a pain relieving spray that contains fluro-methane available at a pharmacy) or an ice cube to freeze the spot, so that there is light frosting over it (this should take two or three minutes only—you don't want to cause frostbite!).
5. While it is intensely cold, gently stretch the scar tissue as if to pull the wound apart four or five times. Stretch round scars from the center out.
6. Warm it up and retest. The indicator muscle should now be strong.

CARPAL TUNNEL AND GUYON TUNNEL SYNDROMES

These are both nerve compression syndromes. They cause weakness, tingling, and pain in the hand. Carpal tunnel syndrome is often associated with an overflexed wrist position, such as when playing above the tenth position on the violin or viola. It may also be made worse by the shape of the upper bouts of the instrument, the set of the neck, and the height of the bridge, all of which affect the amount of pressure needed to depress the strings. Diabetics, young women with slender wrists, pregnant women, and small people are most at risk, due to overuse and lack of space within the wrist. Overuse causes irritation to the nerve sheath and it swells, leaving even less room for the nerve. The median nerve passes through the carpal tunnel and affects working of the thumb, index, and sometimes part of the middle finger. The ulna nerve passes between the pisiform and the hook of the hammate—two wristbones at the base of the little finger, which make the tunnel of Guyon, causing problems with the ring and little fingers. If either of these syndromes keeps recurring, the sufferer should buy a wrist splint or support from the pharmacist, seriously look at their playing hand position, and/or consider a smaller size fingerboard or instrument. To correct these conditions, first do the General Hand Test (fig. 11.1):

1. The Testee holds the tip of the thumb and little finger together, making a ring. The Tester then gently tests them by pulling them apart, using single fingers only, by hooking one finger around the Testee's thumb and one around the little finger.
2. There may be some "give" because there are so many joints involved. However, the muscles should still lock.
3. Correct any weakness as follows (refer to chapter 10). Massage points: (a) Under the pubic bone on the front of the pelvis. (b) Between the seventh and eighth ribs in the cartilage on the left side of the breastbone. (c) The most prominent bumps on the top back of the pelvis. (d) Either side of the spine, level with the bottom of the shoulder blades. Holding points: (a) The frontal eminences—above the center of each eye halfway between the eyebrows and the hairline. (b) Center back of the head on a straight line that starts at the corner of the eye, and passes through the top of the ear, both sides. (c) Acupoints Sp-2 and H-9. Sp-2 is on the nail side of the large joint at the base of the big toe. Hold it with H-8, which is on the palm, on the crease under the ring finger. This will eliminate confusing weakness of the intrinsic muscles of the hand.
4. The Testee now encircles the wrist with thumb and index finger of the other hand, holding it very gently as though it was very precious, fragile, and not to be squeezed. And the muscle test is performed as above again, both with palm up and again with palm down.
5. Watch to see whether the thumb or little finger weakens most, and with palm up or palm down. Thumb weakening means carpal tunnel syndrome, little finger weakening means Guyon tunnel. If weakness is caused only in the palm down position (as it frequently is with pianists), check that the hand muscles are not reactive to pronator teres. If there is weakness only in the palm up position (as in upper strings) then the hand muscles may be reactive to supinator (see reactive muscle technique described earlier).

With carpal tunnel syndrome, it is the median nerve that is impinged under the tough flexor retinaculum or ligament that binds the wristbones

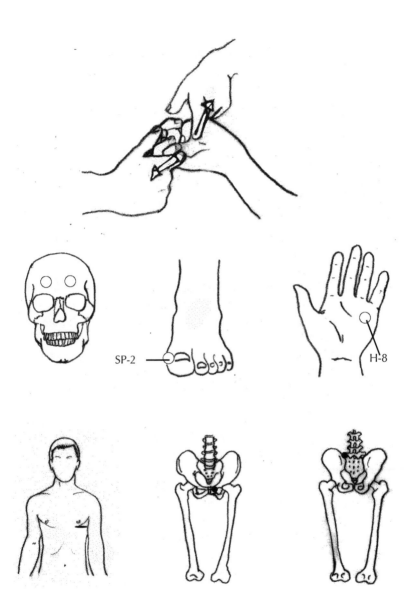

SP-2

H-8

Figure 11.1   General hand test.

together. Correction of weakness is affected by altering the relationship between the bones that tension this ligament. A definitive test is if pressure on the base of the palm just beyond the wrist crease causes a worsening of the problem in the fingers. (There may also be signs of muscle wasting in the ball of the thumb.)

1. The Tester holds the Testee's hand palm up in the fingers of his two hands, and with his thumbs above the wrist joint along the forearm.
2. Establish the direction of adjustment by lightly brushing the thumbs together and retesting, or brushing thumbs apart and retesting. If the thumbs together strengthen the general hand test, then the correction needed is to squeeze the two splayed forearm bones together. However, I have found far more frequently that the forearm bones are jammed together, and need to be eased apart with pressure from the Tester's thumbs on the inside edges of the Testee's forearm bones, pushing them out sideways all the way to the elbow. An overtight watchstrap may well be the cause of the problem.
3. Helpful acupoints are LI-4 and H-3. LI-4 is on the back of the hand halfway along the thumb side of the bone below the index finger. Hold it with H-3, which is at the inner end of the crease on the inside of the elbow.
4. If the wrist is sensitive, support it for two weeks with a support bandage, splint, or "tubigrip." Don't make it too tight, and release it several times a day to let the area breathe and reestablish good blood flow.
5. Eating foods high in vitamin B complex and B6 will help.
6. Gentle use rather than complete cessation of playing can speed return to normal use. However, if there is a lot of swelling and inflammation, do some ice massage before and after attempting any stage in the rehabilitation ladder (see description later). After the swelling has gone, then use heat beforehand, ice afterward. Careful use of this technique may prevent the necessity for surgery.

The ring and little finger malfunction and weakness associated with Guyon tunnel syndrome is corrected as follows:

1. The general hand test is strong (see earlier).
2. With the Testee's hand palm up, pressure is put on the base of the palm, little finger side, to push the knobbly pea-sized pisiform bone away from the thumb and against the hammate bone.
3. Repeat with Testee's hand palm down. Pressure is now put just inside the bump at the end of the forearm bone, little finger side.
4. Correction is in whichever direction causes the general hand test to become strong (little finger side).
5. Take hold of the two sides of the Testee's hand, palm up or palm down as just decided above, and place both thumbs on the bone you are correcting at the little finger side of the wrist. The Testee's arm should be totally relaxed as you pull very gently and press sharply with your thumbs, giving the arm a quick flick like a small whip from the contact point of your thumbs. Speed is more important than pressure.
6. Retest with the general hand muscle test, which should now be strong. This syndrome will benefit also from an increase in intake of vitamin B. Pushing heavy swing doors and leaning on outstretched palms should be avoided for two weeks.

MERIDIAN RUNNING

To "run" each meridian accurately, a complete map is needed. However, a wonderful energizer, and particularly helpful midconcert "perkup" is achieved by running the hand over the body in large sweeps as follows:

1. Run one hand down the inside of your arm from the front of the shoulder, past the armpit to inside elbow, palm, and fingers. Do the other arm.
2. Run one hand up the back of the other arm from fingers, past elbow point, around the back of the shoulder to the back of the ear. Repeat with other arm.
3. Place your hands on your big toes and sweep up the inside of your legs. Continue up the front of the body to the collarbones.
4. Place your hands on your ribs and sweep down the sides of your body and outsides of your legs to the little toes.

5. "Zip up" the front of your body from crotch to lower lip, and up
    the neck from the tailbone, up the spine, over the top of the head
    and down the nose to the upper lip. Each sweep, except the last
    zip up, enhances and emphasizes the correct flow of three meridi-
    ans at once. Ending on the lips will remind you to finish with a
    smile. The whole exercise takes less that ten seconds to do.

OTHER USEFUL ACUPOINTS

These are points to hold or rub gently to relieve a specified problem.
Each point is valid on its own.

Migraine. LU-7—on the inner forearm, four fingers' widths up from
the wrist crease, thumb side.

Frontal headache and sinus pain. GB-14—above the center of each
eye halfway between the eyebrow and hairline; also GV-23—1
inch (2.5 cm) above the natural hairline on the midline of the head.

Headache. BI-67—on the outer edge of the nail of the little toe.

Head and neck pain. LI-4—at the end of the crease when the thumb
and index finger are held together.

Headaches in the back of the head and neck. GB-21—on the base of
the skull halfway between the back of the ear and the small dip
center top of the neck.

Infections. St-36—a hands' width below the kneecap, two finger
widths' to the outer side of the leg.

Hormone and menstrual problems. Sp-6—on the inside calf, one
hands' width above the inside ankle.

Emotional stress. Ht-3—at the inside end of the elbow crease.

Hearing, tinnitus, and jaw problems. SI-19—just in front of the ear
in the dip that appears when the mouth is open; and GB-2—in
front of the ear and level with the lowest part of the ear hole above
the ear lobe.

Eye problems. BI-1—immediately above the inner corner of the eye;
and GB-1—at the outer corner of the eye.

Low back and leg pain. BI-60—halfway between the outer anklebone
and the Achilles tendon; and GB-30—in the dimple in the middle
of each buttock.

Chronic pain and hypertension. K-1—on the sole of the foot, at the heel end of the crease between the ball of the big toe, and the other toes.

Stress from fear or neurosis. Cx-6—three fingers above the inner wrist crease, thumb side, between forearm bone and tendons.

Shoulder, elbow, wrist, and finger problems. Tw-5—three fingers above the wrist crease on the back of the forearm, between the two forearm bones.

General muscle relaxing point. Lv-2—where the skin joins the big toe and the toe next to it.

RIGHT/LEFT BRAIN COORDINATION

Adults as well as children can become subject to minor neurological disorganization. In children, the most common symptoms are reading and learning difficulties, dyslexia, and clumsiness. It is commonly thought to be that the child missed a stage in neurological development between six months and one year, such as at the crawling stage between shuffling along on the bottom and walking. However, this is not the only cause. Upsets in the neurological organization can be caused by opposing brain-hand, brain-ear, and brain-eye dominance, an unbalanced bite and heavy dental work, as well as foot problems and allergies.

In adults, who mostly have found a way to manage without obvious dyslexic symptoms, it shows up as clumsiness, inability to march in step with others (or lifting the same leg as arm when marching, instead of opposite arm and leg, consequently having a rolling instead of a straight gait). There may also be unsynchronized arm/leg swing, or even no arm swing at all. Channeled thinking is another symptom. People with this problem are either thinking spatially or analytically, and are unable to integrate the two skills. They may be very good at one and very poor at the other; good at sport, for example, but unable to spell or write a reasoned letter or essay, despite obvious intelligence and having received a similar level of tuition in both. They may also fail to understand an instruction properly.

The problems of a dyslexic child learning a musical instrument were already discussed. However, we can all benefit from movements that will integrate the two sides of the brain and destress areas of difficulty due to neurological disorganization caused by playing a one-sided instrument, recent dental work, new shoes, or acquired food sensitivity.

Cross-crawl patterning was introduced into applied kinesiology by George Goodheart from Doman and Delacato's work. It is a way of reasserting the normal pattern and integrating right and left brain into good coordination and clear thinking. It raises energy levels, because you are not always fighting yourself to achieve good coordination.

1. With a strong indicator muscle, look at a cross (as in noughts and crosses) and then at vertical parallel lines. If the indicator muscle goes weak when looking at the cross and stays strong when looking at the parallel lines then you need this technique. Any other combination is fine.
2. The Testee lies face up. Legs straight.
3. Assess side of weakness by turning both feet in. The side that turns in most is the side to which the head needs to be turned at stage 5.
4. Simultaneously lift right arm and bend up left leg. Lower both limbs and repeat the other side.
5. Turn the head to the chosen side when the same-side arm is lifted. When the opposite arm is lifted, the head should face up normally (e.g., if stage 3 indicated that the head should be turned to the right, then it will be right arm lift plus head turn to right; left arm lift plus face up normally).
6. Thirty cycles a day is a good number, until it becomes second nature. It is also helpful to do this when tired, and before practicing a particularly difficult technical passage.
7. If the problem persists or you still feel worse after a month of daily cross-crawl, see an applied kinesiologist to sort out the underlying cause.
8. Cross-patterning can also be done standing (marching on the spot), but it is far easier (until you are used to it) to lose the sense of coordination when upright.
9. Another less obvious way to help yourself with integration of complicated comprehension is to draw an infinity sign (infinity or "lazy-eight"—an eight on its side with the right "end" open), making sure you draw up the middle and down the sides). This also integrates right and left brain. Finish by holding the frontal

eminences—points over the center of each eye halfway between the eyebrow and hairline—thirty seconds.

REFLEXOLOGY POINTS

Reflexology points are well worth working on even though you may not be a skilled practitioner. The relevant places will be sore. If you have a problem in any of the areas in the following list, rub deeply with the tip of your thumb for about thirty seconds at the specified point on the foot. The areas listed are those particularly useful to musicians.

1. Eyes—between the second and third toes in the webbing.
2. Ears—between the third, fourth, and fifth toes in the webbing.
3. Shoulder points—on the outside of the little toe where it meets the foot.
4. Neck and jaw—all around the base of the big toe where it meets the foot, and the next joint away.
5. Sinuses—the top of all toes.
6. Spine—from the neck points on the base of the big toe, which represents the top of the neck, all the way down the inside of the longitudinal arch of the foot, to the inner ankle, which represents the sacrum and coccyx.
7. Lungs—on the ball of the foot except under the big toe.
8. Chest—on the top of the foot near the toes. This will be puffy and tender if the chest is congested.

The rest of the points are either harder to find or relate to organs and thus require some knowledge of their function. They should only be worked on by a practitioner or under instruction.

FIVE-MINUTE WONDERS

This is a short list of things you can while waiting somewhere for something for five minutes. Some you can do in public, but for some you need to be alone.

1. Stretch and wiggle and write the letters of the alphabet with the joints that feel stiff.
2. Recharge your energy by meridian running (see earlier).
3. Neck squeeze and facial massage (see earlier), then wring out a face cloth or towel in very hot water and put it over your face or stiff muscles. Then brush your hair 100 times to increase the circulation to the head.
4. If you stand to play, give yourself a foot massage and then soak your feet in warm water.
5. Do a general stretch routine (see chapter 4) and do some deep breathing.
6. Do the relevant massage and holding points for your most used muscles.
7. Do a visualization of happiness, remembering a time you played brilliantly well, then plan your next leisure time for maximum enjoyment.
8. Do a memory rehearsal (see chapter 3).
9. Think through a difficult passage and visualize the exact technique needed to play it with perfect clarity.
10. Take a Five-Minute Holiday. (Close your eyes. Think of your favorite, happiest, most restful place. Take yourself there as a short visualization. Hear the sounds, feel the warmth, smell the scents.)

QUESTIONS FOR MEDICS (DOCTORS, DENTISTS, AND PHYSIOTHERAPISTS)

If you think you need medical help, it's useful to know who is good for what. Ask around locally, but realize that your friends are not experts on your problems, only on theirs, and they may not be musicians. Because of the way doctors are trained, they tend to look only at the problem area and not at the whole person; they may perhaps fail to realize the problem's special significance to you as a musician. They want to help you but only have time to treat you as Mr. Average, not as the specialist artist you are. Use time available maximally by providing accurate information and asking relevant questions. They are the medical experts and you are the musical expert. Both have specialist knowledge the other has not. Respect that. Both ways!

When you see your GP, don't waste time on minor matters. Dive in with what's really worrying you immediately; don't leave it until just before you go out the door, when you sense time's up and you might easily be hurried into forgetting salient facts. Your GP will have follow-up questions, too, but he or she can only ask those if given all the facts, and enough time, hence the need for a prepared symptom list before your appointment.

Remember, too, that medics are trained in scientific methodology (reductionism), which looks for statistical proof about the quantity or proportion of those treated (of the average member of the public) who get reduced symptoms (i.e., that it "works"). Reductionism depends on the least amount of variables to the questions asked that produce viable statistics at the development stage of each pharmaceutical drug. There is no room in such methodology for obscure variables such as the quality of their ability to help you perform muscially. Your symptoms are also scrutinized to see if they fit into the slot of a specific medical diagnosis such as carpal tunnel syndrome or thoracic outlet syndrome. Then there is a specific treatment for such a diagnosis—usually symptom suppression. Such diagnoses assume that all the symptoms arise (a) from one cause, or (b) arise from the place where the symptoms are felt. This is often not the case. Patients have the right to more than one problem, one problem may have several contributory causes; pain may only be felt in the area of weakness that is exhausted trying to compensate for another area of malfunction elsewhere in the body. Medical terminology means nothing to a musician. You need to ask what it means, translate it into what's gone wrong in plain English, and then work out how it got that way and how you can help yourself not to make that mistake again.

Doctors tend to deal with the problems brought to them mainly from a chemical point of view, with the aim of suppressing the symptoms chemically rather than solving the cause of the symptoms. While medical drugs are usually effective for damping symptoms down, it's as well to remember that there isn't a drug in existence that doesn't have side effects for somebody and to which you may or may not be susceptible. (Check for these by asking when given your prescription (see later or look in Mimms or Data Sheet compendium at your local library). If you are taking a drug for something, even if you bought it over the counter, but you are getting side effects, see your GP as soon as possible and ask for an alternative. Do not pretend you are taking a drug when you are not because you don't like the side effects. If you are on tour, recommended websites include www.nhs.org.uk, www.netdoctor.co.uk, and www.patient.co.uk; these may be helpful, but remember they are for the average person, not for specialist musicians.

Doctors are an extremely good source of referral to specialists such as surgeons, physiotherapists, counselors, and some alternative practitioners such as osteopaths and chiropractors. You may then be able to claim fees on your medical insurance if you have one. British Association for Performing Arts Medicine (BAPAM) has a list of doctors who are musicians' specialists.

Before visiting your doctor/dentist/physician, prepare your information and questions so it is as all rounded as possible:

1. Ask yourself all the questions defining the area and degree of pain and dysfunction in chapter 4 to clarify the exact nature of the problem.
2. If your doctor prescribes any pharmaceutical drug for any symptom, whether it has to do with your playing or not, always ask if it will (a) cause drowsiness (i.e., affect your concentration), (b) affect hearing or sight, or (c) affect dexterity. Anything that carries a "do not drive" warning will probably affect all three. Ask what other side effects have been known from the drug (you may have to check this in your local library).
3. If your doctor recommends surgery, always get a second opinion from another surgeon. Ask about success rates. If possible, find another musician who has had that operation and coped with the aftereffects. Remember all surgery leaves scar tissue, which is less flexible than muscle tissue, and often more vulnerable.
4. Since most doctors/dentists/physicians are not usually trained to your standards musically, they may need to see you with your instrument so you can demonstrate exactly what is not working. They will also have little idea about retraining and reintegration into playing again, or expect to see you for follow-up sessions several weeks later. You can help yourself best by building a rehabilitation ladder, possibly in consultation with your physiotherapist (although

his or her main aim is to get you back to "normal" movement, and playing an instrument is way beyond that).

REHABILITATION LADDERS

Rehabilitation ladders are extremely useful to show you how bad the injury is, and to show your progress back to health as a musician. If you have to stop playing for any reason, even an extended holiday, you may need to remedy the disuse by strengthening exercises. A return to health rarely occurs in a steady progressive line, and playing is no exception. Far more common is a small progression, a plateau, then another small progression, and so on. It's important to remember this in your impatience to get back to playing, so that you don't push yourself too fast and too far, and undo all the good already done.

A rehabilitation ladder is a graded series of exercises that can be used for general fitness or for specific injuries. Both are useful to musicians, but each instrument will have its own set of likely injuries and therefore its own specific rehabilitation ladder. It is of no use for me to give one for each instrument, as age, style, and amount of playing as well as techniques vary enormously. All I can do is give you an example, with principles and rules so that you can devise your own. Think for yourself and of yourself in terms of a beginner. What basic exercises would you teach? Then make a progress chart, bridging the gap between the "beginner" and level of professional proficiency you wish to attain. Think of it as a form of accelerated learning. Plan your work, then work your plan with tender care. If pain reappears after progressing to the next level, drop back at least two levels, lengthen rest periods or stop for a day. Expect setbacks due to overeagerness, but don't look for them. Keep positive.

Always begin with gentle stretching exercises (see under warm-up). Start at the bottom of the ladder, even if you can do better, as it will act as a form of warm up for what follows.

At the first sign of pain, STOP. If the pain goes within twenty seconds you may continue, but with caution. If the pain doesn't go, leave it for twenty-four hours and start at the bottom again. Progress from gross or whole body movements, through strength or speed, to stamina or fine movement. Put it all together.

While you are stuck on the lower rungs of the ladder, do not neglect the mental side of playing—do plenty of score reading, memory, and technique visualization, and attend rehearsals so that you don't miss out on the camaraderie of your section, and the chance of marking your part, even if you are paying someone to stand in for you. And don't neglect your general fitness.

General Sports and Fitness Ladder

1. After injury rest, use ice in a cloth ten minutes on, ten minutes off. Repeat three times. Support the area with a bandage and hold it up with a sling or similar for twenty-four hours to stop swelling.
2. Stretch gently. No bouncing! Stretch until it just starts to feel stretched. Hold it at just less than that level and then, in fifteen to twenty seconds, reach a little more. Healing muscles scar because they tear easily and scars shorten muscles. Shortened muscles tear again, so always stretch first before you exercise, even when fit.
3. Isometrics using the muscle in the middle of its range only. Isometrics mean that you push against the opposite hand/arm/leg, without either one winning. That way you won't go beyond your natural strength. Hold ten seconds, relax ten seconds. Repeat for two to three minutes only. Do not push through pain!
4. Isometrics using normal muscles length and contraction.
5. Isometrics using full range of motion.
6. Use light weights—this means light enough to produce no pain, while moving the weight from one extreme range of the muscle to the other over a five-second time span, and back over the same time. Rest for ten seconds and repeat the exercise for two to three minutes.
7. Do the earlier exercises in the list with a slightly increased weight.
8. Start technical skills slowly (e.g., running, swimming, etc.).
9. Increase force, practicing techniques at half maximum effort.
10. Use maximum effort in practice only.

Start to play in easy low-grade matches with easy opposition.
Back to normal grade playing.

Injured Finger Ladder

1. If you are not a string player, translate this ladder into your own terms, using the same principles. If you see someone else in trouble, share what you have learned and tactfully, privately, suggest they do the same.

2. For an injured left finger, start with 1 and 2 as from the earlier list. Wear a sling or immobilize the finger by strapping it to an adjacent one for a few days, to prevent you using it in daily living activities.

3. Move it about gently. Meanwhile, consider refingering your music for when and if you absolutely have to play. Recognize the risk of reinjury if you do.

4. Concentrate on right-hand exercises and mental practice, also attend rehearsals. Alternate ice and heat over the area. Keep up your general fitness levels by swimming, doing t'ai chi, Pilates, or whatever you usually do.

5. While supporting the left hand with the right, do gentle exercises, miming in the air without your instrument. Stop at the first sign of pain or tiredness. Work on flexibility, not strength. Using the injured joint, write the alphabet in the air, with letters at first small, then as large as possible.

6. Do some five-finger exercises (or similar as appropriate to your instrument) on a table—still without your instrument, and still "miming" without any strength. You may still need to use ice afterward for ten minutes to stop any swelling.

7. When you can mime exercise 6 in this list quickly and easily with no strength, then use half strength. Meanwhile, build general strength either by squeezing a squash ball or a ball of newspaper, or putting a rubber band around the outsides of all the fingers and thumb and stretching it out wide, depending on the direction of weakness. Keep exercise times shorter than the rests between them.

8. Now use the finger board but with instrument resting in your lap so there is minimum twist, and still with only half strength (keyboard players could use a light-action pianissimo). Keep doing exercise 7.

9. Full stretch in your lap, half strength in normal playing position, do five minutes at a time and rest five.

10. Do some easy Sevcik, Czerny, or other tongue-twister type exercises for flexibility and speed. Use a metronome to build speed gradually and a video camera with slow-motion playback, to analyze your technique and postural errors. Continue to take frequent breaks, playing ten to fifteen minutes, resting five.
11. Do some harder exercises, some double-stops, and an easy study for strength and intonation. Begin to build playing time.
12. Do a harder study and use vibrato, going for coordination and strength.
13. Play through a whole movement—choose easy ones at first.
14. Play through a whole concerto to build stamina.
15. Do half a rehearsal, or a whole one if the program is not taxing.
16. Return to normal playing.

After each session do some warm-down exercises!
GOOD LUCK.

REFERENCES

Dennison, P. *Switching on: The Holistic Answer to Dyslexia*. Glendale, Calif.: Edu-Kinesthetics Inc.

Fry, H. *The Lancet* (September 27, 1986): 728–731.

Goodrich, J. *Natural Vision Improvement*. Newton Abbot, Devon England: David and Charles Publishers, 1987.

Lautie, R. *Aromatherapy. The Use of Plant Essences in Healing*. Wellingburgh, England: Thorsons, 1982.

Index

Bold indicates the section in which the term is described. Italic indicates an illustration.

About the Author

Having two careers has given Elizabeth Andrews, Bsc Hons, DC, FMCA, LGSM, FRSA, enormous insight into the needs of practicing musicians, particularly their physical stresses and strains and the need for self-help and injury prevention.

As Elizabeh Polunin, she began late on both piano and violin, changing to viola at age seventeen. For five years she was the only pupil of Peter Schidlof of the Amadeus Quartet. This led her to an ensemble with Jaqueline du Pré and Peter Thomas under William Pleeth. She played principal violist with Ballet Rambert and Capriole Orchestras and was offered the same position with Zurcher Kammerorkest. She played with Nederlands Kamerorkest for two years before winning the only British Council postgraduate instrumental scholarship to Moscow Conservatorium. On her return, she freelanced with most of the London chamber orchestras and West End shows. She taught at various public schools, was part of the resident quartet for Waltham Forest, and was a member of London Bach Orchestra for eighteen years.

Elizabeth Andrews has studied many forms of alternative medicine but has concentrated mainly on applied kinesiology and chiropractic. As trackside therapist for the Nottingham Ultra Marathon, she was inspired to publish *Muscle Management* (Thorsons 1991) and then took part in several exchange visits to Moscow, Kiev, and St. Petersburg to demonstrate kinesiology and chiropractic. She has lectured extensively for ILEA (Inner London Education Authority), McTimoney Chiropractic College, and to trainee general practitioners at Hammersmith Hospital, London. As Chair of MCA (McTimoney Chiropractic Association), she helped bridge the gap between chiropractic ideologies.

She wrote a series of articles for *Classical Music* magazine, since reprinted in *ESTA* (European String Teachers Association) and *Pan* magazines. In 1997 she published *Healthy Practice for Musicians* (Rhinegold). This led to lectures at music and chiropractic colleges for five years on treating musicians. She also gave lectures on injury prevention and self-help to many branches of ISM, the ISM (Incorporated Society of Musicians) Mtpp (Music Teachers in Private Practice Initiative) course, and a lecture tour of New Zealand and the Yehudi Menuhin and Purcell Schools. Yehudi Menuhin wrote, "Her advice is first-rate and comes from great, first-hand experience and much study and an all-encompasing mind."